T0330213

Keynes's *General Theory* for Today

Keynes's *General Theory* for Today

Contemporary Perspectives

Edited by

Jesper Jespersen

Professor of Economics, Roskilde University, Denmark

Mogens Ove Madsen

Associate Professor of Economics, Aalborg University, Denmark

Edward Elgar

Cheltenham, UK • Northampton, MA, USA

Published by
Edward Elgar Publishing Limited
The Lypiatts
15 Lansdown Road
Cheltenham
Glos GL50 2JA
UK

Edward Elgar Publishing, Inc.
William Pratt House
9 Dewey Court
Northampton
Massachusetts 01060
USA

A catalogue record for this book
is available from the British Library

Library of Congress Control Number: 2012939928

MIX
Paper from
responsible sources
FSC® C018575
www.fsc.org

ISBN 978 1 78100 951 2

Typeset by Servis Filmsetting Ltd, Stockport, Cheshire
Printed and bound by MPG Books Group, UK

Contents

Contributors

Elisabetta De Antoni, University of Trento, Italy

Anna Carabelli, Universitá del Piemonte Orientale, Italy

Eladio Febrero, University of Castilla–La Mancha, Cuenca, Spain

James Galbraith, The University of Texas at Austin, USA

M.G. Hayes, Robinson College, Cambridge, UK

Jesper Jespersen, Roskilde University, Denmark

Michael Lainé, Bordeaux 4 University, France

Noemi Levy-Orlik, Faculty of Economics, Universidad Nacional Autónoma de México (UNAM), México

Mogens Ove Madsen, Aalborg University, Denmark

Jesús Paúl, CEU San Pablo University, Madrid, Spain

Gregor Semieniuk, Macroeconomic Policy Institute (IMK) in the Hans Boeckler Foundation, Germany

Teodoro Dario Togati, Universitá di Torino, Italy

Till van Treeck, Macroeconomic Policy Institute (IMK) in the Hans Boeckler Foundation, Germany

Achim Truger, Berlin School of Economics and Law, Germany

Jorge Uxó, University of Castilla–La Mancha, Cuenca, Spain

Stefan Voss, Analyst in the investment banking sector for a major financial institution in Munich, Germany

Figures

Tables

Acknowledgements

Selected extracts from Volumes 1–14 of John Maynard Keynes, Edited by Elizabeth Johnson and Donald Moggridge, *The Collected Writings of John Maynard Keynes*, © The Royal Economic Society, published by Cambridge University Press, reproduced with permission.

Introduction

Jesper Jespersen and Mogens Ove Madsen

ABOUT *THE GENERAL THEORY* FOR TODAY

In 2011 it was 75 years since the publication of *The General Theory of Employment Interest and Money*. It was published on 4 February 1936 in the middle of the economic depression. Politicians were groping in the dark with rather little help from the economic profession. People were queuing to buy the book as soon as it was released. Expectations were high.

There are many similarities between then and now: unemployment, low growth and mounting public debt. Unfortunately, no new 'General Theory' has been advertised, which may be a reason for a re-read and an up-dated reflection on Keynes's seminal book.

At the brink of the 21st century a number of academic economists were asked which economist they considered had had the largest impact in the 20th century. A majority pointed at Keynes, many with reference to *The General Theory*; but this voting was about the past. Today one hardly sees a reference to Keynes in the most-used macroeconomic textbooks – perhaps a passing remark related to the case of rigid wages in the labour market (which only demonstrates that the author has not read *The General Theory*). That is all. How can that be? Given the number of similarities between the economic crisis of the 1930s and the recent one, we considered this an obvious reason to gather Keynes-scholars from all over the world to discuss and exchange views on the 'relevance and perspectives' of *The General Theory* for this century.

Three themes were particularly mentioned in the call for the conference, which took place at Roskilde University in May 2011.

The first theme of the conference was the relevance of *The General Theory* for macroeconomic theory related to societies in which we happen to live today. The participants in the conference were asked to give an assessment of what parts of *The General Theory* they found wanting with respect to bringing Keynes's ground-breaking macroeconomic contributions up to date. A number of these conference papers are included in this volume.

This theme is introduced by two invited lectures, followed by papers emphasizing a number of distinct characteristics of Keynes's macroeconomics as opposed to 'Keynesian' economics: methodology, the analytical importance of understanding time, uncertainty and dynamics, the principle of effective demand and the importance of finance for real activity and instability.

The second theme concentrated on recent economic development and the role of Keynes's macroeconomic framework, characterized by capturing the *economy as a whole*. The economic crises in the US and Europe were high on the agenda. How could the crises be understood through the theoretical lenses set up and discussed under theme one? In addition, contributors were asked to give an assessment of economic policies pursued in Western countries to overcome the crises. Many high quality papers were presented during the conference, but due to narrow limits on the number of chapters within this volume of conference proceedings, we were forced to be very selective in our choice of papers analyzing the actual economic situation and decided to focus on the neglected importance of the balance of payments within a monetary union.

The third theme, which will be given a separate conference volume, is teaching the economics of Keynes. This theme is considered very important, because the original contributions from *The General Theory* are no longer present in the syllabuses which are taught in most universities. In many ways, it can be questioned if these original elements contained in *the General Theory* and described in theme one have ever been a true part of the syllabus in macroeconomics, even in the 1950s and 1960s. During the conference it was made clear that so-called Keynesian economics, as we knew it from Paul Samuelson's textbook *Economics*, first published in 1948, is not really the economics of *The General Theory*. The methodology, the emphasis on equilibrium and the role of inflexibility of prices and wages in explaining unemployment are features which Samuelson, together with many other neoclassical synthesizers, developed in the 1950s and 1960s with inspiration from Hicks's ISLM diagram. This macroeconomic teaching was easy to undertake in the classroom and to use for constructing the new macroeconometric models that for a while dominated the macroeconomic debate and were at that time mainstream macroeconomics – as long as it lasted. In the 1980s this approach in macroeconomics was swept aside by the claim that it was not 'scientific', because a rigorous microeconomic foundation was lacking and the theory of expectations was *ad hoc* – not grounded in rational choice theory. This is, in fact, where the teaching in macroeconomics stands today. Only textbooks assuming general equilibrium and using the microeconomic foundation of rational choice theory are widely available. This version of macroeconomics is of little help in understanding the present economic crisis: what caused it, why is it dragging on, and how to get out of it. These are questions which cannot be answered within a general equilibrium model, where crises are caused by exogenous shocks and the macroeconomy is self-adjusting. This teaching situation is, of course, especially embarrassing for those macroeconomists who think that Keynes and *The General Theory* have an important insight and could give students a better understanding of the world in which they live.

At this stage we feel tempted to quote directly from Keynes, who anticipated this situation of difficulties with teaching new ideas. He was in his time up against what he called Ricardian Theory. It was represented in Cambridge by the only professor in economics, Arthur Cecil Pigou, who had just published his view of macroeconomics in the book *Unemployment* (1933). Keynes asked, in *The General Theory*, how it could be that:

> Ricardo conquered England as completely as the Holy Inquisition conquered Spain' . . . The completeness of the Ricardian victory is something of a curiosity and a mystery. It must have been due to a complex of suitabilities in the doctrine to the environment into which it was projected. That it reached conclusions quite different from what the ordinary uninstructed person would expect, added, I suppose, to its intellectual prestige. That its teaching, translated into practice, was austere and often unpalatable, lent it virtue. (Keynes, 1936: 32–3)

VOLUME 1: RELEVANCE AND PRACTICES

There were three invited speakers at the conference, who each initiated one of the themes: Volume 1: Mark Hayes (theory), James Galbraith (practices) and Volume 2: Marc Lavoie (teaching).

Relevance for Today

Mark Hayes gave the opening lecture on '*The General Theory:* a neglected work?!'. Reading his chapter, it becomes evident that it is the exclamation mark which the speaker put emphasis on. According to his reading, *The General Theory* today is a neglected work. He poses the question: how to change that situation in an environment where scholars have stopped reading the classics. The knowledge of Keynes's economics is today for most economists at best second hand, through the work of Keynes-scholars, but quite often neoclassical textbooks are the main source of knowledge about the economics of Keynes.

Mark Hayes argues that to change the neoclassical dominance you have to attack the citadel which they have created through their main gateway.

Keynes held the same opinion; therefore he addressed *The General Theory* to 'my fellow economists'. He thought that by persuasion and reasoning and references to the real world he would be able to change the macroeconomic understanding. A modern reader of *The General Theory* should keep in mind that the book was written for a very specific audience, which had been brought up in the tradition of Marshall. Keynes added arguments related to the *economy as a whole*. The main novelty is that expectations related to the economy as a whole have to be uncertain. No one knows the future with certainty. The macroeconomic system is characterized by imperfect information. Equilibrium is established when nobody has an economic incentive to change his or her behaviour. Unemployment is not caused by rigid wages or prices, but by lack of incentives to increase production, in the short run due to lack of effective demand, and in the longer run due to lack of knowledge of the future. If the neoclassical economists can understand these simple conclusions, the chasm between the neoclassical economists and post-Keynesian economists could perhaps be reduced, to the benefit of both parties.

James Galbraith, giving the second invited lecture, was asked to focus on the present economic and political situation in US and Europe. He was less optimistic about the possibilities for the economics of Keynes to make any impact on the real understanding of the macroeconomic dynamics and by that on economic policy with regard to reducing unemployment. Initially he takes issue with Paul Krugman's (2009) statement that 'Economists got it so wrong'.[1] Galbraith responded rhetorically, 'which economists?', because he could mention a number of outstanding economists who had explicitly warned, or according to his reading would have warned, against the development in the financial markets and on the balance of payments for years: Keynes, Wynne Godley, Hyman Minsky and Galbraith *père*. They had all worked on the implications of increasingly complex market systems: 'Complexity defeats the market'. In this situation, deregulation, especially of the financial markets, is asking for instability. If you add reduced social control, which opened a way for corporate and financial fraud in many layers of society, you have the recipe for increased inequality and credit expansion without limit.

James Galbraith concludes that economic arguments (and theory) cannot be separated from society and the political environment at large. Although a new US administration took office in 2009, the economic thinking is quite similar to the previous one. It was still 'False Keynesianism' (at best) that dominated macroeconomic policy, without any real change in the structures of the financial sector. At the end of the chapter he sets out a list of seven points which should be taken into consideration before one can claim that one is dealing with a realistic theory of macroeconomics as a necessary background for changing the macroeconomic development. It is not lack of economic insight but lack of political will that prevents a reduction in unemployment.

Teodoro Dario Togati's chapter makes a criticism of Keynes's *General Theory* based on the distinction between what he calls a modernist approach and his preferred 'post-modernism'. He characterizes the former as a 'static approach', by which he means something different from the economists' usual meaning: he means an approach that does not take into account the two-way interaction between private agents and policy-makers. He calls the latter 'interactionism', which comes close to the term 'reflexivity' used by other authors – for instance, George Soros. He doubts that Keynes (or post-Keynesian economists for that matter) could win the argument of today unless these insights from post- and neo-modernism are incorporated into macroeconomic analysis.

Reason and references to empirical results are, according to the author, not really appropriate remedies to persuade the audience. The postmodern approach considers all theory as a kind of social construction: if people believe that the theory is the true explanation, then contrary to science it becomes the true argument of today. Ricardo conquered the economic teaching in the 19th century by incomprehensible arguments and recommendation of austerity policy – a combination of metaphysics and bad conscience due to indulgence. Ricardian economists of today argue in favour of austerity policy with reference to the superiority of the market mechanism, to politicians' self-seeking behaviour and to common sense that one should not live beyond one's own means. This is the plausible story of today's individualism, which has become the mainstream argument taught in economics classes and subscribed to by most economists.

The challenge of Keynes's macroeconomics is to construct a story where the fundamental insight from *The General Theory* is combined with the individualistic political arguments. Post-Keynesian economists should search for a microeconomic story which people of the 21st century will subscribe to. The New Classical story of rational economic man has fallen out of fashion in the wake of the financial crisis, increasing inequality and fraud. The author concludes the chapter by suggesting that the neo-modernist microeconomic foundation of Keynes's macroeconomics could be an elaborated theory of 'interactionism' or 'reflexivity', which people might find convincing for their daily life.

Relevance for Macro Methodology

Keynes began studying philosophy and mathematics in 1902 at the University of Cambridge. He could not have studied economics proper, because that study was not established until 1903: we cannot know if he would have chosen economics. His chosen subjects of study do signal his interest in society and in methodology.

There are three papers on macro methodology, which take their departure from Keynes's own struggles with the question, how to understand macroeconomics as different from aggregated microeconomics.

Michael Lainé's chapter is entitled 'Keynes on Method: Is Economics a Moral Science?' If we accept the hypothesis that macroeconomics is a social science, what Keynes called a moral science, we have a scientific problem. Social science, in contrast to natural sciences, does not have a specific purpose. There is no specific outcome that is the preferred one; value judgments are all over the place within and outside the social sciences. Further, we cannot know what people think or how they behave individually. The author is primarily taking issue with the claim that positivism could be helpful in this matter.

If the topic is (hardly) observable then positivism is of no use. Hence, using a number of arguments taken from Keynes, he is sceptical towards Friedman's claim that the quality of an economic theory lies in its ability to predict. He is equally sceptical towards Popper's method of falsification. If one cannot measure the relevant variables and, furthermore, one cannot put into a formal equation the relevant relationship, then empirical testing falls apart. On the other hand, the lack of any correspondence to the real world opens a gateway for all (even post-modern) arguments. Most post-Keynesian economists endorse a realist epistemology, but the author is somewhat sceptical towards critical realism in its more simplistic form. If in the spirit of Keynes the ethical and unknowable aspects of macroeconomics became more explicit however, then an elaborated form of critical realism might 'constitute a sound basis upon which to build a genuinely Keynesian theoretical framework'.

Anna Carabelli follows the same line of reasoning in her chapter 'A new methodological approach to economic theory', that Keynes's macroeconomics requires a special methodology. Her claim is that *The General Theory* can be read as a manual in macroeconomic methodology rather that in macroeconomic theory. That is her conclusion 'from 30 years research on Keynes'. She goes all the way back to *A Treatise on Probability* (Keynes 1921), which she considers Keynes's 'essay on method'. In that book Keynes spelled out principles of rational individual behaviour under the conditions of uncertainty. To Keynes, economics was a 'branch of logic', a way to establish consistent arguments which create probable relationships between uncertain (partly unknowable) expectations and human actions. This kind of reasoning has to be open-ended at the individual level and at the social level. Even more difficulties arise when the aim of the activity is not measurable, for instance utility, goodness, beauty and love, which were Keynes's focal points in his early writings as well as in his later essays.

The complexity of the methodology increases when the focus shifts from individual behaviour to society as a whole. This is what Keynes struggles with in his major books. Procedures to make a consistent reasoning within an interdependent system are extremely demanding. Already in the introduction to *Cambridge Economic Handbooks* (1922/23) (reprinted in *CWK*) he listed five logical fallacies which should be avoided. The best known fallacy in macroeconomics is the 'fallacy of composition' between individual activities and the outcome for the economy as a whole (for instance, the 'paradox of savings'). The chapter concludes with a call to 'post-Keynesian economists to be less reluctant to investigate the potential of Keynes's economic method as a tool to develop a complexity approach to economics'.

Macroeconomics is a dynamic subject. It evolves through time. Any relevant macroeconomic method has to incorporate aspects of time. Mogens Ove Madsen's chapter 'Keynes's early cognition of the concept of time' takes issue with Keynes's awareness of the importance of time in the understanding of social phenomena. Keynes studied philosophy and was taught by G.E. Moore and J.M.E. McTaggart. It is well known from the Keynes biographies that Keynes was, especially in the early Cambridge years, a student of Moore. This is evident in his attempts to break away from the Victorian social norms and conventions and his firm contact with the Bloomsbury group for many years. But the author's claim is that with regard to a number of more abstract philosophical issues Keynes might have been influenced more than is usually acknowledged by ideas put forward by McTaggart.

The teaching of McTaggart especially brought Keynes a vital introduction to an ontological difference between two theories of time. The same fundamental difference is known from contemporary philosophical discussions. One view is the dynamic approach according to which the essential notions are past, present and future. In this view, time is seen 'from the inside'. Secondly, there is the static view of time where time is understood as a set of instants (or durations) ordered by the before-after relation. Keynes's early paper on the concept of time is about the awareness of change, and change requires that at least one aspect differs with respect to what is happening, i.e. whether the event is future, present or past. The idea of adequately incorporating aspects of time as 'economic theory in time' in contrast to 'economic theory out of time' was after Keynes followed in the works of, for example, Joan Robinson, Nicholas Kaldor, G.L.S. Shackle, Nicholas Georgescu-Roegen and John Hicks. This effort to use a dynamic concept of time can still seek inspiration, as Keynes did, from the current philosophical debate on time.

RELEVANCE FOR MACRO THEORY

In a condensed form one can say that it is the explicit treatment of uncertainty which separates Keynes's macroeconomics from neoclassical economics. It is a necessary aspect if one has the aspiration of explaining real world economics. That is a part of the methodology and the analytical outcome of *The General Theory*. Four chapters take up the role of uncertainty for modern financial macroeconomic theory. This is done with inspiration from *The General Theory* as well as *A Treatise on Money* (*TM*) (Keynes 1930). It was in *TM* that Keynes made an elaborate presentation of his new theory of liquidity preference, which cannot be understood without an explicit treatment of uncertainty.

The first chapter of this section is Stefan Voss's '*When Keynes and Minsky meet Mandelbrot. . .*'. This chapter gives an overview of how the phenomenon of uncertainty has been treated by a few leading macroeconomists. The distinction between uncertainty and risk is quite often referred back to Chicago economist Frank Knight (1885–1972) rather than Keynes. This is unfortunate, because Knight only relates uncertainty to individual experiment and, according to the author, claimed that at the macro level uncertainty could be treated as risk due to the law of large numbers. Here, Knight and Keynes separate: in Keynes's 1937 paper 'The General Theory of Employment'[2] especially, it becomes clear that macroeconomics cannot be understood without taking uncertainty, which cannot be calculated by any mathematical method, seriously at the macro level.

Fundamental uncertainty is explaining why the macroeconomic system must be non-ergodic, which means that the future is not predictable in statistical terms. Time is not a linear function and not reversible, because the flow of events is not homogenous and not stable. This conclusion is further enforced by Hyman Minsky's 'Financial Instability Hypothesis', which explains why modern macroeconomic system is inherently unstable in a way Keynes only hinted at in Chapter 12 of *GT*.

These theoretical considerations are empirically substantiated by Benoit Mandelbrot, who concludes his investigation the following way:

> I [Mandelbrot] analyzed more than a century of data on U.S. cotton prices and studied the way they had varied daily, monthly, and yearly. The results were clear and irrefutable. Far away from being well-behaved and normal as the standard theory then predicted, cotton prices jumped wildly around. Their

variance, rather than holding steady as expected, gyrated a hundred-fold and never settled down to a constant value. In the world of financial theory that was a bombshell . . . (Mandelbrot 2008: 95)

Later Mandelbrot extended his research to stocks and currencies and found the same results (Mandelbrot 2008: 96–97). So, there is empirical evidence that market processes are not following any normal distribution and that they are non-ergodic. Unfortunately, the risk models of modern financial theory assume that market processes are ergodic, where uncertainty is reduced to quantifiable risk. The chapter concludes with a plea never to lose sight of the role of uncertainty in macroeconomic analysis.

The importance of getting uncertainty right for the understanding of macroeconomics is further discussed by Jesper Jespersen in 'Keynes's *General Theory* after 75 years'. His focus is the 'principle of effective demand', which is widely considered the analytically distinct novelty of *The General Theory*. But from his point of view, emphasis on *demand* has caused a barrier to communicating Keynes's fundamental new insight of how production and employment are determined. It is important instead to stress the word *effective*, which really is a modifier. According to the author's interpretation, effective means all relevant matters which have an influence on the entrepreneurs' decision on how much to produce and how many people to employ in the coming period. Keynes had no objection to the assumption that entrepreneurs try to maximize profit given the available information. Here the concept of 'rational beliefs' developed in *A Treatise of Probability* becomes relevant. Entrepreneurs have to establish rational beliefs on the firm's future sales dependent on expectations of aggregate demand. Each firm has a market share which is relatively stable from one period to the next. Further, production has to be profitable, which is a necessary but not sufficient condition for producing anything. In addition, access to credit has become demonstrably important. If you cannot get extra credit/finance it is difficult to expand production at the micro level and impossible at the macro level. Hence, effective demand cannot be understood at the macro level independently of uncertain expectations, expected profits, and available credit as well as the more traditional factors of production, qualified labour and real capital.

Hence, the principle of effective demand encompasses a broad-ranging set of arguments which have relevance for entrepreneurs' production and employment decisions. The decision process is based on rational beliefs and influenced by a variety of relevant demand and supply factors where the information is in a varying degree uncertain.

A casual reading of *The General Theory* could leave the impression that finance and credit is not that important for the macroeconomic development. If anything the current economic crisis has demonstrated the relevance of the financial instability hypothesis (FIH) and the importance of availability of credit. Elisabetta De Antoni has made a reassessment of these claims in her chapter '*The General Theory* after the Sub-Prime Crisis: A Minskyan Perspective'. Minsky's analysis of the dynamics of the financial sector and its impact on the real economy is an important supplement to analysis within *The General Theory*. Minsky's FIH is an important extra argument for the inherent trade cycle discussed by Keynes in Chapter 22. The trade cycle is unavoidable especially when the psychology for bankers (and other financial actors) is understood. In fact one could argue that the FIH could rather easily be integrated into Keynes's theory of liquidity preference. It is in this perspective naïve to believe that a modern macroeconomic system ever could get rid of trade cycles. Keynes was struggling with a theoretical explanation of *persistent* unemployment of 10 percent or even more, which in fact is the same magnitude of unemployment which has characterized European economies since the early 1980s. Right now the rate of unemployment is close to 11 percent and the average has been around 9 percent for several decades.

The author takes issue at this point with Chapter 12 in *The General Theory*, asking if the organization of the financial sector with ample room for financial speculation adds to the persistent deficient effective demand. If the capitalist system has developed into a full flush casino which is soaking up a substantial amount of available credit and where the trend of asset prices is derailed from the fundamentals, then a case for persistent underemployment is at hand. The author concludes that the organization of national and international financial markets allows the predominance of speculation over entrepreneurship. For these reasons the macroeconomic system, not only the trade cycle, has an inherent element of macroinstability in the short run but even more importantly in the long run. Only an open-system analysis could make this fact comprehensible for the politicians.

Private banks did not play a significant role in *The General Theory*. This is discussed and expanded by Noemi Levy-Orlik in her chapter 'Keynes's Views in Financing Economic Growth: The Role of Capital Markets in the Process of Funding'. The author outlines three important aspects of banking and finance in modern growth societies, where the stock of real capital and the flow of output are constantly growing except for periods of economic crisis. In *The General Theory* Keynes focused on the low level of real investment. One of the great novelties was his demonstration that 'investment creates its own savings'. Hence, the key to prosperity is private investment. For that reason he made a thorough discussion of the determinants of the rate of interest and of entrepreneurs' long-term expectations. The author acknowledges the importance of Keynes's arguments but wants to put more emphasis on the role of the banking system as the provider of the credit which is a necessity for production plans to be realized. Growth in GDP requires a continuous expansion of bank credit. Hence, the functioning of the banking system is important for any expansionary economic policy to be successful. The author recommends that the theory of endogenous money supply, the monetary circuit and the working of the inter-bank market get a more prominent position within Post Keynesian macroeconomics in the future.

RELEVANCE FOR MACRO POLITICS

The final two chapters are directed towards economic policy in the Euro area. Making a macroeconomic analysis of the *economy as a whole* today means looking at the European economy as a whole. This statement is obvious with regard to trade and capital flows; but when it comes to economic policies each country is treated as a separate entity. Especially within the European Monetary Union this partial approach hardly makes sense. One could say that an analytical *fallacy of composition* is committed at the European level. This is the common theme of both papers, that macroeconomic imbalances in one country cannot be corrected independently of the development in the other 16 Euro zone countries. But the Stability and Growth Pact only focuses on the imbalance of the public sector, independently of the corresponding imbalances within the private sector and the balance of payments. As we know from the national accounting principles, these imbalances are linked. The correction of the public sector deficit in any country has an impact on the current account and by that on the other member countries' macroeconomic performance, which will to some extent create a backfire. In some way one could read these two chapters as a modern response to Keynes's 'Notes on Mercantilism' in Chapter 23 of *The General Theory*.

Gregor Semieniuk, Till van Treeck and Achim Truger ask the question 'Nothing Learned from the Crisis? Some remarks on the Stability Programmes 2011–2014 of the Euro Area Governments'. What governments could have learned is that member countries within the Euro area are more closely interrelated than previously realized. Within orthodox theory of 'optimum currency areas' the importance of balance of payments imbalances within a common currency area is hardly mentioned. The theoretical and practical focus has been solely on the public sector deficit. Hence, balance of payments deficits and surpluses were allowed to build up within the Euro area without anyone taking serious notice. This imbalance is a mirror image of the sum of the private and public sector financial deficit/surplus. Not even the financial markets reacted to balance of payments deficits of more than 10 percent of GDP in some countries. Until 2007 the margin of the rate of interest on Greek government bonds compared to German bonds was less than 0.5 percent.

This chapter looks at the adjustments of the individual euro-countries which are planned for 2012–14 and challenges the projections, because according to the authors the euro-interdependence has not been taken into account. The programmes concentrate on the adjustment of the public sector, without any consideration of which sectors domestically or abroad are implicitly assumed to take the corresponding adjustment. And what imbalances may that cause? An improved public sector deficit (increased public savings) means by definition a reduction of the private sector's financial surplus domestically (reduced savings) or abroad (reduced balance of payments deficit). These changes in the private sector financial balance will have further repercussions: attempts to increase private sector indebtedness (which is the case in Southern Europe, the so-called PIGS countries: Portugal, Italy, Greece and Spain) will be difficult to finance. Are the Northern European countries prepared to reduce their current account surpluses? These questions are not addressed within the mutual plan of Stability Programmes for the euro-countries.

Three counterfactual exercises are carried out to demonstrate that the outcome with regard to reduced sector imbalances could easily be less positive if there is some resistance within the private sectors or abroad passively to accept the desired reduction of the public sector deficit. Especially, if the Euro zone as a whole cannot realize a substantial balance of payments surplus, the PIGS cannot improve their national balance of payments as assumed in the Stability Programme, and they will end up with huge – unsustainable – balance of payments and private sector deficits. If the balance of payments between the Euro area and the external world does not improve (which is difficult with a floating euro exchange rate), then the only sustainable adjustment programme within the Euro area is one where the Northern European countries expand their national economies by a more relaxed attitude to the public sector deficit – at least for the time it takes to restart the growth process in the South. According to the calculations this is the only economically viable programme to create stability within the Euro area; but it is hardly politically realistic.

The chapter 'European Economic Policy and the Problem of Current Account Imbalances: The Case of Germany and Spain', written by Jorge Uxó, Jesús Paúl and Eladio Febrero focuses on the impact of balance of payments imbalances within the Euro area. They emphasize that this imbalance is a mutual problem within the European Monetary Union, to a much larger extent than public sector deficits. This interdependency is further enforced by the fact that, since the EMU was established in 1999, there has been, by and large, an external balance. This means that balance of payments deficits and surpluses with the Euro area as a whole have cancelled out. Deficit countries, mainly the PIGS countries plus to a lesser extent Italy and France, have exported jobs to the much more competitive Northern countries (especially Germany) and at the same time indebted themselves to Northern investors. When the crisis broke out in 2008 it was overwhelmingly demonstrated that it does not matter much that South shares the same currency as North, because unemployment and high rates of interest were not shared. Year by year it has been demonstrated by the statistics that South and North deviate more and more with regard to overall macroeconomic imbalances. The root of the imbalance is the balance of payments, which cannot be corrected unilaterally. The situation within the Euro area comes close to the one Keynes feared could be the outcome of the Bretton Woods agreement in 1944: that the US economy would dominate due to a strong competitive position and excess savings. Keynes therefore suggested that surplus countries should pay a penalty on their accumulated foreign assets and hereby give an economic incentive to reduce the surplus.

Using Spain and Germany as illustrative cases, the chapter demonstrates that Spain cannot improve on its current account without Germany accepting a reduced surplus and some weakening of its strong competitive position. Unfortunately, the idea that Germany should have any mutual responsibility for the re-establishment of macroeconomic balance within the Euro area as a whole does not occur in the minds of decision-makers of a surplus country. Deficit countries have to 'make order in their own house' but they cannot do that without cooperation from the surplus countries. The claim of the chapter is that the poorest countries within the Euro area cannot grow their way to prosperity at the same level as the Northern countries without being able to increase exports at least as speedily as imports. This is not only a matter of relative competitiveness but also a matter of accepting higher growth rates in the South for a while.

However, it should also be said that Spain might have created some problems of its own by letting the housing bubble grow too high and for too long; but no warning signal was sent from Brussels, because Spain had a surplus on the public sector deficit. In fact, until 2007 Spain was often claimed as a success story within the Euro zone on account of its high growth rates. If anything this demonstrates how badly the euro-institutions are organized. Spain was not really able to break the housing bubble, because monetary policy was directed from Frankfurt with an eye on the weak German (and French) performance. No consideration was paid to the mounting balance of payments deficit, and capital markets were blind and deaf to the huge indebtedness of the private sector.

If these inherent institutional asymmetries are not corrected, the authors are sceptical with regard to any substantial reduction of the macro-economic imbalances within the Euro area.

NOTES

1. See http://www.nytimes.com/2009/09/06/magazine/06Economic-t.html?pagewanted=all (last accessed 13 March 2012).
2. *CWK* XIV: 109–23.

REFERENCES

Keynes, J.M. (1921) *Treatise on Probability*, *CWK*, VIII.
Keynes, J.M. (1930) *A Treatise on Money*, vols. 1 & 2, *CWK*, V & VI.
Keynes, J.M. (1936) *The General Theory of Employment, Interest and Money*, *CWK*, VII.
Keynes, J.M. (1972–89) *The Collected Writings of John Maynard Keynes*, 30 vols, Donald Moggridge (ed.), London: Macmillan and Cambridge: Cambridge University Press for The Royal Economic Society (Literature sources are written as '*CWK*' followed by the volume number in roman and original date of publication is given where relevant).
Mandelbrot, Benoit (2008) *The (Mis)Behavior of Markets*, London: Profile Books Ltd.
Pigou, A.C. (1933) *The Theory of Unemployment*, London: Macmillan.
Samuelson, Paul A. (1948) *Economics: An Introductory Analysis*, New York: McGraw-Hill.

1. *The General Theory*: a neglected work?!

M.G. Hayes[1]

The General Theory (Keynes 1936, hereafter *GT*) a neglected work? Am I joking? Few books have been subject to so much review, criticism and interpretation. Yet I suggest that its impact on modern economic theory, both neo-classical and post Keynesian, has in fact been minimal. This theoretical neglect has also limited Keynes's impact on policy, other than as a poster boy for a traditional policy of public works which predated *The General Theory*. My aim in this lecture is to try to justify these claims.

When I am not in Cambridge, I live just outside the border of an empire, appropriately enough for a post Keynesian economist. My home is just north of Hadrian's Wall, the northern border of the Roman Empire. In a similar way, the wall surrounding the citadel of neo-classical economics is its methodology. Attempts to engage or challenge neo-classical economics by outsiders with different methodologies have been ignored or repelled. Conversely, when the imperial citizens have sought to colonize their neighbours, they have, despite their military discipline, met fierce resistance from the unruly painted tribes. Some of whom I see represented here in Roskilde . . . in this place that, fittingly, was never conquered by the Romans.

The General Theory is the only gateway we know between the neo-classical citadel and the rest of political economy, although the gateway has remained locked for many years and its bolts and hinges are rusty. Keynes claimed that it was a major step forward in the development of the theory of competitive equilibrium, or supply and demand that ought to have transformed that tradition and increased its scientific value. For many historical reasons, *The General Theory* was not received as a platform for development, but as a revolution that has fractured the study of economics for three generations. The wholesale rejection of 'supply and demand theory' by many of Keynes's followers was, I think, premature, and the subsequent counter-reformation has merely reinstated an intellectually more powerful version of the *status quo ante* Keynes.

The implications of *The General Theory* for neo-classical theory are indeed fairly devastating. One can understand why the immediate followers of Keynes sought to rebuild economic theory on entirely different foundations. One can also understand the refusal of neo-classical scholars to accept that the previous century of formalization of economic thinking since Ricardo had been fundamentally misguided. In the ensuing cacophony, Keynes's own voice has been drowned out.

There is, on the one hand, a great deal more common ground between the formal methods of Keynes and the modern Classics than is generally allowed. That is the main area I wish to address in this chapter. Nevertheless, *The General Theory* demonstrates that neo-classical theory depends upon the special assumption of a constant and reliable state of expectation. Therefore the re-unification of political economy requires movement on both sides. Neo-classicals would need to accept, for example, that competitive equilibrium theory has no place in the theory of growth over time. Post Keynesians and other heterodox economists would need to accept that equilibrium theory remains useful as a theory of value at a point in time, the present. This is still very much unfinished business, despite the passage of 75 years.

When I say that *The General Theory* has had minimal impact on modern theory, I cannot avoid the need to state what I think *The General Theory* is. The neglect stems from the fact that each school thinks it has Keynes taped. It is well known that neither neo-classical Keynesian synthesis nor post Keynesian economics, let alone the current New Keynesian consensus, are the economics of Keynes. Each school has taken from Keynes what they think is important and left the rest. It is my contention that we are much the poorer for that. There is still much to be gained from reading *The General Theory* and using it as a starting point for research.

I have boiled down my own understanding of *The General Theory* to five propositions (see Box 1.1) that have helped me to make sense of Keynes, and I hope will help you. This is, of course, yet another interpretation and a contentious one at that, which is set out in full in my book *The Economics of Keynes* (Hayes 2006). Yet the history of science tells us that it can take several generations for truly original thinkers like Keynes to be fully understood. For my part, I do not think we are finished with *The General Theory*.

My five propositions relate to key concepts in economic theory. They relate to matters on which Keynes was either silent or cryptic, I think because of an implicit framework that he inherited from Alfred Marshall and believed would be shared by his readers. This belief turned out to be, for the most part, quite wrong.

BOX 1.1   FIVE PROPOSITIONS OF *THE GENERAL THEORY*

EQUILIBRIUM
Employment is in continuous 'daily' equilibrium corresponding to the point of effective demand, although equilibrium does not mean that all available labour and capital goods are employed and factor markets clear, nor that expectations are fulfilled.

COMPETITION
Competition in supply and demand is the motivating force which holds the system in equilibrium. Agents take prices in each market to be independent of their own actions. The degree of competition is not the same as the degree of monopoly.

MONEY
Equilibrium reflects decisions to incur money-expense by employers, investors and consumers, and not the optimal allocation of factors of production. Money is integral to production and income is intrinsically monetary. The wage unit is not an equilibrium value.

EXPECTATION
Decisions to produce, consume and invest are based on expectation. Effective demand corresponds to the state of expectation at any time. The long and short term are not the same as the long and short equilibrium periods. The future is unknown and long-term expectations are fundamentally uncertain.

LIQUIDITY
Liquidity means more than convertibility and includes invariance of value to changes in the state of expectation. Assets possess this property in different degrees, so that money is more liquid than bonds, and both are more liquid than capital goods.

EQUILIBRIUM

There are at least four ways of defining equilibrium and a clash between them produces terminal confusion. Keynes is a Marshallian, he believes in equilibrium analysis but he uses it in a highly original and quite unique fashion. For the most part, *The General Theory* is good old mechanical comparative statics, with some dynamics between different static equilibria, for reasons that will become clear.

Accordingly, the first important, almost certainly contentious, idea to establish is that the key variables in *The General Theory* are continuous equilibrium values. Income, effective demand and employment are in continuous equilibrium.

This may be because Keynes recognizes that equilibrium must be observable if equilibrium analysis is to be of any scientific value. Curiously he shares this conviction with Lucas, of all people, although their notions of equilibrium are quite different. Yet how can the system be in continuous equilibrium, in a theory which contains disequilibrium dynamics and, of course, unemployment?

Here it is Keynes's treatment of time that is crucial. He takes up Marshall's distinction between the market, short and long periods and resolves how these should relate to calendar time. Recall that in Marshall, market-period equilibrium is based on stocks of finished goods on hand; short-period equilibrium allows for employment and production to change, given the aggregate capital stock; and long-period equilibrium allows for the adjustment of the aggregate capital stock by the production of new capital-goods, i.e. investment. In both Marshall and Keynes market prices are the only prices that are actually observable. The short-period and long-period prices are expectations in the minds of entrepreneurs.

Now Marshall linked the market period to a calendar day, the short period to a calendar period of months and the long period to a calendar period of years. Yet both the short and the long period are for him of indefinite length, merely logical constructions showing the way things are heading. Marshall is quite realistic that we may never reach a given short- or long-period equilibrium; expectations may be disappointed on the way. Yet he retains a faith in the full employment stationary state as the long-term anchor of the dynamic adjustment.

Keynes introduces greater rigour into Marshall's approach. First of all, think of the terms market-period, short-period and long-period as adjectives, not substantives. Thus, each term refers to a type of equilibrium adjustment. The market period relates mainly to the clearing of goods markets, and income. The short period relates to the employment of labour and the other existing factors of production, and effective demand. The long period relates to the production of new capital goods, and the capital stock. It is a subtle point, but we need to distinguish the nature of the adjustment to equilibrium from the interval of time in which the adjustment takes place. We also need to distinguish the nature of the adjustment from the time horizon of the expectations which prompt the adjustment.

In *The General Theory*, the production and employment decision involves two separate units of calendar time, which Keynes defines as the *day* and the *period of production*, which is a number of *days*. The day is Keynes's quantum unit of time, 'the shortest interval after which the firm is free to revise its decision as to how much employment to offer' (*GT*: 47, fn 1). It does no harm to think of this as a calendar day. The *period of production* is the macroeconomic counterpart of the period between starting and finishing an individual production process, or *production period*.

In terms of equilibrium, the day has two aspects, the market-period and the short-period aspects. Each day, equilibrium market prices are struck for the finished goods delivered, thus determining current income. Also each day, equilibrium expected prices are struck for the production in which today's labour is employed. The principle of effective demand is itself a theory of the formation of expected prices as equilibrium values. The prices are necessarily expected prices because today's output of various products will not be finished until the end of their various production periods. These expected prices correspond to the effective demand, meaning the income expected to result from today's employment. Employment is adjusted in accordance with the expected prices, so that effective demand determines employment. Current income and effective demand are not the same thing, yet both income and employment are separately in equilibrium each day, which for all practical purposes means, continuously.

In a further departure from Marshall, Keynes defines the long period in a unique and strictly *short-term* technical sense, to mean the equilibrium on which employment will in theory converge, if a new state of expectation persists for the full length of the period of production. Note that this long period is *not* the same as the long term.

Finally, how can we have an equilibrium with unemployment? In what I will now follow Keynes in calling the classical sense, unemployment is always a sign of *dis*-equilibrium. This is because the classical notion of general equilibrium is a state in which all parties make their preferred choices, meaning that factor markets clear.

Classical authors (old and new) see disequilibrium in terms of shocks to a long-period equilibrium based on preferences, technology and endowment. In *The General Theory*, the level of employment at any time reflects a position of short-period equilibrium conditional upon not only that standard classical list of parameters, but also upon the state of psychological response of consumers and owners of wealth to an unknown future. In Keynes's equilibrium analysis, these psychological factors are as exogenous as the classical parameters. Furthermore, they are independent *variables*, liable to discontinuous, short-term variation. This is a kind of variation not shared, or fully determined, by the classical parameters. Therefore Keynes's system is not 'closed' like the classical system, in which the level of employment is fully determined by the parameters. Keynes's system is 'open' in the sense that the key independent variables are not endogenous, that is, not part of the equilibrium theory. Nevertheless, *The General Theory* remains a theory of the level of employment as an equilibrium value. Disequilibrium exists only in the sense that a short-period equilibrium position converges to a long-period equilibrium.

Keynes has a notion of general equilibrium, of the equilibrium of industry as a whole as he puts it, which differs from the classical. For Keynes, it is possible for the system as a whole to be in a state of competitive equilibrium even though not everyone is in their preferred position. Entrepreneurs may have no reason to change their employment decisions and labour has no power to make them do so. To avoid confusion, I use the term 'system equilibrium' to cover the still more general case. System equilibrium encompasses both classical full-employment general equilibrium and Keynes's equilibrium of 'industry as a whole', with or without full employment.

COMPETITION

There can be little doubt that Marshall saw competition as a force similar to natural selection and gravity. In mechanical statics, the problem is always related to being *in* equilibrium. Marshall uses the analogy of a basin, containing a number of balls, which is tilted. The balls move smoothly and instantaneously to a new position of equilibrium, without an intervening position of *dis*-equilibrium. In a similar way, Marshall's and Keynes's product prices are always equilibrium prices. Any tendency to diverge from market-period equilibrium is prevented by the countervailing forces of competition, and a change in the conditions of supply or demand leads not to disequilibrium, but to a change in the equilibrium price. Competition in supply and demand is the force that holds the system continuously in equilibrium.

This is easier to see with market prices than with the expected prices of effective demand. Yet the same approach applies: competition holds employment in equilibrium, each day we move instantaneously to a new equilibrium position.

Clearly what I am describing is a state of perfect competition with instantaneous price adjustment and clearing goods markets, though not, please note, clearing factor markets. What about fixed/sticky prices, nominal and real rigidities preventing adjustment? They are not there, or at least, they are not part of the main story. Much confusion has been caused by reading imperfect competition into *The General Theory*, partly through a misreading of a single phrase, the degree of competition.

What Keynes calls 'the degree of competition' (*GT*: 245) refers to the conditions of supply rather than to the slope of the demand curve faced by an individual firm. Joan Robinson wrote that 'Keynes did not accept the "perfect competition" of the text-books, but some vague old-fashioned notion of competition that he never formulated explicitly' (Sawyer 1992: 107). Taking her slightly barbed words with a due pinch of salt, Keynes's degree of competition refers to competition among entrepreneurs and workers. It is a matter of the obstacles to the free movement of resources into and between industries and occupations. These obstacles are associated with what Keynes calls 'closed shops' (Keynes 1973: 639, fn 1) of either employers or workers, together with the other social and institutional resistances connected with voluntary unemployment. So here are the real rigidities so dear to New Keynesians, but they have nothing to do with Keynes's central argument.

The degree of competition and the degree of monopoly are not the same thing. *Pace* Davidson (1962) and Kregel (1987), *The General Theory* is not compatible with monopolistic competition. *The General Theory* necessarily assumes that the degree of monopoly is zero, so that individuals take prices as given and independent of their own actions. In other words, you must approach *The General Theory* as written on the assumption of perfect competition in the modern sense. Prices are fully flexible, in the short run as well as the long: we will address why factor prices tend to be stable in a moment.

The assumption of perfect competition explains a number of important aspects of *The General Theory*, including its abstraction from financial and industrial structure and the distribution of income. Nowhere is Keynes's method clearer than in his treatment of capital-goods as if they were individually traded on the stock exchange. All finished goods, whether capital or consumption, new or second-hand, have equilibrium market prices that can be realized at any time. Here again I disagree with Paul Davidson. The assumption of perfect competition therefore has implications for the meaning of liquidity in *The General Theory*, and I will return to this later.

In Marshall's theory, it is competition that holds market prices in equilibrium and then drives this temporary equilibrium, as he calls it, towards the short-period and long-period equilibrium positions over time. In respect of competition, Keynes's theory is no different, even though his definitions of the short and long period equilibrium positions are quite different, as we have seen. The microfoundations of *The General Theory* are laid squarely upon those of Marshall, and it was not on the question of competition that Keynes differentiated himself from the classical school.

MONEY

If *The General Theory* is a theory of continuous equilibrium under perfect competition, how and why does it differ from classical theory? If what I have said is true, should we not always be in the classical long run, where only relative prices matter in the allocation of resources, and money is neutral in real terms? Why does *The General Theory* not lead to the same 'classical dichotomy', if it shares with classical theory the concept of competitive equilibrium?

Well, as we have already noted, Keynes's system equilibrium is different from the classical general equilibrium. In Keynes's equilibrium, entrepreneurs are centre-stage. The equilibrium position is determined by the spending decisions of employers, investors and consumers, and not by the optimal allocation of factors of production. Put another way, it is entrepreneurs who make the hiring decisions, not the owners of the factors of production. Unemployed factors cannot insist on being employed in return for the value of their marginal product.

There are good reasons for preferring Keynes's concept of equilibrium. The existence of a wage-dependent workforce is a sufficient condition. The monetary economy is an entrepreneur economy, not a cooperative or self-employed economy. It is a monetary production economy, meaning that production depends on the payment of wages and wages must be paid in money. The heterogeneity of output makes it unacceptable to pay workers in final product. Heterogeneity is not a minor detail of *The General Theory*, it is a direct consequence of the division of labour. Income is intrinsically monetary outside a corn model. This is why the appropriate concept of system equilibrium for a monetary production economy is the principle of effective demand.

Furthermore, there is a subtle, but far-reaching inconsistency in classical theory. The current orthodoxy is that classical theory describes the long-run equilibrium, which would be reached immediately if prices were perfectly flexible and agents fully competitive, while Keynesian or 'business cycle' theory describes the short run, since prices are in practice sticky. The stickiness of prices, we are told, reflects both nominal and real rigidities, the latter including obstacles to competition, slow adjustment of expectations, and in more recent theory, asymmetric information. This view of things should be called New Pigovian, not New Keynesian.

On the contrary, Keynes's principle of effective demand also assumes competitive, flexible prices in goods and asset markets. Only relative prices matter in the determination of employment; the problem is that the relative prices are 'wrong' as Leijonhufvud (1968) pointed out. The principle of effective demand can be (and is) worked out using the money-wage of a standard unit of labour as the unit of account: the employment of labour is determined completely independently of the price of labour.

Keynes devotes most of Chapter 2 of *The General Theory* to refuting, on entirely classical grounds, the idea that involuntary unemployment is the result of a failure to allow money-wages to clear the market. Keynes's notion of system equilibrium does not include the clearing of factor markets as a necessary condition. If it did, *The General Theory* would no longer be a theory of a monetary economy.

The inconsistency is not in Keynes's definition of equilibrium, but in classical theory. The basic tenet of classical theory is that money is neutral; yet how are markets to clear, except through changes in money-prices? Relative prices are ratios of prices in more than one market, and there is no reason to think that a change in one price will leave prices in other markets unchanged.

The perception of sticky factor prices (there is nothing in *The General Theory* to suggest sticky goods or asset prices) reflects their exogeneity from Keynes's equilibrium model. Exogenous wages are not rigid or sticky wages; on this point Keynes is quite explicit, both in Chapter 2 and the *whole* of Chapter 19. Yet, in a monetary economy, there has to be an anchor for the price level if the price system is not to break down. Since the quantity theory assumes away the problem of involuntary unemployment, it cannot be invoked to explain the price level. Classical theory does not take supply and demand seriously enough.

EXPECTATION

So far I have argued that *The General Theory* is an extension of essentially classical competitive equilibrium analysis, i.e. supply and demand theory, to a monetary economy. Taking money seriously means taking time seriously, and I have already set out the importance of Keynes's redefinition of Marshall's equilibrium periods.

The understanding of time as irreversible has profound implications for equilibrium analysis. If today's decision to produce, consume or invest is to be described as an equilibrium outcome, the competitive forces bringing about this equilibrium must also act today, in the present. Past decisions and future outcomes are strictly irrelevant.

However, most production takes time. The decision to employ labour or invest in a new capital-good today depends on market prices that are expected to rule in the future. In the absence of a forward contract, decisions must be made on the strength of an expectation, something which already plays an important part in Marshall's system. Keynes makes a subtle, but important, addition to the classical scheme by distinguishing between short-term expectation, which governs the level of production and employment, and long-term expectation, which governs the investment decision. The state of short-term expectation turns out to depend upon the state of long-term expectation, so we can follow Keynes in often referring simply to the state of expectation as a whole, but this shorthand must not obscure its compound nature.

This use of the long and short term does *not* correspond to the long and short equilibrium periods. Keynes's long-period equilibrium is based on short-term expectation and relates to a state of expectation which remains unchanged long enough to allow the capital stock to adjust fully to that state of expectation. Although Keynes's long-period equilibrium is important for theoretical completeness, it is rather unlikely to be observed, since the state of expectation is liable to constant change, far more so than the parameters of the classical system. Nevertheless, however much the state of expectation may shift from day to day, today's state of expectation determines *in the present* the point of effective demand and the level of employment, as a position of short-period equilibrium, a shifting equilibrium. It is of theoretical, but less practical, importance that the state of expectation also defines today a position of long-period equilibrium, on which the short-period equilibrium will converge if today's state of expectation continues unchanged.

Keynes treats the state of short-term expectation as reliable, or at least discoverable by trial and error – what we now call 'rational' – given the state of long-term expectation; but the state of long-term expectation itself is an entirely different matter. Keynes does not assume long-term expectations are fulfilled even in his long-period equilibrium (where they are merely unchanged), and indeed considers disappointment more than likely. I suggest that the period over which competitive equilibrium analysis is of scientific value relates directly to the time horizon within which expectations can reasonably be treated as determinate. The method cannot be applied to the long term, thus wholly undermining the classical concept of long-period competitive equilibrium, i.e. mainstream intertemporal macroeconomics.

To assume 'rational expectations' in the long term is heroically to assume a very unheroic world, in which knowledge of the present and the past is a reliable guide to the future. The state of long-term expectation is as exogenous in *The General Theory* as the endowment and other classical system parameters, meaning that it is beyond the reach of equilibrium theory. It is a close cousin to the propensity to consume and the preference for liquidity, both of which also reflect the historical nature of time. These three psychological states represent reasonable responses by purposeful individuals to the problems of time, in the real world where the classical long-period equilibrium is *logically* unattainable, and therefore an objectively optimal response is physically impossible.

So now we are moving into the mysterious area of the forces of time and ignorance, whose analysis falls outside the equilibrium model on which I have so far placed so much emphasis. The particular point I address in the next section is the nature of liquidity, and how different Keynes's treatment is to what you might expect.

LIQUIDITY

These days, a liquid asset is understood to be one that can readily be exchanged or converted into money at a well-defined market price. My claim is that this does not capture the full meaning of liquidity in *The General Theory*, and that Keynes distinguishes between the attributes of convertibility and liquidity. There is more to his conception of liquidity than convertibility. In principle, an asset with low convertibility may have high liquidity, and vice versa, however counter-intuitive this may now seem. Liquidity is intimately related with expectation in *The General Theory*, and its meaning is fundamental to the understanding of the book as a whole.

The paradox of *The General Theory* is that Keynes so emphasizes the liquidity of money within a theoretical framework, based on perfect competition, in which *all* assets are equally marketable or convertible. Why does he then discuss *degrees* of liquidity and, furthermore, suggest that in certain historic environments *land* has 'ruled the roost' in the hierarchy of liquidity (*GT*: 223, 241, 358)? Land can never have been preferred for its convertibility, let alone as the medium of exchange. Keynes claims that historically land has possessed high liquidity, despite low convertibility. Conversely, in his discussion of organized investment markets, which come closest in practice to the ideal of perfect competition in terms of transaction costs and uniformity of price, he treats their 'liquidity' (which he places in inverted commas on no less than five occasions during his discussion in Chapter 12) as an illusion and something distinct from true liquidity. Listed equity securities have high convertibility, but low liquidity.

Although Keynes does not provide an explicit definition of liquidity in *The General Theory*, he comes close towards the end of Chapter 17

(*GT*: 240). My view is that Keynes's implicit definition of liquidity is the degree to which the value of an asset, measured in any given standard, is independent of changes in the state of expectation, as we defined it a few moments ago. Liquidity risk is therefore the possible – not the probable or expected – the *possible* loss of value as a result of a change in the state of expectation, which includes the state of confidence. A constantly shifting and precarious state of expectation means a high liquidity risk.

In *The General Theory* there is a hierarchy of liquidity risk, in which bonds are superior to capital-goods (for which read equities), and money is superior to bonds. This hierarchy, which later theory has neglected, is of crucial importance to Keynes's division between consumption and different types of investment decisions. I have argued elsewhere that the hierarchy provides a solid basis for Kalecki's principle of increasing risk and for the dependence of industrial investment on accumulation. Yet very little research has started from Chapter 17 in which Keynes expressed his most subtle insights. Hansen (1953), of course, reckoned Keynes should not have bothered.

Keynes's conception of liquidity is intimately bound up with his conceptions of the state of expectation and of the historical nature of time. Liquidity has value only because the future is unknown, and its value increases with our fear of what might happen, that we cannot prevent or insure against. In *The General Theory*, money is *the* liquid asset and dominant store of value, as well as the standard of value, and money's liquidity is the foundation of its non-neutrality.

In summary, I have attributed a number of propositions to *The General Theory* that will, I'm sure, not go uncontested, but that I have found to resolve most of the puzzles and paradoxes that have bedevilled the reading of this book. These propositions would shock anyone accustomed to the New Keynesian interpretation of Keynes: continuous equilibrium, perfect competition, flexible prices, rational short-term expectations, and liquidity as something more than convertibility.

Let me conclude by relating this understanding of *The General Theory* back to my initial claim that Keynes's work has been neglected in both theory and policy. It has taken several decades for neo-classical economists to rediscover, without attribution of course, two concepts that are central to the principle of effective demand: continuous equilibrium and rational expectations. However they have never come to grips with the need to redefine equilibrium in a monetary economy. Still less have they recognized the need to distinguish short from long term expectation. While it is plausible to model short-term expectations as rational equilibrium values, it is nonsense to attempt this with long-term expectation.

As for the post Keynesians, well, by and large we have abandoned supply and demand theory, following in the footsteps of Joan Robinson and Nicholas Kaldor. Joan always maintained that Kalecki had made a better job of effective demand than Keynes. What maintains the unity of the post Keynesian school is the recognition that, under either formulation, demand matters in the long run. What we have lost by abandoning supply and demand theory is any hope of breaching the citadel. We have ranged ourselves with the other heretics, outside the wall.

What does this understanding of *The General Theory* mean for policy? Very briefly indeed, consider the following major classical doctrines: flexible labour markets, floating exchange rates, and financial liberalization, in terms of both free capital movement and prudential regulation. Underpinning the doctrine of flexible labour markets is the concept of a natural rate of unemployment. In other words, observed unemployment is said to be what Keynes called frictional or voluntary unemployment. Any temporary departure from the natural rate is held to be the result of wage stickiness, so that flexible labour markets are a euphemism for the traditional policy of wage cuts. Keynes's proof that flexible money wages cannot clear the labour market as a whole has been ignored. His policy conclusions are ignored because his concept of equilibrium is not understood, let alone accepted.

The classical notion of equilibrium also underpins the doctrine of floating exchange rates. Competition is supposed to drive the economy to full employment with balance of payments equilibrium. Without the recognition that competition alone cannot do this and that demand matters in the long run, the concept of balance of payments constrained growth is incomprehensible. The case for a return to a managed exchange rate system, including an onus of adjustment on countries in trade surplus, cannot be made within the classical framework. The same applies to the case for the management of commodity prices, let alone for more radical ideas such as an international commodity reserve currency.

Furthermore these policy ideas clash with the third doctrine, of the free movement of financial capital. In all the recent public debate about the role of Wall Street and the City of London, I have heard no challenge to the claim that equity markets allocate capital to best advantage. The incontrovertible evidence that physical industrial investment is almost entirely financed by accumulation is simply dismissed as a spurious correlation. Lacking a solid grasp of the concepts of long-term expectation and liquidity, classical theory cannot explain convincingly why corporations depend on accumulation. Nor can it explain why equity markets provide an exit for entrepreneurs, a convenience for rentiers, a hunting ground for corporate raiders, and a plaything for speculators, anything indeed, other than an intermediary through which savings are channelled into investment. Yet the social case for the free movement of financial capital depends upon the last.

And finally we come to financial regulation. The carnage of the last three years should have prompted a fundamental rethink. Yet without Keynes's concepts of long-term expectation and liquidity at their disposal, governments are proving unable to resist the demands of powerful banks to maintain unfettered financial liberalization on the strength of the flawed concept of Value at Risk underpinning Basel III.

This chapter has been about theory rather than policy, because bad theory makes bad policy, as I have just outlined, and also because I do think it is true in economics that it takes a theory to beat a theory. This is particularly so in macroeconomics, where contrary evidence is so easily explained away or ignored. *The General Theory* is a gateway into the citadel, a careful attempt to refute classical theory on its own terms and rules of engagement. I believe it has still so far been underestimated, by both friend and foe alike.

I have said little or nothing about the many positive post Keynesian policy ideas; I by no means deny the value of working out these ideas. Yet the truth is, that I entertain little hope of their gaining a hearing in the corridors of power at present. Not until the theoretical climate changes, or else the economic system collapses – not something I would wish on anyone, least of all a would-be post Keynesian policy-maker.

Empires do fall and defensive walls are abandoned and tumble down. Perhaps some of you await the internal collapse of mainstream economics. Yet it has weathered the 2008 crisis by keeping its head down. After a brief nod to Keynes from the foxhole, economic policy-makers are safely back in the clutches of the classicals. Keynes did not want to set up a rival school of economic thought, he wanted to transform economics. I think his view, and mine, is that the only way to change policy is to change fundamental theory. Seventy-five years on, there is still a long way to go.

NOTE

1. This chapter is based on an invited lecture given at the 5th Post Keynesian 'Dijon-Conference', Roskilde, May 2011.

REFERENCES

Davidson, P. (1962) 'More on the aggregate supply function', *Economic Journal*, 72(286): 452–7.

Davidson, P. (2002) *Financial Markets, Money and the Real World*, Cheltenham UK and Northampton MA: Edward Elgar.

Hansen, A.H. (1953) *A Guide to Keynes*, New York: McGraw-Hill.

Hayes, M.G. (2006) *The Economics of Keynes: A New Guide to The General Theory*, Cheltenham UK and Northampton MA: Edward Elgar.

Keynes, J.M. (1936) *The General Theory of Employment, Interest and Money*, reprinted as Vol. VII of *The Collected Writings of John Maynard Keynes* (D. Moggridge, ed.), London: Macmillan for the Royal Economic Society.

Keynes, J.M. (1973) *The Collected Writings of John Maynard Keynes* (D. Moggridge, ed.), Vol. XIII: The General Theory and After, Part I: Preparation. London: Macmillan for the Royal Economic Society.

Kregel, J.A. (1987) 'Keynes's given degree of competition: Comment on McKenna and Zannoni'. *Journal of Post Keynesian Economics*, 9(4): 490–5.

Leijonhufvud, A. (1968) *On Keynesian Economics and the Economics of Keynes*, New York: Oxford University Press.

Sawyer, M.C. (1992) 'The relationship between Keynes's macroeconomic analysis and theories of imperfect competition', in B. Gerrard and J. Hillard (eds) *The Philosophy and Economics of J.M. Keynes*, Cheltenham UK and Northampton MA: Edward Elgar, 107–28.

2. The final death and next life of Maynard Keynes

James Galbraith[1]

Back in 2009, you may recall, the economics profession enjoyed a moment of ferment. Economists who had built their careers on inflation target-ing, rational expectations, representative agents, the efficient markets hypothesis, dynamic-stochastic-general-equilibrium models, the virtues of deregulation and privatization and the Great Moderation were forced by events momentarily to shut up. The fact that they had been absurdly, conspicuously and even in some cases admittedly wrong even imposed a little humility on a few. One senior American legal policy intellectual – a fellow-traveller of the Chicago School – announced his conversion to Keynesianism as though it were news.

The apogee of this moment was the publication in the *New York Times Sunday Magazine* of Paul Krugman's essay, 'How did Economists get it so Wrong'. There Krugman admitted that:

> a few economists challenged the assumption of rational behavior, questioned the belief that financial markets can be trusted and pointed to the long history of financial crises that had devastating economic consequences. But they were swimming against the tide, unable to make much headway against a pervasive and, in retrospect, foolish complacency.

In keeping with mainstream practice, Krugman named almost nobody. So in a reply essay entitled 'Who Were Those Economists Anyway?' I described the neglected, ignored or denied second- and third-generation work, mostly but not entirely in the tradition of Keynes, who did get it right. I could have named many more than I did including quite a few in this room.

Let me begin here by distinguishing between the three major lines of Keynesian thought that did get it right. I will honour the well-remembered and beloved by identifying these lines with the late Wynne Godley, Hyman Minsky, and Galbraith *père*.

Godley worked in the Keynes-Kuznets-Kalecki-Kaldor tradition of macro models attentive to the national income accounting identities and to consistency between stocks and flows. The virtue of this approach is clarity and a comparative lack of overreaching ambition. Models of this type say nothing false, a huge advantage over the mainstream starting position which consists of nothing true. And the models direct you to check whether factual claims make sense given everything that they may imply. That federal surpluses implied unsustainable private debt was clear to Godleyans in the 1990s, just as the fact that household debt burdens were again unsustainable was clear to them in the 2000s. In contrast the Congressional Budget Office today asks no such consistency questions, and makes nonsense forecasts for that reason – in which for instance the ratio of net interest payments to GDP rises manifold with no effect on growth or inflation.

Hyman Minsky developed an economics of financial instability, of instability bred by stability itself, the intrinsic consequence of over-confidence mixed with ambition and greed. Minsky's approach is mainly conceptual, rather than statistical. A key virtue is that it puts finance at the centre of economics, analytically inseparable from real economic activity for the simple reason that capitalist economies are run by banks. And his second great insight is into the dynamics of phase transitions – hedge to speculative to Ponzi – arising from within the system and subject to for-malization in the endogenous instabilities of non-linear dynamical models.

To grasp Minsky is to go immediately beyond the coarse notion of 'Minsky Moments' – a concept which implies falsely that there are also 'non-Minsky moments'. It is to recognize that the financial system is *both* necessary and dangerous, that strict financial regulation is *both* indispensa-ble and imperfect. Right away the idiocy of a 'Great Moderation' becomes clear. Just as with a nuclear reactor (or any machinery, for that matter) a long record of stable performance does not prove that the controls and backup systems are perfect, any more than it can show that they are unnecessary. Either position, even when taken by authors of the Stability and Growth Pact, the leaders of the Federal Reserve System, or by appli-cants for license renewal before the Nuclear Regulatory Commission, is the mark of a crank.

The Galbraith line is allied and descended from Keynes in the same sense that my father was, accepting the central role of aggregate effective demand, the national income accounts, the credit-circuit view of economic life, and the financial instability hypothesis. But it is also embedded in a legal-institutionalist framework, rooted in pragmatism, framed by Veblen and Commons, forged in the political economy of the New Deal. This tradition emphasizes the role played in financial crisis by the breakdown of law and the failure of governance and regulation – and the role played by technology as a tool in the hands of finance for breaking down the law.

I stress this line not just for family reasons but because it remains the least familiar. When you engage the mainstream on the national income accounts, at least they know what the damn things are. And these days you can even get – though who knows for how much longer – a respectful mention of Minsky even from Larry Summers, if not any sign that he has, actually, read him.

What you cannot get – not at a meeting at the IMF, not from the participants at INET – is any serious discussion of contract, law and fraud. I know, because I've tried. No one will deny the role of fraud in the financial debacle – how could they? But they won't discuss it either.

Why not? Personal complicity plays a role, among present and former government officials, regulators, consultants and the academic ideologues who advised them and those who either played the markets or took fees from those who did. At the 2011 meeting of the Institute for New Economic Thinking at Bretton Woods, New Hampshire, Lawrence Summers, the former Treasury Secretary and instigator of the repeal of Glass-Steagall, stated that he was 'not among those who regard financial innovation as necessarily evil'. There is a vast web of negligence and culpability here, deeply abetted by the way universities (and especially business schools) are funded and by what they teach.

But it's more than any of that. The commodity is the foundation-stone of conventional economics. The theory of exchange requires the commodification of tradable artifacts. Without that, there is no supply and demand. A world of contracts, each backed by a separate and distinct set of promises, each only as good as the commitments specifically made the ability of the laws and courts to enforce them, is a different sort of world altogether. Just because you can call a set of such contracts 'collateralized debt obligations' or 'credit default swaps' – and just because you can create something called an 'exchange' to trade them on – does not make them into commodities with a meaningful 'market price'.

Complexity defeats the market. With infinite variability in principle, and in practice more distinct features than one can keep up with, in great volume, contracts of these kinds are hyper-vulnerable to fraud. Examples range from the New Jersey phone company that printed made-up fees on its bills, to the fact that almost no one at AIG realized that the CDS contracts they were selling contained a cash-collateral clause. They range from the unnoticed provisions permitting CDO managers to substitute worse for better mortgages in previously-sold packages without notifying the investors, to the Mortgage Electronic Registration System and the pervasive incentive to document fraud in the foreclosure process.

The concession that 'fraud was present' is like the phrase 'Minsky Moment': though true it doesn't begin to cover the case. Even to say that 'fraud overwhelmed the system' doesn't go far enough. Read the Financial Crisis Inquiry Commission Report, the Report of the Senate Permanent Subcommittee on Investigations, and the many reports of the Congressional Oversight Panel and the Special Inspector General for the Troubled Asset Relief Program. It's plain as day: fraud was not a bug, but a feature. The word itself, along with 'abusive,' 'egregious,' 'reckless' and even 'criminogenic', suffuses these reports.

Wynne Godley taught that stocks cannot be separated from flows. Hyman Minsky taught that finance cannot be separated from reality. My father's tradition teaches that the legal and the technological are one. The financial world as it exists has nothing to do with the commodity-world of real-exchange economics, with its delicate balance of interacting forces. It is the world of technology in the form of quasi-mass-produced legal instruments of uncontrolled complexity. It is the world of evolutionary specialization in the never-ending dance of predator and prey. In nature when the predators achieve an overwhelming advantage the prey suffer a population crash, from which the predators in turn suffer later on. In economics, it's a financial crash – but the dynamics are essentially the same.

Corporate fraud is not new. Financial fraud is also not new. What was new here was the scale and complexity of debt obligations backed by mortgages. Mortgages are not like common stocks, which though also issued in the millions are each an identical claim on company's net worth. Mortgages are each a claim on the revenue stream of a different household, backed by homes of a diversity made irreducible by the simple fact that each one is in a different place. Long-term mortgages have existed since the New Deal, but they were rendered manageable by their simple uniform structure, their substantial margin of safety, and the fact that the secondary markets were public and imposed public standards.

All of this meant that supervision was possible. There could be a well-understood code covering what was right and what was wrong, alongside practitioners who understood professional ethics and enforcement officers who could work with them smoothly for the most part.

With computers we entered the world of private-label securitization of the negative-amortization payment-optional Adjustable Rate Mortgage with a piggy-back to cover the down-payment. Oh, and . . . documentation optional. There was a private vocabulary covering these loans and related financial products – liars' loans, NINJA loans, neutron loans, toxic waste – which tells you that those who sold them knew their line of work was not 100 percent honest. To learn that at the mortgage originator Ameriquest office chiefs fed their sales staff crystal methamphetamine adds just a touch of telling detail.

Rendering such complex and numberless debt instruments comparable requires a statistical approach, based on indicators. And that launches us into a world not imaginable in (say) 1927: a world of credit scores, algorithms and ratings, and a world of derivative and super-derivative instruments, of sliced-and-diced Residential Mortgage Backed Securities, of collateralized debt obligations, of synthetic CDOs and of credit default swaps – all designed to secure that AAA rating and to place the instruments – *counterfeited, laundered* and *fenced* – into the hands of the *mark*, who as Michael Lewis has told us (in *The Big Short*) was known to the industry by the nickname *Düsseldorf*.

The Texas institutionalist Clarence Ayres stressed most strongly the role of technology and the irreversible contribution of new tools to the production process. In finance, the algorithm is that new tool – a radically-cheap substitute for underwriting, a device for converting the financial game into a computerized casino in the strict sense, where one can never be sure by how much the house is bending the rules. We only observe that RMBS ratings models did not factor in the default risk when teaser rates reset; nor did the holders of synthetic CDOs know that the managers could substitute sure-to-default 2006–7 vintage mortgages for the slightly-better 2005 vintages without notification.

I think Keynes understood these issues as far as they went in his time, and they led him to argue that the speculative markets should be small, expensive and restricted to those who could afford to play and lose – but that they should not repressed, on the famous grounds that it is far better for a man to tyrannize over his bank balance than over his fellow man. And in Keynesian terms, what we've seen since the financial crash is no surprise at all. Absolute distrust, leading to absolute liquidity preference, is the incurable consequence of overwhelming financial fraud.

I say incurable because – it is so. The diagnosis is of an irreversible disease. The corruption and collapse of the rule of law in the financial sphere is irreparable. It is not just that restoring trust takes a long time. It's that under the new technologies it cannot be done. The technologies are designed to sow distrust and that is the consequence of their use. Recent experience is the proof. And therefore there can be no return to the way things were before. It's the true end of illusions – the illusion of a marketplace in the financial sphere.

Let me extend this analysis into Europe. It is commonplace to speak these days of the 'Greek debt crisis', the 'Irish crisis', the 'Portuguese crisis' and so forth as though these were distinct financial events. This fosters the impression that each can be resolved by appropriate agreement between the creditors – headquartered in Frankfurt, Brussels, Berlin and Paris – and the debtors taken one by one. Good behaviour, taking the form of suitable austerity, will be rewarded by a return to normal credit conditions and market access. The 'financial market' in this imagery is severe but fair: she cracks the whip on the profligate, but praises and rewards the prim.

But that Greece has a weak tax system and a big civil service was not news. It was a fact overlooked in the good times and surfaced when convenient. The initial shock to Europe came from the American mortgage markets. When European banks and others realized the extent of their losses there, beginning in late 2008, they looked for ways to protect themselves. They did this by selling weak assets and buying strong. That is why yields rose on all the small peripheral countries despite their very different circumstances but fell for the large.

Greece cannot implement the cuts demanded of it without crashing its GDP. But even if it could, any event affecting any European country could sink Greece again, irrespective of what Greece does. So obviously there is no national policy solution, and no financial market solution. That is the meaning of the negotiations now underway. There will be a restructuring or a default. And there must be an economic and not merely a financial rescue, and a new European architecture not built around the banks and the credit markets. Either that or the depression in Europe will simply go on until the European Union falls apart. This is the practical meaning of an incurable disease.

Our challenge as Keynesians now is to work out the practical implications of this reality and to spell out a course of action. And the first aspect of this challenge is to condemn clearly the False Keynesianism that came briefly to power with the new administration in America in 2009.

In January 2009, as you recall the new US Administration announced the need for a 'stimulus' or recovery programme. Without it, they calculated, unemployment might rise as high as 9 percent by 2010 before beginning to decline again. With it, they forecast, the rise in unemployment would be held to 8 percent, recovery could begin in mid-2009, and by early 2011 unemployment would be down to 7 percent, on its way back to 5 percent by 2013.

The forecast was a political and economic disaster. But in retrospect it's most interesting for what it tells us about those who made it. Plainly, they did not understand – perhaps they did not wish to understand – what was going on. The assumption of a glide path back to 5 percent unemployment meant that the natural rate of unemployment was built into the mentality and the computer model – the only issue was speed of adjustment. And the stimulus package was meant to increase that speed slightly.

There was, in short, no real crisis in the minds of those who took office in 2009. There was, rather, just an unusually deep recession – a Great Recession, it came to be called. But the recession would end – Chairman Bernanke said so from the beginning – and when it did, things would return to the normal prosperity of the mid-2000s. It was the mindlessness of estimated output gaps, of consensus business cycle forecasting, of 'Okun's Law'. The 'Minsky Moment' would surely pass.

We have of course seen this bad movie before. Recall that in 1960 Larry Summers' uncle co-invented the Phillips Curve, stipulating on weak empirical evidence and no clear theory a relationship between unemployment rates and inflation. True Keynesians including Nicholas Kaldor, Joan Robinson, Robert Eisner and my father were appalled. The construct was doomed to collapse, and when it did after 1970 the school that most people thought of as 'Keynesian' was swept away in the backwash.

Today the failure of the forecast behind the recovery package is conflated with the failure of the 'stimulus' itself, and so the same thing is happening again. Those who failed most miserably to forewarn against the financial crisis have regained their voices as the scourges of deficits and public debt. There is a chorus of doom, as those who once thought the New Paradigm could go on forever now inveigh against 'living beyond our means' and foretell federal bankruptcy and the collapse of the dollar and the world monetary system. This includes such luminaries as the leadership of the International Monetary Fund and the analytical division of Standard & Poor's. It would be pathetic if it were not so dangerous, but the fact is, these forces are moving down a highway cleared of obstacles by the retreat of the False Keynesians.

It is our task – whatever the odds against us – to build a new line of resistance.

I think that line must have at least the following elements within it.

First, an understanding of the money accounting relationships that pertain, within societies and between them, so that we cannot be panicked by mere financial ratios into self-destructive social policies or condemn ourselves to lives of economic stagnation and human waste.

Second, an effective analysis of the ongoing debt-deflation, banking debacle and of the inadequate fiscal and illusory monetary-policy responses so far. In America and in Europe this is a crisis primarily of banks, not of governments, and it is for us to call attention to this fact.

Third, a full analysis of the criminal activity that destroyed the banking sector, including its technological foundation, so as to quell the illusion that these markets can be made to work again. As part of this, there must be a renewed commitment to expose crime, punish the guilty and enforce the laws.

Fourth, an understanding of the way in which financial markets interact with the changing geophysics of energy – especially oil – to choke off economic recovery, unless the energy problem is addressed squarely.

Fifth, a new strategic direction, to redesign and rebuild our societies for the challenges of aging, infrastructure, energy, climate change and shared development that we all face, and to create the institutions required to make this happen.

Sixth, a commitment to achieve these goals by mobilizing human brains and muscles, to overcome unemployment and to assure a widely-shared, decent and reasonably egalitarian society according to the most successful and enduring social models.

Seventh, the reconstruction of the instruments of state power – the power to spend, the power to tax, the money power and regulation – so as effectively to pursue these goals, with democratic checks and balances to help prevent the capture of new state institutions by predatory forces. I will not pretend, as Keynes did, that nothing stands in the way but a few old gentlemen in frock coats, who require only to be bowled over like ninepins and who might enjoy it if they were. We should take on this challenge simply as a matter of conscience. We are not contestants for power. It is for us a matter of professional responsibility and civic duty.

As Bill Black likes to say, and in the words of William of Orange, it is not necessary to hope, in order to persevere.

NOTE

1. This chapter is based on an invited lecture given at the 5th Post-Keynesian 'Dijon-Conference', Roskilde, May 2011.

REFERENCES

Ayres, Clarence E. (1978) *The Theory of Economic Progress: A Study of the Fundamentals of Economic Development and Cultural Change*, Kalamazoo: New Issues Press, Western Michigan University.
Black, William K. (2005) *The Best Way to Rob a Bank is to Own One: How Corporate Executives and Politicians Looted the S&L Industry*, Austin: University of Texas Press.
Congressional Oversight Panel (2011) 'March Oversight Report: The Final Report of the Congressional Oversight Panel', available at http://cybercemetery.unt.edu/archive/cop/20110401223205/http:/www.cop.senate.gov/ (last accessed May 30, 2012).
Congressional Budget Office (2011) 'The Economic and Budget Outlook: Fiscal Years 2011–2021' (CBO Publication No. 4236), Washington, DC: US Government Printing Office, available at http://www.cbo.gov/sites/default/files/cbofiles/ftpdocs/120xx/doc12039/01-26_fy2011outlook.pdf (last accessed March 4, 2012).
Congressional Budget Office (2011) 'Table 1–1 Projected Deficits and Surpluses in CBO's Baseline, Current Budget Projections: Selected Tables From CBO's

Economic and Budget Outlook', Washington, DC: US Government Printing Office, available at http://www.cbo.gov/sites/default/files/cbofiles/ftpdocs/120 xx/doc12039/budgettables.pdf (last accessed March 4, 2012).

Congressional Budget Office (2011) 'Table 1–4 CBO's Baseline Budget Projections, Current Budget Projections: Selected Tables From CBO's Economic and Budget Outlook', Washington, DC: US Government Printing Office, p. 2, available at http://www.cbo.gov/sites/default/files/cbofiles/ftpdocs/120xx/doc12039/ budgettables.pdf (last accessed March 4, 2012).

Congressional Budget Office (2011) 'Table 1–6 CBO's Baseline Projections of Federal Debt, Current Budget Projections: Selected Tables From CBO's Economic and Budget Outlook, Washington, DC: US Government Printing Office, p. 3, available at http://www.cbo.gov/sites/default/files/cbofiles/ftp docs/120xx/doc12039/budgettables.pdf (last accessed March 4, 2012).

Galbraith, James K. (2009) 'Who Were Those Economists, Anyway?', *Thought & Action*, Fall 2009: 85–97, available at http://www.nea.org/assets/docs/HE/ TA09EconomistGalbraith.pdf (last accessed March 3, 2012).

Galbraith, John Kenneth (1967) *The New Industrial State*, Cambridge: Houghton-Miffflin.

Godley, Wynne (1999) 'Seven Unsustainable Processes', January, Levy Economics Institute, *Strategic Analysis Series*, available at http://www.levyinstitute.org/ pubs/sevenproc.pdf (last accessed May 30, 2012).

Godley, Wynne (2000) 'Interim Report', January, Levy Economics Institute, *Strategic Analysis Series*, available at http://www.levyinstitute.org/pubs/stratan. pdf (last accessed May 30, 2012).

Godley, Wynne (2002) 'Strategic Prospects and Policies for the US Economy', April, Levy Economics Institute, *Strategic Analysis Series*, available at http:// www.levyinstitute.org/pubs/prospects.pdf (last accessed May 30, 2012).

Godley, Wynne (2003) 'A Changing Strange Predicament', March, Levy Economics Institute, *Strategic Analysis Series*, available at http://www.levyinsti- tute.org/pubs/stratpred.pdf (last accessed May 30, 2012).

Godley, Wynne and Izurieta, Alex (2001) 'The Developing US Recession and Guidelines for Policy', October, Levy Economics Institute, *Strategic Analysis Series*, available at http://www.levyinstitute.org/pubs/recess.pdf (last accessed May 30, 2012).

Godley, Wynne and Izurieta, Alex (2001) 'As the Implosion Begins . . .?', August, Levy Economics Institute, *Strategic Analysis Series*, available at http://www. levyinstitute.org/pubs/implos_rej.pdf (last accessed May 30, 2012).

Godley, Wynne, Izurieta, Alex and Zezza, Gennaro (2004) 'Why Net Exports Must Now Be the Motor for U.S. Growth', August, Levy Economics Institute, *Strategic Analysis Series*, available at http://www.levyinstitute.org/pubs/stratan- jul-04.pdf (last accessed May 30, 2012).

Godley, Wynne, Papadimitriou, Dimitri B., Dos Santos, Claudio H. and Zezza, Gennaro (2005) 'Can the Symbiosis Last?', September, Levy Economics Institute, *Strategic Analysis Series*, available at http://www.levyinstitute.org/ pubs/sa_sep_05.pdf (last accessed May 30, 2012).

Godley, Wynne, Papadimitriou, Dimitri B., Hannsgen, Greg and Zezza, Gennaro (2007) 'The US Economy: Is There a Way Out of the Woods?', November, Levy Economics Institute, *Strategic Analysis Series*, available at http://www.levyinsti tute.org/pubs/sa_nov_07.pdf (last accessed May 30, 2012).

Godley, Wynne, Papadimitriou, Dimitri B., and Gennaro Zezza (2008) 'Prospects for the United States and the World: A Crisis That Conventional Remedies Cannot Resolve', December, Levy Economics Institute, *Strategic Analysis Series*, available at http://www.levyinstitute.org/pubs/sa_dec_08.pdf (last accessed May 30, 2012).

Keynes, John Maynard (1963) *Essays in Persuasion*, New York: W.W. Norton & Company.

Krugman, Paul (2009) 'How did Economists get it so Wrong?', *New York Times Sunday Magazine*, September 2.

Levin, Carl and Tom A. Coburn (2011) *Wall Street and the Financial Crisis: Anatomy of a Financial Collapse.* New York: Cosimo Reports, United States Senate Committee on Homeland Securities and Governmental Affairs. Permanent Subcommittee on Investigations, available at http://www.levin. senate.gov/imo/media/doc/supporting/2011/PSI_WallStreetCrisis_041311.pdf (last accessed March 4, 2012).

Lewis, Michael (2010) *The Big Short: Inside the Doomsday Machine*, New York: W.W.Norton.

McLean, Bethany and Joe Nocera (2010) *All the Devils Are Here: The Hidden History of the Financial Crisis*, New York: Penguin Group Inc.

Minsky, Hyman (2008) *Stabilizing an Unstable Economy*, New York: McGraw-Hill Companies.

Troubled Asset Relief Program (US) & United States (2009) 'Initial Report to Congress', Sigtarp, Office of the Special Inspector General for the Troubled Asset Relief Program, United States Government Printing Office.

Troubled Asset Relief Program (US) & United States (2009–2012) 'Quarterly Report to Congress', Washington, DC: Office of the Special Inspector General for the Troubled Asset Relief Program, available at: http://www.sigtarp.gov/ reports.shtml (last accessed March 4, 2012).

Troubled Asset Relief Program (US) & United States (2009–2012) 'Audit Reports', Washington, DC: Office of the Special Inspector General for the Troubled Asset Relief Program, available at: http://www.sigtarp.gov/reports.shtml (last accessed March 4, 2012).

Troubled Asset Relief Program (US) & United States (2012) 'Quarterly Report to Congress', Washington, DC: Office of the Special Inspector General for the Troubled Asset Relief Program, available at http://www.sigtarp.gov/reports/ congress/2012/January_26_2012_Report_to_Congress.pdf (last accessed March 4, 2012).

United States (2011) 'The Financial Crisis Inquiry Report: Final Report of the National Commission on the Causes of the Financial and Economic Crisis in the United States', Washington, DC: Financial Crisis Inquiry Commission.

3. The crisis in macro and the limitations of the economics of Keynes – or why the master will not return unless his *General Theory* is dressed up in neo-modern clothes

Teodoro Dario Togati

INTRODUCTION

This chapter addresses the crisis in macro and the possibility that this could lead to a revival of the *General Theory*, both in teaching and policy advice, as explicitly advocated by many recent books (see for example, Lance Taylor's *Maynard's Revenge*, Robert Skidelsky's *Keynes: The Return of the Master* or Paul Davidson's *The Keynes Solution*).

In my view, this is unlikely to happen. The *General Theory* will not come back into fashion without substantial amendment. Like it or not, even in the face of a deep crisis such as the present one, most economists simply regard Keynesian economics either as the source of some ad hoc or last resort policy remedies devoid of intellectual appeal (such as the need to fix the economy by running budget deficits) or, from the theoretical point of view, as synonymous with a vast array of 'sub-optimal results' caused by market imperfections which often turn out to be little more than sophisticated versions of pre-Keynesian stories.

I suggest that to become really fashionable again – in both policy and theoretical terms, in such a way as to inspire new research programmes – those believing in the potential of 'Keynesian theory in the spirit of Keynes' should not just rely on the (necessary) critique of standard theories but also come to terms with some key defects in both the *General Theory* and in post-Keynesian approaches.

In order to understand the limitations of the *General Theory* (as well as its actual achievements) better, it is useful to adopt an evolutionary view of theories and place this book in its historical and cultural context, rather than to consider it as a stand-alone product. Using the modernist/post-modernist labels proposed by Phelps in his book on schools of thought (see Phelps 1990, Dow 1991), Keynes can be regarded as belonging to the stage of 'high modernism' in economic theory, in line with other key contemporary revolutionary thinkers, such as Picasso or Einstein (for a similar view, see Klaes 2006). To avoid misunderstanding, it should be clear that economic theories or paradigms do not uniquely correspond to such broad, and even hard-to-define, cultural labels. For example, it is possible to interpret Keynes as either a modernist or a post-modernist (see, for example, Dow 2002: 124; Dow 2001:73);[1] the same applies to general equilibrium theory. However, in my view these labels help clarify which interpretation of theories are bound to prevail in different times as well as define their limitations.

When seen in this light, Keynes appears inadequate to contemporary eyes for a number of reasons. To label him as modernist means, for example, that he is committed to a static, economicist approach placing the emphasis on the 'intrinsic' anatomic features of capitalism rather than 'interactionist' dynamic properties: that is, features which are not 'spontaneous' but result from the evolving interaction between institutions and agents' behaviour. These properties reflect post-modern trends and are at least partly captured by anti-Keynesian post-war developments in macroeconomics, such as the famous Lucas critique, which stresses an interaction between policy-makers and agents, calling into question the simplicity or linearity of modernist policy recipes.

On the basis of all this, what I ultimately hold in this chapter is that a restatement of the Keynesian stance can only succeed if it is able to absorb the lessons taught by these more recent developments. This means that we have to follow something like a 'neo-modern' perspective, seeking to combine both modernist and post-modern features[2] and suggesting a new simile to describe the economists' task: they should be more like neurologists than dentists, as Keynes suggested: that is, more concerned with dynamic connections than with simple anatomic considerations.

The aim of this chapter is not to provide a full-blown account of this alternative paradigm but simply to indicate its basic ideas, such as the need to pursue a more explicit 'dynamic' perspective, considering the Keynesian propensities to consume, invest and hold money as malleable, conventional and historically-contingent variables rather than mere psychological data. In this way it is possible to account for changes in aggregate demand due to factors such as *endogenous changes* in collective confidence and income and wealth distribution.

To deal with these issues, this chapter is organized as follows. Section 1 presents an overview of Keynes's modernist claims. Section 2 discusses the links between standard macro and post-modernist views. Section 3 focuses instead on the neo-modern perspective.

KEYNES'S 'HIGH' MODERNIST APPROACH

As noted by Phelps (1990), Keynes can be regarded as belonging to the stage of 'high' modernism in the early 20th century. Modernism refers to a vast cultural movement that flourished between the end of the 19th and the early decades of the 20th centuries and that criticized the trend towards modernization. Strictly speaking, it is also a heterogeneous movement. On the one hand, as noted by McCloskey (1986), it is related to the Age of Enlightenment and its positivistic methodology (inspired by philosophers such as Descartes, Hume and Comte) and was concerned with establishing the foundations of knowledge and certainty (we can label this as 'official' modernism). Among its leaders, McCloskey lists Russell and Hempel. On the other hand, modernism also includes quite different (i.e., non-positivist) landmarks, such as the critique of old rationalism, positivism and utilitarianism carried out by Nietzsche, Freud, Weber in philosophy, psychology and sociology, the musical innovations produced by Schoenberg, the Cubist revolution in painting and sculpture, the international style in architecture and the subjectivist turn in literature where writers such as Strindberg, Ibsen, Pirandello and Brecht, for example, emphasise that individuals do not possess a unifying character but exhibit a multiplicity and contradictory nature of levels of consciousness (see, e.g., Kumar 1995: Ch. 4). In regard to these contributions, we can speak of 'high' modernism.[3]

In the light of these remarks, it seems that Phelps is right to regard Keynes's emphasis on the sharp rejection of classical doctrines, the irreducible multiplicity of perspectives, the end of 'objective truth' and the system's disequilibrium as being in line with these revolutionary, 'high modernist' thinkers (1990: Ch. 1). This view has also been recently confirmed by Klaes (2006), who stresses that Keynes was at the core of the most prominent British modernist movement of the time – i.e. the Bloomsbury group – and 'his work displays the central hallmarks of literary and artistic modernism' (2006: 258). Among the features of the movement mentioned by Klaes, the following are especially relevant to Keynes: a) emphasis on avant-garde, revolutionary views; b) linguistic innovations and stylistic changes; c) an attempt to break with history; d) rejection of realist models of representation; e) preoccupation with form and technique; f) striving towards uncovering invariant structures of reality; g) belief in progress.[4]

Avant-garde, Revolutionary Views

In the *General Theory*, Keynes attempts a bold generalization in various respects. Like Picasso with his cubist painting, for example, Keynes considers 'all sides at once' in his analysis of stability (e.g. regular business cycles, states of depression and long-run growth concerns). Moreover, he overcomes the dichotomy between the monetary and the real sector of the economy in order to account for its internal instability.

Linguistic Innovations/Stylistic Changes

In line with several strands of modernism that sought to proceed to autonomous analysis of subsets of social or natural science based on different principles, Keynes fights to establish the peculiarity of his macro approach, dealing with the economy as a whole, in contrast with Marshallian microeconomics, based on the partial equilibrium approach. This struggle is clearly reflected in the linguistic innovations he adopted, such as his anti-reductionist metaphors or the view that the economist should be like a dentist, which well reflects his systemic approach as well as its scientific and therapeutic nature.

Attempt to Break with History

Keynes's attempt to emancipate himself from the Marshallian orthodoxy leads him to break with history, in the hope of achieving a high degree of applicability to most contexts. He provides an essentially abstract or *a priori* account of the working of the economy. In his analysis of the role of money and banks he admits, for example, that institutional details fall into the background. Moreover, he focuses on actual observation of markets and business psychology only when discussing notions such as expectations and the state of confidence in Chapter 12 of his book (see e.g. Keynes 1936: 149).

Rejection of Realist Models of Representation

When compared to the institutionalist and historical school, the *General Theory* shows a more reflexive and inward-looking concern with representation. In line with Woolf's rejection of the realistic novel and the refusal of naturalistic data in modernist painting, Keynes rejects one kind of realism, namely descriptive realism, to embrace a psychological perspective. In contrast with the 'rational economic man' of standard theory, Keynes emphasizes the fragmented nature of individual identity and experience in an uncertain context: he stresses both the key role played by irrational moves in agents' decisions and the stabilizing role of conventions (Klaes 2006: 262).

Preoccupation with Form and Technique

There is no doubting that the *General Theory* greatly contributes to the development of macro and national accounting as technical disciplines. This is so because it provides a model, i.e. a coherent framework, including precise definitions of the core concepts. As he makes clear in Chapter 18 of his book, Keynes – not unlike contemporary revolutionary theorists in other fields, such as Einstein, who stressed the non-homogeneity of time – develops a seemingly 'static' approach. He focuses mainly on how the key causal factors involved by the principle of effective demand give rise to momentary positions of rest in the system. While always applying in the determination of income at any given moment, this principle cannot be regarded as generating natural laws concerning the evolution of income through time.

Striving Towards Uncovering the Invariant Structures of Reality

In line with contemporary modernist movements, Keynes too fails to pursue formalism and abstraction as ends in themselves; they are needed not to depart from reality *tout court* but to capture its essential part beyond contingent or transient elements. Indeed Keynes can be regarded as adhering to the canons of modernist avant-garde painters, according to whom reality has an objective existence and unifying forces await discovery so that the basic aim of abstraction is to isolate the fundamental invariant or deep structures that underlie appearances:

> Representation of the invariant structure required, it was believed, the development of abstract and formal methods. If the abstract, geometric paintings of Piet Mondrian and Malevitch seem removed from reality, they actually are intended to be realistic in the sense that they probe and represent 'deep' reality. (Klamer 1995: 321)

In particular, not unlike Kandinsky's 1911 manifesto stressing that the move towards abstraction 'liberated the artist from the constraints of figurative representation, towards an exploration of the symbolic primitives of the visual field . . .' (quoted by Klaes 2006: 266), the *General Theory* seeks to isolate the primitives of the macroeconomic field. According to Keynes, these consist of the intrinsic properties of a monetary economy, in which money and expectations play an essential role and make sense of the principle of effective demand. It can be argued that his fundamental contribution is to provide the anatomy of modern capitalism, an analysis of its basic elements at a given moment in time. From this standpoint, his work parallels the achievements of Einstein's relativity theory, which introduces time as an essential dimension of the analysis (see Togati 1998: 45–61).

Belief in Progress

Keynes certainly shares another basic ideal of the modernist movements, which is aptly described by Klamer as follows: 'Far from retreating into an abstract world removed from the real one, these early modernists were utopian ... [They] strove for ideals of emancipation and liberation and worked for a better world.' (Klamer 1995: 321) In line with the dentist metaphor, Keynes quite optimistically regarded his theory as being the right tool in the hands of policy-makers to cure the 'toothaches' of the economy most effectively. This sort of belief has often been translated by both academics and journalists in simplified policy formulas, such as the possibility to jump-start the economy or the 'pump-priming' concept.

THE NEW NEO-CLASSICAL SYNTHESIS AND POST-MODERNISM: SOME PLAUSIBLE LINKS

Post-modernism can be seen as the cultural correlate of a post-industrial society, in which knowledge has become the principal force of production (see Lyotard 1984: 5; also Preston 2001: 82). Many authors suggest that post-modernism has not much affected economics (see e.g. Dow 2001, 2002; Jackson 2009) and certainly neo-classical theory may appear very far from its influence. The general equilibrium approach is widely regarded as an application of modernist principles in economics. As clearly stated in Samuelson's 1947 contribution, for example, this approach aims to build a universal model around the unifying principle of maximization under constraint (see, e.g., Dow 2001: 67). However, general equilibrium can also be given a post-modern interpretation. As Phelps suggests, for example, the Real Business Cycle model – which lies at the heart of today's dominant macro paradigm, i.e. the New Neo-classical Synthesis (NNS) – can actually be seen in this light. In this section, I will justify this view by singling out some of the most plausible links between the NNS and post-modernism.

Eclecticism

Following its refusal of grand meta-narratives, such as Marxian theory, post-modernism favours eclectic tendencies that attempt to combine new and past features. The NNS appears to be in line with this move as it combines new formal tools with past theoretical beliefs and methods. It reverses Keynes's 'all-sides-at-once' approach to pursue segmentation of the whole macro discipline, not just between business cycle and long-run growth theory, but also within an increasing number of uncoordinated, partially autonomous subfields, such as labour, money and finance. More generally, it can be argued that much of mainstream economics is characterised by a certain amount of fragmentation; macroeconomists apply the standard assumption of rationality in piecemeal fashion in a variety of contexts, quite outside any unifying logic of a Walrasian kind. This is especially evident in the literature on the search for the microfoundations of macro. This has led many to emphasize a variety of partial equilibrium stories based on a plethora of special assumptions that defy generalization (see, e.g., Blanchard and Fisher 1989: 27–8; Caballero 2010).

Linguistic Innovations

One of the key aspects of post-modernism is its calling into question the autonomy of various subsets of social science and the lines of demarcation between various realms of society or between nature and society or culture. This accounts for key tendencies in post-modern culture, such as reductionism and the increasing role of advertising. In line with this stance, the various strands of neo-classical macro theory and the NNS have now dropped Keynes's systemic thinking and persistently advocated the search for the microfoundations of macro as the basic criterion for producing acceptable economic science, not unlike advertising campaigns stressing, for example, the virtues of a particular electronic device to enhance the quality of life. Indeed, it can be argued that the marketing strategist, rather than the dentist, has become the relevant metaphor for the economist. The aim is not so much to solve or cure specific problems, for it is difficult to know whether a specific remedy works or not (deregulation may fail because it is not implemented properly etc.). Rather, the aim is to discover the right rhetorical arguments to 'impose' the model upon the economy in a soft way through a fundamental 'interaction' between theorists and agents; that is, by shaping their expectations by reassuring or convincing them that the standard model is the only 'true' model of the economy, the only acceptable grammar or correct framework for thinking as economists and deriving plausible normative conclusions.

Attempt to Account for History

Another feature of post-modernism which is somehow captured by the NNS is its concern for the historical dimension. While still committed to abstract axiomatic theory and even claiming to search for natural laws governing market economies – in particular by deducing business cycle theory (not just long-run or growth theory) from the correct neo-classical postulates – standard macro theorists have ceased, for example, to regard the economy as a kind of self-contained machine, separated from the institutional set-up. The market system can only work if there are adequate institutional premises, such as law enforcement and property rights, or institutional anchors, such as a certain academic set-up capable of popularising or imposing the 'true model' of the economy to coordinate agents' expectations, as implied by the rational expectations hypothesis. Institutional differences between countries may account for their divergent economic performances.

Appreciation of Descriptive Realism

In line with post-modernism's appreciation of elements that comprise pure surface (i.e., the view that 'surface is everything'), standard macro theorists often subscribe to a form of descriptive realism. While relying on patently and descriptively false abstractions or assumptions and even defending them as virtuous in line with Friedman's 'as if' stance, Lucas, for example, argues that the task of his model is to mimic actual co-movements; i.e. those invariable regularities or stable patterns among data series. Another 'descriptive' feature that modern macro has in common with the original general equilibrium theory of the 19th century is its focus on 'observable' elements, such as individual agents, as the key ontological feature of the economy.

Technique/Form as 'Ends in Themselves'

In line with the 'linguistic turn' emphasized by post-modern thought and the so-called 'rhetorical' approach to understanding economics developed by McCloskey (1986), the NNS – in comparison with modernist authors – certainly does not drop formal models, but it changes their interpretation. While sticking to the same Walrasian paradigm as the older generation of neo-classical theorists, it tends to consider its general equilibrium models as narrative elements, as 'tales' rather than 'true' representations of the economy as Walras himself or Samuelson would (see e.g. the latter's emphasis on the realism of assumptions). In other words, it is possible to see NNS models as reflecting a 'linguistic' or technical turn, according to which what matters is not the 'true' representation, but simple internal consistency or the technical ability to construct tales. It should be clear that a degree of indeterminacy inevitably follows from this perspective. On what grounds should we prefer one model to the other? Simple reference to basic postulates is not the decisive criterion. The point is that analytical results are obtained mainly due to the use of technical assumptions that are not uniquely related to such postulates. For example, like Real Business Cycle theory, the NNS places the emphasis on real shocks. But in the recent past, similar representative-agent based models emphasizing monetary shocks instead (e.g. Lucas's models) were also popular. It is difficult to say that the former is 'better' than the latter in some objective sense, apart from conformity to conventional criteria such as rigour, simplicity, parsimony etc.

Are There Any Invariant Structures?

As already noted, according to popular accounts post-modernism puts forward the view that 'surface is everything'. Moreover, it also contrasts the use of discourse analysis as a search for 'meaning' (inevitably context-dependent) with the modernist programme of searching for 'truth'. In our view, however, these claims should not be taken at face value, especially when dealing with the influence of broad post-modern culture upon scientific subjects, such as economics. The obvious fact that NNS authors continue to use modernist concepts, such as the 'deep' parameters or 'truth', does not mean *per se* that they are immune from post-modernism; in my view, the latter does influence the interpretation of such concepts.

First, while the NNS approach does not rule out the emphasis on 'deep' parameters, in line with the modernists' search for the unchanging primitives of the economic field, on close scrutiny, however, it does call into question their invariant nature. One can note, for example, that in standard macro approaches, institutions influence individual behaviour at least in the long run (growth theory) (see e.g. Rodrik 2003: 1). Moreover, the rational expectations hypothesis introduces some dynamic, interactionist elements in standard models, such as the fact that people react to policy. Now, according to this hypothesis, it is because agents' preferences remain stable in the face of policy changes that one can rely on standard models to predict agents' reactions to such changes. However, there is also a further dynamic element to consider: namely, that the scenario just described is true only if all agents know the standard model. But if this model is to be applicable to the real world populated by heterogeneous agents, one imperative question naturally arises: how do they manage to learn this model? To address this issue implies recognizing the full potential of the interactionist perspective as 'deconstruction', to use a post-modern term, of the notion of the 'rational economic man' as an autonomous or context-independent entity underlying the modernist versions of neo-classical theory.

Second, while the NNS approach, like the modernist one, does not drop the term 'truth' (and reference to external reality) altogether from its language kit, it does use it in a quite different sense. The linguistic turn for the NNS does not literally mean what post-modernist authors such as Roland Barthes have in mind; namely, that no fundamental reality exists outside language and discourse, i.e., the view according to which 'everything which we encounter or experience as 'reality' is only (or primarily) a matter of language or text or discourse – that is essentially forms of information – rather than external things (there is no 'out there', as it were) (Preston 2001: 87). It does mean, however, that the relationship with external reality is much more tenuous and is mediated by technical language in an essential way.

On the one hand, provided they can be interpreted as essential structures underlying reality, deep parameters must carry the weight of an enormous analytical superstructure built upon them. Indeed, it is true that in the process of deriving analytical conclusions, all the work is done by technical assumptions which introduce wide margins of manipulation in modelling procedures (see e.g. Lawson 1997). On the other, the 'empirical evidence' for such theorists is not synonymous with 'brute facts': it is only what econometric techniques identify as such (e.g. statistical correlations or regularities behind the chaotic surface, i.e., the mass of actual data). The combination and overlap of theory and econometric techniques along these manipulative, technical lines lead Lucas, for example, to regard the so-called co-movements as the only characteristics of the business cycle worth considering in the analysis. Moreover, they justify reliance on calibration approaches, according to which evidence can be chosen to satisfy the theoretical value of parameters,[5] an approach which makes theories almost unfalsifiable, despite the formal appeal to empirical testing as the ultimate judge, and attaches a strong conventionalist connotation to the notion of 'true model' of the economy.

Weakening of the Concept of Progress

Another feature of post-modernism is the emphasis on the 'negative' aspects of phenomena from the start, asserting that they do not possess linear outlines in our society, and that simple accounts for them may not hold (see e.g. Cullemberg et al 2001: 9). This clearly undermines the modernists' optimistic belief in the possibility of achieving progress through intervention. Following this stance, the NNS raises serious doubts about Keynes's optimistic belief that governments are able to steer the economy.[6] By assuming that agents think in terms of the standard model, it stresses that agents react to the implementation of Keynesian demand policies, thus undermining their effect at the aggregate level (for example, if more debt-financed public expenditure occurs, rational consumers may discount future taxes to cover it by reducing current consumption). In this way, a fundamental interaction between agents and policy-makers is recognized, in line with the view that the market economy is not a self-contained mechanism. It follows from here that, in order to grant macro stability, policy-makers need to commit themselves to clear policy rules, such as balanced budget or inflation targeting, that minimize the risk of agents' adverse reactions.

THE LIMITATIONS OF KEYNES IN THE LIGHT OF THE NEO-MODERN APPROACH

The key suggestion of my chapter is that to deal with current macroeconomic problems simple reference to Keynes is insufficient; there are significant limitations to his approach. This is clearly not a new claim *per se*. Critiques have been raised on his *General Theory* ever since it was published, by friends and foes alike.[7] Below, I do not discuss such critiques; I only suggest that they are often partial or limited to particular aspects. My basic concern here is to indicate a novel perspective from which Keynes's limitations can be more easily understood in a *comprehensive* way. I label this perspective as 'neo-modern' since it combines both modernist and post-modern features. In a nutshell, what I hold is that while Keynes's approach is a milestone of macro, its key achievement is to uncover the anatomy of capitalism. It fails to provide instead a sufficient account of its dynamic properties, such as the 'internal relation' between policy-makers and agents (for example, the fact that the latter react to policy moves), partly emphasized by post-modern macroeconomics. In this section, I provide only a brief sketch rather than a complete account of this perspective; my aim is to show that it is potentially fruitful and constructive: namely, that it can help to pursue 'macroeconomics in the spirit of Keynes'.

What General Theory?

First of all, the neo-modern perspective involves a critique of Keynes's generalization effort. His 'all-sides-at-once' approach is certainly more useful than the neo-classical eclectic approach based on segmentation and partial equilibrium stories. However, it would work better if its limits were clearly specified. Keynes, for example, apparently attaches the same weight to the general principle of effective demand or the multiplier, which are part of his 'static' model, and command a wide consensus among economists and to 'dynamic' claims, such as those concerning prices and costs changes, which reflect particular assumptions (e.g. decreasing returns) that appear more questionable. In other words, I feel that we must somehow take into account the post-modern critique, that some degree of segmentation in Keynes's original theory is needed, though of a different kind from the one usually suggested in the literature. In particular, I hold that we should make a hierarchical distinction between the two above sets of propositions. Although I cannot fully justify my labels here, I would simply regard the static core of the *General Theory* as Keynes's 'True Model' and the other part as his 'Hypothetical Model'.

Linguistic Innovations/Stylistic Changes

To describe how the neo-modern perspective differs from Keynes's, it is useful to adopt a new metaphor for describing the economist's task. While sticking to the basic medical metaphor, I hold that economists should regard themselves as neurologists rather than dentists. In their view, the brain appears more complex than other organs. It has not just an objective, out-there, existence, like a tooth: it is not, for example, just an aggregate of cells (as one could expect by looking at it at a given instant of time); it is also about dynamic connections, which are partly constructed through the interaction with the external environment in 'real' time. Such connections cannot be derived from the knowledge of static properties alone and are not the spontaneous result of evolution; that is, they could not exist without human intervention or cultural influence. In other words, the brain appears to be the part of the body for which 'self-contained' anatomic analysis is most insufficient; indeed, it is not easy to tell the boundary between biological 'spontaneous' evolution and external or cultural influences. Neurology therefore appears as the realm of autonomy of the dynamic connections from simple anatomic structure, partly due to cultural influences or 'learning'. While this introduces a degree of indeterminacy in science (the brain is mostly unknown, like economic growth), it does not amount to 'anything goes' (we have at least a sufficient static knowledge of the brain).

History and Theory as Compatible Bedfellows

A further feature of the *General Theory* that the neo-modern perspective invites us to call into question is its relatively abstract or a-historical approach. The novelty of this perspective, however, is the belief that accounting for the proper role of history and institutions as advocated by post-modern developments does not necessarily involve the rejection of Keynes's generality claim. On the contrary, it is the ability to 'generalize' the NNS interactionist insights that opens the way to a successful restatement of that claim.

To make this point clear, let us first note that the key limitation of Keynes is that he subscribes to a 'self-contained' or economicist stance. While allowing for the internal instability of the economy, he fails to consider the 'internal relation' between policy-makers and agents or what happens when the factors which he takes as given in his static model are allowed to change. As for the first point, it can be argued that what Keynes fails to notice is that, under the fiat money regime, institutional premises or anchors need be established because agents may lack a sufficient amount of confidence in the working of the economy and the basis of their decisions. In particular, while stressing the fragility of the conventional background, Keynes does not provide a dynamic account of 'confidence' and the institutional response which occurs when it breaks down.

This is the key step that neo-modernists should take to restate Keynes's original generality claim. For this purpose, it is vital to single out the relevant anchors granting stability in real world economies. Indeed, ever since the Great Depression these have increasingly been 'tamed' by intervention in the shape of internal anchors, which have become endogenous, built into the system. While Keynes was thinking mainly in terms of quite reversible discretionary demand policy moves, many systemic stabilizers have become structural, almost a 'natural' or uncontroversial part of the institutional landscape. I refer to 'official' mechanisms, such as given money wages, the pledge of central banks to defend the value of money, key features of the welfare system, such as unemployment benefits or public health services, deposit insurance etc. – which have accounted for the structural rise of public expenditure over GDP in all advanced countries ever since the 1930s – as well as to some more subtle or tacit mechanisms through which institutions shape aggregate behaviour. We can think, for example, of 'popular' models or theories that are 'institutional' in the sense that they are strongly supported by academia and influence policy-makers to the point that they provide almost common-sense accounts or policy solutions. There is no doubting that people's unconditional belief in most sophisticated models claiming to provide a scientific analysis of risk is one of the key factors that led to the recent expansion of financial markets and the subsequent crisis.

On these grounds, our generality claim can now be made clear. When seen through neo-modern lenses, Keynesian theory is more general than its neo-classical counterpart because it advocates a broader range of institutional anchors or stabilizers. Standard theory actually implies that the economy is internally stable, and that 'right' institutional set-ups and policy regimes as well as the standard model itself are sufficient to support agents' confidence. Based on Keynes's view that the economy is not internally stable, the neo-modern stance underlines instead that there is no guarantee that institutional anchors can actually succeed in this confidence-restoring task. Ever new forms of anchors need to be devised for this purpose.

What Kind of Realism?

Another feature of Keynes's approach that appears questionable in the light of the neo-modern stance is that he formulated his principle of effective demand by appealing to explanatory factors, such as psychological and conventional terms, unsuitable to account for the evolution of the economy. The point is that they seem, to a large extent, descriptive terms which have no clear ontological status, as they fit neither a full-blown individualist ontology (Keynes's aggregates defy the canons of individual rationality), nor a full-blown aggregate ontology insofar as he makes reference to maximization and 'animal spirits' that are ultimately in tune with an individualist ontology and a narrow notion of structure.[8]

The neo-modern stance advocates a way out of Keynes's ambiguity in the opposite direction to the microfoundations strategy: that is, it regards aggregates as distinct ontological entities relating to concepts, such as 'collective confidence', which acquire a special status and do not result from the aggregation of individual mental states. This is possible because while endorsing his view that conventions stabilize somehow animal spirits – a feature that accounts for his claim that the system is not violently unstable but only moderately so – I regard the relative stability of the conventional background itself, however, not as an intrinsic property of the system but as a result of the institutional anchors or what I label as the 'internal relation' between agents and policy-makers.[9]

Placing the emphasis on this relationship actually makes it possible to recast Keynesian theory in dynamic terms. Indeed, the key drivers of the theory; i.e. agents' propensities underlying aggregate demand now appear as malleable variables because the 'collective confidence' influencing them does not have a static nature, but must be continuously reproduced by appropriate institutional mechanisms. Once this step is taken, one can discuss the evolution of aggregate demand in terms of determinants of 'collective confidence', including objective factors, such as trends in globalization, technological change and finance, that affect income and wealth distribution. This is possible because 'collective confidence' appears more as a structural rather than a simple psychological feature. For example, it is not just about waves of pessimism or optimism but about structural changes, such as people's tendency in the New Economy to use less paper money, which reduce their propensity to save or increase their propensity to go into debt as a consequence of financial innovations.

What Role for Formal Models and Story-telling?

The neo-modern perspective also involves a critique of Keynes's literary form of exposition. This is not effective mainly because Keynes fails to specify the boundaries between his 'True Model' and the 'Hypothetical Model', a feature which undermines his dynamic analysis; he gives the impression, for example, that this could consist of *a priori* claims, such as the tendencies of the propensity to consume or the marginal efficiency of capital to fall. To remedy this flaw, neo-moderns advocate a two-step approach. The first step is to provide a formal representation of his True Model (for example, in terms of a fixed price IS-LM model)[10] in order to isolate the primitives of macro and thus the role of aggregate demand at a given point in time. The second step, in line with Keynes's non-homogeneity view, together with our emphasis about the 'internal relation', is to recognize that dynamic analysis does not lend itself to formal treatment and thus regard Hypothetical Models in general as a form of story-telling, concerning how the 'primitives' singled out in the True Model are influenced by the combination of trends mentioned above.

Deep but Changing Structures

The neo-modern stance subscribes to Keynes's modernist project whereby we should single out deep structures, such as the primitives of effective demand. However, following post-modern views, it regards such deep structures as being changeable. In particular, while Keynes affirms the possibility of a lack of effective demand as an anatomic feature of capitalism, the result of some 'generic' features of capitalism, such as money and uncertainty, in the neo-modern perspective a lack of effective demand is not a static phenomenon which can be discussed simply in terms of under-employment equilibrium, but should be analyzed in dynamic terms. This means, for example, that it is important to understand its origins, how it results from changes in the primitives of effective demand brought about by some key trends or phenomena occurring in historical time (e.g., those features that characterize the New Economy, see Togati 2006). Moreover, a lack of effective demand also implies that a confidence crisis is under way which must be checked by appropriate institutional stabilizers and expectation-coordinating devices. This internal relation between agents and institutions thus implies that economic data are not 'objective' in the sense that they are not entirely spontaneous or 'natural' but incorporate a policy response.

For these reasons, dynamic analysis can only be about plausible 'stories' aimed at discussing broad qualitative features or tendencies of the economy rather than precise quantitative relations. The 'story' label suggests that there is a degree of creative selection or manipulation of evidence involved in this representation of reality, which is the post-modern heritage that survives in the neo-modern stance. Such dynamic stories should be mainly concerned with one major point: namely, how to split up the overall aggregate evidence into more or less 'spontaneous' trends; i.e. tendencies of the economy irrespective of policy influence (this is needed to substantiate claims about endogenous instability) on the one hand, and counteracting policy moves on the other. In principle, many stories are possible and many different combinations of these trends can be produced (I provided an instance of such combinations in Togati 2006).

A More Roundabout Approach to Progress

The last feature of Keynes's approach that the neo-modern approach calls into question is his belief that 'progress' (in particular, the possibility to remedy the lack of effective demand and the existence of involuntary unemployment) is relatively easy to achieve. Using his dentist simile, it can be argued that in his view demand policy is not unlike a tooth which can be pulled out at a relatively minor cost (as compared to other types of surgical operations). According to the neo-modern stance, instead, progress can still be achieved but in a more roundabout way.

This claim is justified by the fact that, following the neurologist metaphor, we seek to go beyond a simple anatomic account in order to understand better the actual evolution of the economy. There is no doubting that the latter has undergone major changes ever since the 1930s. In particular, it has been increasingly 'tamed' by intervention in the shape of internal anchors, which have become endogenous, built into the system. Now the reason why this change makes the road to progress much more impervious is that it has been generally misinterpreted by academics and policy-makers alike, generating a curious paradox. Instead of having been regarded as an intellectual victory of the Keynesian paradigm, according to which stability is not intrinsic to the system but can only be achieved by intervention, the relative stability of post-war capitalism has been seen in opposite terms, that is, as a justification of the standard paradigm affirming the intrinsic stability of the economy in which problems are due to excessive state interventions. Indeed even the recent crisis – in which an unprecedented creation of liquidity and public deficits has so far avoided something like the Great Depression happening again – has now created the conditions for the intellectual resurgence of standard theory in the shape of orthodox policy recipes, such as the drastic welfare cuts advocated by US tea party movements or many European leaders and the punishment of profligate countries by financial markets.

In this context, sustainable progress can then only be achieved by adapting the Keynesian paradigm to these new conditions (in particular, making it able to capture the relevant interactionist properties) in such a way that it becomes easier for people to believe the stories it is able to tell.

CONCLUSION

The basic conclusion of this chapter is that to understand both the achievements and the limitations of the *General Theory* we need to rely on a new paradigm, such as the neo-modern perspective proposed here, which invites us to combine the insights of previous modern and post-modern stages of macroeconomics in order to improve the analysis of global stability. This perspective, which leads us to adopt the neurologist as the relevant metaphor for economics, makes clear, for example, why Keynes's work is a scientific landmark in the history of economics: it is an invaluable contribution to unveiling the anatomy of capitalism. However, it also helps us to understand his weaknesses in dynamic analysis. Just as the brain is not only about anatomy, so capitalism cannot be entirely understood in terms of a static model of instantaneous equilibrium such as that underlying the *General Theory*. In particular, we have noted that Keynes's work fails to highlight the dynamic implications of the working of an economy based on fiat money, which are relevant for assessing the stability of real world economies. For these purposes, it is necessary to take into account not just some spontaneous trends that can be inferred from anatomy as he did (such as the tendency of the propensity to consume or invest to fall), but also the systematic 'internal relation' between policy-makers and agents, which undermines the possibility to talk about the dynamics of capitalism in an objectivist, abstract or high-brow theoretical way. In particular, to study this relation two steps need to be taken. The first is to consider collective confidence as an autonomous structural (rather than simply individual and psychological) feature which responds to changes in objective factors. It has been noted, for example, that financialization (combined with other trends) has increased confidence in the stability of the financial system and has brought about structural changes in people's behaviour (as distinct from simple waves or optimism or pessimism), such as the tendency to use less paper money and reduce their propensity to save. The second is to single out the relevant endogenous anchors which have been granting stability in the real world economies ever since the Great Depression.

NOTES

1. For an interpretation of Keynes as a post-modernist, see, for example, Cullemberg, Amariglio and Ruccio 2001, Ruccio and Amariglio 2006, Klamer 1995.
2. This perspective is discussed at greater length in Togati 2006.
3. 'Official' modernism has prevailed in the literature; i.e., the label has been associated mainly with positivist views justifying the emphasis on linearity, stability and steady progress. For example, McCloskey (1986) suggests that modernism is anti-historical in its preoccupation with foundations or certainty, endorsing scientism in holding that the boundaries of genuine knowledge coincide with those of science, relying on old-fashioned paradigms of physics and the understanding of science in axiomatic terms, with a primary focus on prediction, control, observation, experimentation and measurement. Among the commandments of modernist methodology, McCloskey also includes explanation in terms of covering laws and a clear distinction between ends and means (see also Boylan and O'Gorman 1995: 39).
4. These features also have a counterpart in contemporary scientific breakthroughs, such as relativity theory. Significant analogies can be found for example between Keynes and Einstein (see in particular, Galbraith 1996, Togati 1998, 2001).
5. As rightly noted by Jespersen, 'the deep parameters . . . were calibrated, that is, given empirically plausible values, without necessarily being anchored by formal statistical tests. It is considered more important that parameter values respect the theoretical requirements of a well-behaved general equilibrium model' (Jespersen 2009: 28).
6. As Dow points out (2002: 123–5), post-modernism thus justifies the new wave of liberalism and this results in a shift from demand management towards the privatization of public sector activity. It also validates the critique made by the rational expectations theory of the idea that government has superior access to knowledge that would warrant government activism.
7. For example, Jespersen (2009: 37–50) mentions a long list of weaknesses of Keynes. This book provides a very useful background analysis for this section.
8. The debate which has occurred since the publication of Akerlof and Shiller's 2009 book on animal spirits cannot be addressed here. For interesting comments, see e.g. Dow and Dow (2011).
9. This explains why the neo-modern stance advocates a macrofoundations perspective: this amounts to stressing the existence of irreducible systemic or institutional determinants of individual behaviour, so that one cannot derive conclusions about macro stability from micro analysis alone.
10. I cannot justify this claim here. For a more detailed argument see Togati 2012.

REFERENCES

Akerlof, G.A. and Shiller, R.J. (2009) *Animal Spirits: How Human Psychology Drives the Economy and Why It Matters for Global Capitalism*, Princeton: Princeton University Press.

Blanchard, O. and Fischer, S. (1989) *Lectures on Macroeconomics*, Cambridge, Mass. and London: MIT Press.

Boylan, T.A. and O'Gorman, P.F. (1995) *Beyond Rhetoric and Realism in Economics. Towards a Reformulation of Economic Methodology*, London: Routledge.

Caballero, R. (2010) 'Macroeconomics After The Crisis: Time To Deal With The Pretense-Of-Knowledge Syndrome', *Journal of Economic Perspectives*, 24 (4), Fall, 85–102.

Cullemberg, S., Amariglio, J. and Ruccio, D.F. (eds) (2001) *Post-modernism, Economics and Knowledge*, London: Routledge.

Davidson, P. (2009) *The Keynes Solution. The Path to Global Economic Prosperity*, London: Palgrave Macmillan.

Dow, S.C. (1991) 'Are there signs of postmodernism in economics?', *Methodus*, 3, 81–5.

Dow, S.C. (2001) 'Modernism and Postmodernism: A dialectical analysis', in S. Cullemberg, J. Amariglio and D.F. Ruccio (eds) *Post-modernism, Economics and Knowledge*, London: Routledge.

Dow, S.C. (2002) *Economic Methodology: An Inquiry*, Oxford: Oxford University Press.

Dow, A. and Dow, S.C. (2011) 'Animal Spirits Revisited', *Capitalism and Society*, 6 (2), 1–23.

Galbraith, J.K. (1996) 'Keynes, Einstein and Scientific Revolution', in P. Arestis (ed.) *Keynes, Money and the Open Economy*, Cheltenham UK and Northampton MA: Edward Elgar.

Jackson, W.A (2009) *Economics, Culture and Social Theory*, Cheltenham UK and Northampton MA: Edward Elgar.

Jameson, F. (1992) *Postmodernism, or The Cultural Logic of Late Capitalism*, London: Verso.

Jespersen, J. (2009) *Macroeconomic Methodology: A Post-Keynesian Perspective*, Cheltenham UK and Northampton MA: Edward Elgar.

Keynes, J.M. (1936) *The General Theory of Employment Interest and Money*, London: Macmillan.

Klaes M. (2006) 'Keynes between modernism and post-modernism', in R.E. Backhouse and B.W. Bateman, *The Cambridge Companion to Keynes*, Cambridge: Cambridge University Press.

Klamer, A. (1995) 'The conception of modernism in economics: Samuelson, Keynes and Harrod', in S. Dow and J. Hillard (eds) *Keynes, Knowledge and Uncertainty*, Cheltenham UK and Northampton MA: Edward Elgar.

Kumar, K. (1995) *From Post-Industrial to Post-modern Society. New Theories of the Contemporary World*, London: Routledge.

Lawson, T. (1997) *Economics and Reality*, London: Routledge.

Lyotard, J.F. (1984) 'Answering the Question: What is Postmodernism?', in *The Postmodern Condition. A Report on Knowledge*, Manchester: Manchester University Press.

McCloskey, D. (1986) *The Rhetoric of Economics*, Brighton: Wheatsheaf.
Phelps, E.S. (1990) *Seven Schools of Macroeconomic Thought*, Oxford: Clarendon Press.
Preston, P. (2001) *Reshaping Communications*, London: Sage.
Rodrik, D. (2003) 'Introduction', in D. Rodrick (ed.) *In Search of Prosperity: Analytic Narratives on Economic Growth*, Princeton. Princeton University Press
Ruccio, D.F. and Amariglio, J. (2006) *Postmodern Moments in Modern Economics*, Princeton: Princeton University Press.
Skidelsky, R. (2009) *Keynes: The Return of the Master*, London: Penguin Books, Allan Lane.
Taylor, L. (2010) *Maynard's Revenge: The Collapse of Free-Market Macroeconomics*, Harvard: Harvard University Press.
Togati, T.D. (1998) *Keynes and the Neoclassical Synthesis: Einsteinian versus Newtonian Macroeconomics*, London: Routledge.
Togati, T.D. (2001) 'Keynes as the Einstein of Economic Theory', *History of Political Economy*, 33 (1), Spring, 117–138.
Togati, T.D. (2006) *The New Economy and Macroeconomic Stability*: *A neomodern perspective drawing on the complexity approach and Keynesian economics*, London: Routledge.
Togati, T.D. (2012) 'Is there a Keynesian "True Model" of the Economy?', University of Turin, mimeo.

4. Keynes on method: is economics a moral science?

Michael Lainé

In the history of science, Galileo triggered a major breakthrough: by considering mathematics as nature's language, he wiped away the Aristotelian tradition, so far prevalent, according to which mathematics shaped the laws of the sole divine spheres. An enthusiastic proponent of his method, Kepler helped to spread the new scientific gospel. Nowadays, heaven is still on earth and the fact that mathematics is truth's language has become conventional wisdom. As a matter of fact, mainstream economics, buttressed by positivism, relies on an extensive use of mathematical modelling. Despite his mathematical skills, Keynes endorsed a dualist view: in a famous letter to Roy Harrod he put forth that economics should be regarded as a 'moral science', different from natural sciences. Since the main focus of his theories was on psychology and uncertainty, mathematics was of little help. The methodological outlines of *The General Theory* were expounded in Chapter 18, of paramount importance in Shackle's opinion (Sardoni 1989). In fact, owing to these conflicting views, economics has made little progress since the years of high theory, for mainstream is rather impervious to criticisms that do not grow out of the same epistemological ground. According to Lawson (2006), the remaining discrepancies between heterodoxy and mainstream only stem from an epistemological tenet, the latter relying on formal-deductive positivist methods, the former endorsing realism.

The aim of this chapter is threefold: 1) analyzing Keynes's stances on method and epistemology, 2) rebutting positivism, 3) proposing outlines of a general epistemology consistent with Keynes's views.

KEYNESIAN EPISTEMOLOGICAL REVOLUTION

Keynes's creeds could be found, either throughout *The General Theory*, or in Chapter 18. They are: an ontology based on radical uncertainty, safe generalization from experience, logical necessity, an organicist standpoint, a moral duty to fight unnecessary laws.

From Ontology to Epistemology

Keynes's epistemology (i.e. his theory of the limits and conditions of knowledge) stems from his ontology (i.e. his theory of the nature of the universe). His concept of radical uncertainty mixes both, but it should be emphasized that some of his epistemological stances stem from *a priori* ontological assumptions. 'The outstanding fact is the extreme precariousness of the basis of knowledge', he stated in the so-famous Chapter 12. Note the terms used: 'basis of knowledge', that is not knowledge herself but nature combined with our imperfect logical insights. 'Although nature has her habits, due to the recurrence of causes, they are general, not invariable.' (Keynes 1973 (henceforth *TP*): 402) In *TP*, Keynes castigated the standard probability theory for relying on the tacit ontological assumption that 'constant causes are always at work and assert themselves in the long run' (*TP*: 366), which was an egregious error for him. Nature is thus constantly altering (ontology) rendering it impossible to derive sound knowledge from observation (epistemology), a position well summarized by Davidson, who put forth that, according to Keynes, economics pertains to a non-ergodic world (i.e. unique and non-repetitive) (Davidson 1991, 1996).

Furthermore, Keynes warned in Chapter 18: 'we must not conclude that' there is something like 'the mean position thus determined by "natural" tendencies, namely, by those tendencies which are likely to persist' (*GT*: 229). Indeed, there is no such thing as laws of necessity as in natural science: 'The unimpeded rule of the above conditions is a fact of observation concerning the world as it is or has been, and not a necessary principle which cannot be changed' (*GT*: 229). Thus, economics has to put psychology at the very core of its analyses. 'Unlike the typical natural science, the material to which [economics] is applied is, in too many respects, not homogeneous through time', he wrote in a letter to Roy Harrod (Keynes 1987b: 296). He added: economics

> deals with introspection and with values. I might have added that it deals with motives, expectations, psychological uncertainties. One has to be constantly on guard against treating the material as constant and homogeneous. It is as though the fall of the apple to the ground depended on the apple's motives, on whether it is worth while falling to the ground, and whether the ground wanted the apple to fall, and on mistaken calculations on the part of the apple as to how far it was from the centre of the earth. (Keynes 1987b: 300)

Let's summarize Keynes's claims as to moral science (the old term for 'social science'), deriving from a radical uncertainty ontology: 1) the material is heterogeneous and constantly altering, 2) laws are unnecessary and non-natural, therefore, 3) there is room for human agency.

Safe Generalization from Experience

It was one of Chapter 18's most compelling pleas: one should rest on 'safe generalization from experience'. This might sound somewhat odd, to put it mildly, if not vague and confusing. What could a 'safe generalization' mean? And what would be the difference between a safe one and a normal one?

To find an answer to these questions, one should revert to the *Treatise on Probability* (TP). There, Keynes expounded his views on probability, considered as a branch of logic. Probability deals with uncertain, incomplete knowledge, allowing us to entertain a certain degree of rational belief. Thus, probability is not a question of degrees of truth, but rather of degrees of truth according to the knowledge at hand. Hence the term *'rational* belief', and not *mere* belief.

> The probability of the same statement varies with the evidence presented, which is, as it were, its origin of reference ... It would be as absurd to deny that an opinion *was* probable, when at a later stage certain objections have come to light, as to deny, when we have reached our destination, that it was ever three miles distant.(*TP*: 7–8).

Such probability stems from induction. Induction consists of inferring causes by observing consequences or, in other terms, to draw general conclusions on the basis of particular events. On the basis of observation, one is able to apprehend similarities and discrepancies (what Keynes called 'analogy'). Does the event or proposition currently at hand resemble one that occurred in the past? Is the basic question one is constantly trying to answer, whether consciously or not. The first step is to shape categories (e.g. 'eggs'). A category musters events or objects thanks to a certain number of common characteristics (e.g. 'shape', 'size', 'color', and so on). The second step consists of deriving a causality relation from those characteristics (e.g. 'the fact that eggs break has nothing to do with their size or color, but it is rather due to the very structure of its tiny envelope and to the laws of gravity'). The third is to multiply experiments ('pure induction'), so as to vary the circumstances (e.g. 'eggs break, no matter how high they fall'). Then, one is able to entertain some degrees of belief between a conclusion and a premise, that is, to make a 'safe' generalization. An inductive argument necessarily involves some synthetic *a priori* assumption, among which is the existence of a finite probability of a finite set of independent variables (labeled 'limited independent variety' by Keynes). There are two kinds of induction: universal and statistical (Bateman, 1990), the former being the probability that a general law or statement is correct (i.e. it is of a binary kind: true/false), the second pertaining to a frequency, 'asserting a characteristic of a *series* of proposition, rather than of a particular proposition' (*TP*: 444) – e.g. 'out of 100 such kind of investments, how many will fail?'

On his way from the *TP* to the *GT*, Keynes acknowledged to have evolved toward a subjectivist theory of probability (Keynes 2010), that is a theory of degrees of *mere* rather than rational belief. Thus, it has often been asserted that, to some extent, he abandoned the analyses expounded in *TP* (Bateman 1991; Davis 1994). But one should not overemphasize the changes in his thoughts, for the very core of his theory is left untouched (in his controversy with Tinbergen, he stressed that his thoughts on the topic remained consistent since *TP*): probability is a relation between a conclusion and a premise, whether the latter is true or not, and not a relation between two events. Therefore, there is little using probability or mathematics as a guide for action, as with the subjective expected utility theory. Recall that the latter theory, still prevalent nowadays in studies about rationality and decision-making, consists of multiplying quantitative probabilities by quantitative utility assessments with a view to maximizing such a result. Indeed, the flaws of such a theory are numerous: it does not heed the weight of arguments (later on, in *GT*, labeled 'state of confidence'), a comparison is often not possible, even just in respect of more or less, and it 'ignores the element of "risk" and assumes that an even chance of heaven or hell is precisely as much desired as a certain attainment of a state of mediocrity' (*TP*: 344).

Logical Necessity

'The possible contingencies are too numerous to be covered by a finite number of experiments, and *exact calculation is therefore out of the question*.' (*TP*: 402, author's emphasis)

Indeed, as O'Donnell accurately pointed out, for Keynes, mathematics is the servant and logic the master (O'Donnell 1990b). No wonder, then, that he would keep on castigating 'the mathematical charlatanry' (*TP*: 356) of those using 'pseudo-mathematics'. 'Too large a proportion of recent "mathematical" economics are merely concoctions . . . which allow the author to lose sight of the complexities and interdependencies of the real world in a maze of pretentious and unhelpful symbols.' (*GT*: 298)

The casual use of mathematics leads to a vicious circle. The scholars are then lured by aesthetic and virtuosic purposes and lose sight of reality. But the assumptions underlying models should be carefully considered, as well as the incommensurability of certain factors:

What place is allowed to non-numerical factors, such as inventions, politics, labor troubles, wars, earthquakes, financial crises? One feels a suspicion that the choice of factors is influenced (as is indeed only natural) by what statistics are available, and that many vital factors are ignored because they are statistically intractable or unprocurable. (Keynes 1987b: 287)

As a matter of fact, Keynes dubbed the nascent econometrics 'alchemy' in his controversy with Tinbergen, albeit he supported the inception of the Econometrics Society. But there is no contradiction here, for Keynes did not dismiss the use of mathematics; rather, he advocated a proper, limited use (given circumstances and radical uncertainty).

Relevance

From all this, it follows that economics is a moral science. 'The only purpose of (schematic equations) is to elucidate general ideas.' (Keynes 1987a: 484) Of course, one can use mathematics when it is appropriate, but one should not overlook reality. In fact, there are very few equations in *GT*. But the method expounded in Chapter 18 is not deprived of the least resemblance to that of natural science. It is undeniable that his distinguishing between given, independent and dependent variables is very much in tune with the methods of natural science: The aim is to peg some variables so as to be able to elucidate the role of a very few of them. Moreover, the very fact of putting forward some stabilizing factors, however unnecessary and unnatural, has some positive economics flavor. It is abundantly clear that one should use methods imported from natural science when it is possible, and rely on induction and logical necessity most of the time.

'The object of statistical study is not so much to fill in missing variables with a view to prediction, as to test the relevance and validity of the model.' (Keynes 1987b: 296) As a result, a model should explain events and social mechanisms. That's why even assumptions should be realistic (O'Donnell 1990a), and orthodoxy ran the gauntlet of criticism for failing in that respect:

> Our criticism of the accepted classical theory of economics has consisted not so much in finding logical flaws in its analysis as in pointing out that its tacit assumptions are seldom or never satisfied, with the result that it cannot solve the economic problems of the actual world. (*GT*: 346)

Here we must pause a little in order to consider the following controversial issue. Since a prominent scholar puts forth that, according to Keynes, logic supersedes experience, there would be no contending that he endorsed some kind of realism (Carabelli 1988; and also in this volume). In *TP*, Keynes supported the notion of 'logical induction' as opposed to 'mere induction', namely an induction process that does not abide by logical necessities. His endorsement of 'logical induction' does not make him a critic of realism, on the contrary, for realism is the result of such an induction. It is because we make many (more or less) logical inductions everyday that we are able to entertain some sense of realism, so that realism is a form of knowledge. In Keynes's sense, logic is always logic about the world, and not logic without the world. Consequently, there is no making any hierarchy between logic and experience, since both are vital. If Keynes did not think that way, the previous quote would not be understandable. Moreover, one can find a plea for not making any hierarchy between logic and experience in a letter to Harrod: 'The specialist in the manufacture of models will not be successful unless he is constantly correcting his judgment by *intimate and messy acquaintance with the facts* to which his model has to be applied' (Keynes 1987b: 300, author's emphasis). If I may, I would like to make a point as to a possible misconception of Carabelli. She wrote:

In Keynes's view, the elements which gave 'strength' (or 'value' or 'force') to inductive arguments, therefore furnishing them with high probability, were the logical ones, prior to the mere counting of instances. In inductive procedure, the first step was actually the grasping of the qualitative likeness and non-likeness. (Carabelli 1988)

There might be two sources of confusion here. First, experience does not amount to 'mere counting of instances'. Second, judgments of likeness are empirical in nature! One cannot 'grasp the qualitative likeness' of a given object without *observing* it, without trusting to some extent one's senses. For example, the following empirical questions are vital in making a comparison: does the object *actually* have the same shape, colour, or size? Of course, the answer to such question cannot be merely empirical, for it rests *also* on logical assumptions, but it cannot depend on any hierarchy either. Neither logic nor experience can prevail over each other, for they both collapse if one of them turns out to be unsound.

Organicism

Yet there might well be quite different laws for wholes of different degrees of complexity, and laws of connection between complexes which could not be stated in terms of laws connecting individual parts. In this case natural law would be organic and not, as it is generally supposed, atomic. (*TP*: 277)

No doubt that some macro variables of *GT* are not the aggregation of micro ones. For example, effective demand, even if it could be said to have a micro basis (Torr 1981), for the cost of a single entrepreneur is the income of her employees, so that slashed cuts could imply dwindling

revenues as a whole. It should be obvious that state of confidence and conventions are sheer macroeconomic phenomena, since their inception and
momentum is not really a question of individual behaviour. Apart from
this, there are pure microeconomic concepts, such as animal spirits and
liquidity preference, for instance. Thus, macroeconomics has methods and
laws of its own, as microeconomics, and the former is not the aggregation
of social atoms.

Social Philosophy

Although his remarks on the dualism issue were scant in his academic
work, it is safe enough to assert that he rejected the divide between positive and normative economics. Minsky held that Keynes was 'a political
animal throughout his life' (Minsky 2008: 160). Politics, or ethics, was at
the bottom of things. What Keynes dubbed 'social philosophy' in the last
chapter of *GT* is nothing less than the goals ascribed to economic policy.
It should be obvious that, according to him, a scientific stance is entangled
with a moral or ethical commitment. Keynes set two issues to be addressed
by economists: full employment and a less unequal distribution of wealth.
Economics cannot be severed from social philosophy, for its very aim is to
provide tools for action. As early as the first chapter of *GT*, Keynes chas-
tises 'classical economics' not only for being flawed, but for the fact that
'its teaching is misleading and disastrous if we attempt to apply it to the
facts of experience' (*GT*: 3). Put differently, the policies it advocates are
bound to fail. The very name of his masterpiece is a political agenda, and
it is the whole architecture of the book which is devised so as to explain
and solve unemployment.

In fact, throughout his life, he more readily portrayed himself as a
'publicist', rather than an economist. No wonder, then, that the acclaimed
book of Dostaler on his work starts with his ethics (Dostaler 2005).
According to him, ethics lied at the very gist of marginalism, a point he put
forward in his biography of Edgeworth: 'How far the initial assumptions
of the marginal theory stand or fall with the utilitarian ethics and the utilitarian psychology' (Keynes 2010: 260). In 'Economic Perspectives for our
Grand Children', he makes it clear that he wants to get rid of the alleged
'economic problem', i.e. the 'struggle for subsistence', so that mankind
may be able to focus on 'real values': 'live wisely, agreeably and well'.

Finally, it might be up to a point misleading to regard Keynes as a
typical dualism proponent of the 19th century. Albeit he has been, to a
certain extent, swayed by Cambridgians such as Marshall and his father
(Gruchy 1949), it is nonetheless undeniable that his epistemology has
salient features of its own. The fact that his epistemology stems from his

ontology, his views on induction and human agency give his philosophy a specific flavour, palatable to the modern critical realist line of thinking of, say, Roy Bhaskar (Bhaskar 2008). Dualism views were under attack soon after Keynes's death. The works of Popper, although he defined himself as a 'critical rationalist', and Friedman gave rise to a revival of positivism.

AGAINST POSITIVE AND POPPERIAN ECONOMICS

Keynes was poles apart from positivism, or any tenet that would discard the 'moral science' nature of economics. According to Boland, there are four strands of positive economics (Boland 1991). 'Chicago positivism' is influenced by Friedman, whereas 'LSE positivism' has been marked by the seminal work of Popper. The 'MIT positivism', founded by Samuelson, is said to be the loosest, since it only aims at developing models that are 'potentially refutable', without much emphasis on empirical evidence. As for experimental economics, or 'Harvard positivism', save for the fact that it strives to create a world akin to neo-classical theories in a laboratory, it has a lot in common with the other strands. I will mainly focus on Friedman's instrumentalism and Popperianism, because of their being the two most influential economics methodologists ever (Hausman 2008). I conflate them, whereas one might contend that it is controversial. My basic claim here is that, although they both endorse falsifiability, Friedman put his analyses one step further: Popper held that there is no choosing between non-falsified theories and that the question is almost irrelevant; for Friedman, since there only exists a method of disproof, there remains too many competing non-falsified theories, so that one should decide between them with regard to their predictions and not their explanatory power or realism. In this regard, some assumptions appear to be less falsified than the others. Since the method designed to test theories cannot be too precise lest all theories should be discarded, the door is open to interpretation. Somehow, one might argue that Friedman's positivism was more consistent than Popperianism. But one should not exaggerate this discrepancy, for Popper endorsed also a conventionalist view as to basic empirical observations (Boylan and O'Gorman 2008), which seriously mitigates his falsificationism: 'But if it is permissible to include background knowledge among one's premises in order to make conventional *falsifications* possible, then one also makes conventional *verifications* possible' (Hausman 1992: 185). In fact, and despite this narrower scope, both strands share common features. Let's summarize them: falsifiability, deduction (induction is a pseudo-problem), discovery/ justification contexts dichotomy, prediction, independence of any ethical position, individualism. Neither Positivism nor Popperianism can be a valid epistemology for post-Keynesians. My criticisms will hinge around four headings: 1) it is self-defeating; 2) the induction problem should be taken seriously; 3) individualism is a value more than a scientific result; 4) hypothesis and test cannot be independent and realism of assumptions matter.

Self-defeating

'Factual evidence can never "prove" a hypothesis; it can only fail to disprove it', asserts Friedman (Friedman 1953: 8). One cannot conclude from the fact that the sun has always risen that it will rise again tomorrow. It would suffice of one single morning to shatter all certainty. As our experience is finite, facts cannot confirm theories, for we have no guarantee that future will be like the past. Consequently, one should not aim at proving anything, the argument goes, but at testing the resilience of a model. Therefore, if a model or hypothesis cannot be shown to be false, it should be ruled out.

As Hilary Putnam aptly pointed out, falsifiability is self-defeating (Putnam 1981). That is, falsifiability, itself, is not falsifiable. It is a posit. Why should one accept it? There is no decisive argument here. If falsifiability were the alpha and omega of truth, then one should discard the theory, because one is not able to test it. In order to do so, one should take all the theories known to be true and test them on the basis of each and every epistemological theory, but how could we ascertain that a theory is true prior to any method?

Besides, by expatiating upon epistemology one necessarily uses language and arguments outside of the method thereafter expounded. Indeed, it is precisely this kind of argument that succeeds in or fails to convince the reader. To devise epistemology is to rely on an innate ability toward rationality. Put differently: why would anyone spend a single second of one's time writing papers or books if one does not believe that one could be properly understood, at least by some readers? Philosophy or any social science necessarily rests on twin assumptions, prior to any content or statement: Rationality is real, reality is rational.

Absolute skeptics, like Pyrrho, do not bother to write books for, according to them, truth is impossible to grasp (Hadot 1995). Thus, do we need something like an epistemological theory or, put more accurately, can such a theory depart from actual rationality? Falsifiability cannot be said to lie at the very roots of truth, for it would be a contradiction in terms; one has no choice but to acknowledge layman rationality, however limited and unsatisfactory it may appear to be, for grasping truth is a question of good reasoning and not a question of technique or prior theory. This should not be taken to mean that one does not need concepts or theories so as to come closer to the truth, but that, eventually, *they* do not entail conviction.

The Induction Problem

So, it should be asked, what is rationality, then? Apart from the formal rules of consistency (Hacking 1975) and *tertium non datur* (Castel 2000; Kant 2000), one should revert to Keynes's views on induction. According to Popperians, there is nothing but deduction, induction being a misplaced word for describing the same phenomenon (Blaug 1992). It is entirely consistent with the whole theory, for it also distinguishes between a context of discovery and a context of justification, the line of demarcation between science and non-science resting on the latter. I would like to argue, if I may, that the induction problem might be misconceived of by Popperians. They contend that 'in the strict logical sense', induction is 'an argument that employs premises containing information about some members of a class in order to support a generalization about the whole class, thus including some unexamined members of the class' (Blaug 1992: 16). Thus defined, one could wonder whether induction is different from deduction; after all, a deductive argument draws conclusions out of premises. But induction does not stem from premises, rather it stems from observation, from a mix of what Keynes dubbed 'analogy' and 'pure induction'. Such terms should not confuse us. Induction is obtained by means of judgments of similarity: one compares the likeness of a certain object, e.g. 'swans' ('analogy', or 'positive analogy'), with the differences in the same object ('pure induction', or 'negative analogy'). If one has wholly characterized an object (i.e. there is no difference in the features of the numerous objects or phenomena examined), then one draws a universal induction (e.g. 'all swans are white'); otherwise, it should be called a statistical induction (e.g. 'most swans are white'). As Keynes made clear, since one cannot know, prior to any experience, how many relevant features comprise a particular object, one should make as many observations as possible ('pure induction') in order to be sure that there is no variation (*TP*: Chapters 18–22). (Otherwise, provided that the variations are of a regular sort, we pass from a universal induction to a statistical one.) Induction then consists of the very moment when the 'generalization' crops up in the mind of the observer. Hence, 'pure induction' is aimed at proving 'analogy' wrong or right, to test it, so to speak. Were it not confusing, we would maintain that 'pure induction' is tantamount to deduction, save for it is not opposed to induction, since it is part of it. Thus, it would seem that there is but one system of reasoning, deduction being the continuation of induction with other means. Testing a model is only a matter of increasing 'pure induction'. Scientific method is superior to the methods of laypeople in that it tries to control the variables or features comprising an object (exogenous variables) so as to observe the actual effect of one or a very few of them on the others (the endogenous variables). But both rely basically on the same reasoning:

> The first introduction of iron ploughshares into Poland . . . having been followed by a succession of bad harvests, the farmers attributed the badness of the crops to the iron ploughshares, and discarded them for the old wooden ones. The method of reasoning of the farmers is not different from that of science. (*TP*: 273)

Of course, no factual 'truth' can have a probability (defined as a degree of rational belief) of 1, for the number of our experiments can only be finite and constant causes are not always at work. There is nothing but knowledge by argument. But, also, there is no ruling induction out.

Of course, positivists would strongly disagree with such statements. 'Without waiting, passively, for repetitions to impress or impose regularities upon us, we actively try to impose regularities upon the world', asserts Popper (2002: 60). Since some people make generalizations on the basis of a unique experience, and since observations are theory-laden, he holds that there is no such thing as induction. The only existing method is that of trial and error, he contends. 'The problem "Which comes first, the hypothesis (H) or the observation (O)," is soluble; as is the problem, "Which comes first, the hen (H) or the egg (O)". The reply to the latter is, "An earlier kind of egg"; to the former, "An earlier kind of hypothesis"' (Popper 2002: 62): This is a somewhat questionable argument. For the world always spills over our mental outfit; imagination has limits which only reality can go beyond. Observations are made ex-post outside the topics we intended to investigate ex-ante. The possibility of surprise does not only regard our expectations *per se*, but the kind of subject upon which we can form expectations. If it were the hypothesis that comes first, how could we have other topics of interest?

Individualism: Value or Method?

Because individuals comprise society, it could seem somewhat obvious to take individuals as the subject matter of social science. But how should we know, then, that society has no rule or regularity of its own? After all, in natural science, atoms comprise animals, but it would be preposterous to hold that a laughing animal is composed of a bunch of laughing atoms (Passet 2000). Nonetheless, positivists have decided to rule out organicism or holism, with the qualification that social phenomena are the unintended result of intentional human actions (Popper 1991). By thus narrowing the scope of our research, don't we maim truth? Why should we forbid ourselves from entering such territories? The argument goes that there should be no black box, that is, science should refer to reasons and not to causes. 'There is no postulating the existence of hidden forces, whether *psychological, biological* or *cultural*, in order to explain collective beliefs' (Boudon 2003: 63). In fact, 'one should . . . make do with ordinary psychology, the kind of psychology we use in everyday life . . .: the sole to be able to legitimately persuade' (Boudon 2007: 129). Hence, scientists should focus on the 'conscious or semi-conscious reasons' individuals ascribe to themselves. These need not be the actual reasons, but rather the understandable reasons 'that could, in all likelihood, be ascribed to an ideal-type actor' (Boudon 2003: 67). Thus, one is able to reconcile Popper's explicit rejection of psychologism with individualism. Still, the question holds: Why should this be the case? Boudon replies: because it is unnecessary to assume another explanation. Which, in turn, begs the unanswered questions: why should necessity be a sound method to grasp the truth? And how is it different from confirmation, or, put differently, is it still falsifiability? One can't help but conclude that 'methodology is normative' (Udehn 2002).

Can Hypotheses and Tests be Independent?

'The only relevant test of the *validity* of a hypothesis is comparison of its predictions with experience', asserts Friedman (1953: 8–9). But his claims are even bolder than that, since he boasts: 'the more significant the theory, the more unrealistic the assumptions' (1953: 14). Indeed, 'A hypothesis is important if it "explains" much by little' (1953: 14), but it does not follow that it *must* be all the more unrealistic. Thus, Friedman casually discards the cumulativity of knowledge: 'realism' can be the outcome of the testing of many models and theories. Of course, some widely accepted theories might happen to be wrong or misleading, so that one should not refrain oneself from testing hypotheses that depart from them, but it does not entail that one must *always* do that. If science always started from scratch with a change in paradigm, we would know very little about our world. Sometimes, we cannot do 'as if' the assumption to be tested is correct, for our knowledge tells us that it is blatantly false. Popper would have been at odds with Friedman, for he maintained that there can be growth of knowledge (Popper 1989).

Furthermore, the tests are already theory-laden. It appears somewhat questionable to simply rely on a test. Take, for instance, the only example put forward by Friedman in his famous paper. The debatable hypothesis ('enterprises maximize profits') is substantiated by an even more debatable 'test' (there is a natural selection, and survival is only about profit). There is no test, here, but only a ventriloquist theory that is mistaken for an oracle. Indeed, evidence is understood differently depending on the paradigm (Kuhn 1970).

Moreover, in their everyday practice, scientists cannot possibly behave as Popperians or positivists. They have to rely on realism, otherwise they would waste a considerable amount of time. If realism did not matter, then one should test each and every idea that comes through one's mind, haphazardly, most of which would appear totally irrelevant. As Hilary Putnam pointed out with humor, a positivist or Popperian should put his head in a bag and kick it on the table a hundred times to see if, in the end, a devil will pop up (Putnam 1981).

We might wonder, with a famous Popperian, whether mainstream positivist economics is 'playing tennis with the net down' (Blaug 1992: 241). In fact, many theories are non-falsifiable. The plea for unrealistic hypotheses staves off any criticism as to the models devised. And, if results are not conclusive, its proponents see it as an incentive to improve existing models, and not stamp them out. In nowadays econometrics, many models imply theory-laden tests (Cahuc and Zylberberg 2005, 2009). Thus, it is rather unclear whether Popperianism could, in principle, do the job, since it 'is hard to practice in economics: any hypothesis is subject to other things being held constant and these other things are numerous and not always well specified . . .; to test a theory, we must construct a model of the theory and, unfortunately, the same theory may be represented by a variety of models.' (Blaug 1992: xiv) Falsifiability is ambiguous, to put it mildly. If, say, a model predicts that the unemployment rate is 9.2 percent whereas the actual rate is 9.1 percent, should the underlying theory be discarded? When is it sensible to consider it falsified? In that, it might appear that falsifiability is, itself, an 'ad-hoc auxiliary assumptions', an 'immunizing stratagem' (Popper 1972, 2002).

OUTLINES OF A GENERAL EPISTEMOLOGY

Since positivism is mainstream's creed, many post-Keynesians, if not the great bulk of them, following in Keynes's footsteps, have endorsed one version or another of realism, whether 'comprehensive' (Davidson 1994), critical (Lawson 1997, 2003; Lee 2002), or Babylonian (Dow 2001). The views expounded hereafter, however sympathetic they are to such works, differ in some respects. The outlines of a general epistemology I would like to put forward hinge around four headings: 1) ontology, 2) psychology, 3) thick ethical concepts and values, 4) human agency.

From Radical Uncertainty to Social Science

Roy Bhaskar contends that positivism's claims are synonymous with 'dissolution of ontology' (Bhaskar 1998). As a matter of fact, ontology should be put first, for there is no way of ascertaining 'the actuality of causal laws' (Bhaskar 1998). This was precisely Keynes's point, whose epistemology stems from his ontology of radical uncertainty. Economics deals with psychological uncertainties, expectations and values of business men, their animal spirits, and not so much with calculus and certain knowledge. Everything is subject to change, because our senses are not adjusted to the world, nor is our intellect. Intricacies are too numerous, the world is constantly shifting . . . Natural science laws are much more invariable. Fewer parameters come into play . . .

Psychology as an Irreducible Unobservable

The method of natural science is to reduce the number of unobservables. The ideal case is the one in which there is only one unobservable. Of course, this seldom happens. Thus, according to the Duhem-Quine thesis, it is impossible to test an isolate hypothesis, because each assumption involves a background of related, auxiliary hypotheses. This does not entail, as it is sometimes asserted, that there is an infinite regression: so long as we are able to define auxiliary observables, it could be the case that, for example, we have four unknown variables in four or more equations system.

Of course, one should be constantly on guard against overemphasizing the discrepancies between natural and social science. In an ant or robot society, methods would be on a par with that of natural sciences (Yildizoglu 2003; Nelson and Winter 1982). Since humans have imagination, bounded rationality and free-will, things might be different. There is no denying that the human brain causes action. But human thoughts are sealed; one cannot percolate nor penetrate them. Each being is the sole witness of his thoughts. Of course, some of them are visible, but deception, self-deception, misconception are always possible. In social science, there is always, at least, one more observable than in its natural counterpart: psychology. As there are many unobservables that come into play, the Duhem-Quine thesis all the more applies. One is not able to test hypotheses in the positivist or Popperian sense.

Thick Ethical Concepts and Values as Shortcuts

'Positive economics is in principle independent of any particular ethical position or normative judgments' asserts a typical positivist, aka Friedman (1953: 4). In fact, positivists take a firm stance against those who intervene in public affairs. They point out that science has, or at least should have, nothing to do with ethics or values. Very often, their stand is underpinned by appeals to Weber's *Wertfreiheit*, or 'axiological neutrality' (Weber 1965, 1989). In fact, Weber did not contend that scientists should shy away from taking any stance as to public affairs; he himself contributed to the Weimar constitution, and was a prominent member of the Liberal party. Rather, he argued that one should not use it with students, because the struggle is then unequal (Kalinowski 2005): 'To the prophet and the demagogue, it is said: "Go your ways out into the streets and speak openly to the world", that is, where criticism is possible.' (Weber 1989: 21)

Hilary Putnam has shown that science rests on epistemic values (Putnam 1981). For example, when we utter so plain a sentence such as 'The cat is on the doormat', values are involved. We have a 'cat' category, because we think that the distinction between animals and non-animals is *important*. We find it relevant to have a 'doormat' category, because we deem it *interesting* to distinguish artifacts from non-artifacts, and also because we believe it *valuable* to know the nature and function of such artifacts. We have a category 'on', because we surmise it *crucial* to have spatial categories . . . The fact/value dichotomy should be put to an end. There is no neutral language in social science. What Putnam dubs 'thick ethical concepts' are rife (Putnam 2002). Facts and values are entangled, and there is no severing a neutral, descriptive element from a value-ridden element in such adjectives. For instance, the words 'cruel', 'stiff', 'inflexible', 'stubborn', 'firm', 'resolute', 'courageous' could be ascribed to the same policy or person. Why should one cull one of them and disregard the others? Although they can be said to pertain to the same phenomena, they have not the same value content. In fact, none has a neutral content in this regard. At various degrees, 'cruel', 'inflexible', 'stubborn' and 'stiff' have a derogatory flavor, whereas 'firm', 'resolute' and 'courageous' rather have a laudatory flavour. Indeed, their value content is part and parcel of the words themselves. Even apparently scientific concepts such as 'unemployment' are not stripped of any value content. Whether one uses the ILO or the French INSEE standard, the results are not the same. The former tends to improve the image of market-friendly policies, the latter tends to enhance administration interventions and the alleged 'market rigidities'.

Furthermore, I would contend that values are shortcuts towards truth. Action implies pace, and individuals need shortcuts to be able to find their bearings. They lack time to compute all available information. Like Janus, values have two faces: they set goals, and means. They are a guide for action. In fact, means and ends are closely interwoven. What is a means to a specific end can be an end implying another means, in an almost infinite regress. For instance, if an enterprise is to maximize profits (end), it is to invest in China (means). But it could be that it has not invested any sum yet, so that it is also an end to invest in China. For the purpose at hand, it should then study the market (means), which in turn, turns out to be another goal, implying that it hires a pundit or uses the services of a firm specializing in investments in China, or both, or even that it forms a new alliance with other interested companies, since it lacks the cultural expertise that would ensure the success of its plan, and so on. Values can be taught or acquired by immersion (Bourdieu 1980, 1997), but they can also be the result of quick inductive reasoning. The precise role of values in scientific reasoning needs more inquiry, but it appears possible that assumptions, as well as choices of scientific paradigms, or even tests and conclusions drawn from them, may well be influenced by them.

Human Agency

As Keynes accurately pointed out, in natural science, it does not depend on the apple's motives or beliefs to fall onto the ground. A natural law is a necessary cause, and it applies so long as the law itself does not change. Law is universal, and human beings cannot bend it. With social atoms, the situation is quite different. Freedom accounts for human agency. Even if there were no radical uncertainty, people could choose to act regardless of the rules, or bend them. Freedom implies unpredictability. Consciousness makes it possible to alter social laws, at least in part. To illustrate human agency, one could consider the following market paradox. Suppose that one day someone finds the true mathematical model of stock markets. Suppose also that every investor can afford to purchase or copy such a model. Everyone would be able to predict, without mistake, the future indexes of the market. As a result, markets would collapse. Except for the cases of dire need, nobody would be willing to trade. Disagreement is what makes the market possible; if there is genuine consensus, why should one buy at 100 today a stock that is bound to be valued 105 tomorrow? Various (very high) discount rates would be an ad hoc hypothesis, or what Popper would have dubbed an 'immunizing stratagem'. The paradox holds. No one would accept such situation. Then, everyone would be spurred to evade from the variables of the model, to make it obsolete by following other, unpredictable behaviours. By the sole fact that it is true, it is bound to become false.

CONCLUSION?

It appears that positivism or Popperianism is a potent rhetorical tool to dismiss opponents' arguments. For the last decades, empirical, qualitative studies have been either discarded as 'non-scientific', or frowned upon. No doubt that Keynes, had he been alive today, would be the object of much scorn. Another revolution, like the one ignited by Lord Keynes, would be impossible today.

As a matter of fact, most post-Keynesians endorse a realist epistemology. It is worth noticing that critical realism departs from the principles expounded here in that it advocates monism (Bhaskar 2008). Such discrepancy might be ascribed to the non-acknowledgement of thick ethical concepts and to the playing down of values in scientific reasoning. Still, it constitutes a sound basis upon which to build a genuinely Keynesian theoretical framework.

REFERENCES

Bateman, B. (1990) 'Keynes, Induction and Econometrics', *History of Political Economy*, 22, 359–79.

Bateman, B. (1991) 'Das Maynard Keynes Problem', *Cambridge Journal of Economics*, 15(1), 101–111.

Bhaskar, R. (1998[1979]) *The Possibility of Naturalism*, London: Routledge.

Bhaskar, R. (2008) *A Realist Theory of Science*, London: Routledge.

Blaug, M. (1992) *Economic Methodology*, Cambridge: Cambridge University Press.

Boland, L. (1991) 'Current views on economic positivism', in David Greenaway, Michael Bleaney and Ian Stewart (eds) *Companion to Contemporary Economic Thought*, London: Routledge, 88–104.

Boudon, R. (2003) *Raisons, bonnes raisons*, Paris: PUF.

Boudon, R. (2007) *Essais sur la théorie générale de la rationalité*, Paris: PUF.

Bourdieu, P. (1980) *Le Sens pratique*, Paris: Minuit.

Bourdieu, P. (1997) *Méditations pascaliennes*, Paris: Le Seuil.

Boylan, T. and O'Gorman, P. (2008) *Popper & Economic Methodology*, London: Routledge.

Cahuc, P. and Zylberberg, A. (2005) *Le Chômage : fatalité ou nécessité?*, Paris: Flammarion.

Cahuc, P. and Zylberberg, A. (2009) *Les Réformes ratées du président Sarkozy*, Paris: Flammarion.

Carabelli, A. (1988) *On Keynes's Method*, London: MacMillan.

Castel, P.-H. (2000) 'La Vérité', in D. Kambouchner (ed.) *Notions de philosophie*: 1, Paris: Gallimard.

Davidson, P. (1991) 'Is Probability Theory Relevant for Uncertainty? A Post-Keynesian Perspective', *Journal of Economic Perspectives*, 5.

Davidson, P. (1994) *Post Keynesian Macroeconomic Theory: A Foundation for*

Successful Economic Policies for the Twenty-First Century, Cheltenham UK and Northampton MA: Edward Elgar.

Davidson, P. (1996) 'Reality and Economic Theory', *Journal of Post Keynesian Economics*, (18)4, 479–508.

Davis, J. (1994) *Keynes's Philosophical Development*, New York: Cambridge University Press.

Dostaler, G. (2005) *Keynes et ses combats*, Paris: Albin Michel.

Dow, S. (2001) 'Post Keynesian Methodology', in R. Holt and S. Pressman (eds) *A New Guide to Post Keynesian Economics*, London: Routledge, 11–20.

Friedman, M. (1953) 'The Methodology of Positive Economics', in *Essays in Positive Economics*, Chicago: University of Chicago Press, 3–43.

Gruchy, A. (1949) 'J. M. Keynes' Concept of Economic Science', *The Southern Economic Journal*, (XV)3, January.

Hacking, I. (1975) *The Emergence of Probability*, Cambridge: Cambridge University Press.

Hadot, P. (1995) *Qu'est-ce que la philosophie antique ?*, Paris: Gallimard.

Hausman, D. (1992) *The Inexact and Separate Science of Economics*, Cambridge: Cambridge University Press.

Hausman, D. (2008) 'Philosophy of Economics', *Stanford Encyclopedia of Philosophy*, available at http://plato.stanford.edu/entries/economics/ (last accessed January 2011).

Kalinowski, I. (2005) 'Leçons webériennes sur la science et la propagande', in M. Weber, *La Science, profession & vocation*, Marseille: Agone.

Kant, I. (2000[1800]) *Logique*, Paris: Vrin.

Keynes, J.M. (1973[1921]) *A Treatise on Probability*. London: MacMillan.

Keynes, J.M. (1978[1936]) *The General Theory of Employment, Interest and Money*. London: MacMillan.

Keynes, J.M. (1987a[1973]) *Collected Writings, XIII, The General Theory and After: A Preparation*, London: MacMillan.

Keynes, J.M. (1987b[1973]) *Collected Writings, XIV, Defense and Development*, London: MacMillan.

Keynes, J.M. (2010[1972]) *Collected Writings, X, Essays in Biography*, London: MacMillan.

Kuhn, T. (1970[1962]) *The Structure of Scientific Revolutions*, Chicago: University of Chicago Press.

Lawson, T. (1997) *Economics & Reality*, London: Routledge.

Lawson, T. (2003) *Reorienting Economics*, London: Routledge.

Lawson, T. (2006) 'The Nature of Heterodox Economics', *Cambridge Journal of Economics*, 30(4), 483–505.

Lee, F. (2002) 'Theory Creation & the Methodological Foundation of Post Keynesian Economics', *Cambridge Journal of Economics*, 26(4), 789–804.

Minsky, H. (2008[1975]) *John Maynard Keynes*, New York: McGraw.

Nelson, R. and Winter, S. (1982) *An Evolutionary Theory of Economic Change*, Cambridge, MA: Harvard University Press.

O'Donnell, R. (1990a) 'The Epistemology of J.M. Keynes', *British Journal for the Philosophy of Science*, 41, 333–350.

O'Donnell, R. (1990b) 'Keynes on Mathematics: Philosophical Foundations and Economic Applications', *Cambridge Journal of Economics*, 14(1), 29–47.

Passet, R. (2000) *L'Illusion néo-libérale*, Paris: Fayard.

Popper, K. (1957) 'Philosophy of Science: a Personal Report', in C.A. Mace (ed.) *British Philosophy in Mid-Century*, London: MacMillan.

Popper, K. (1972) *Objective Knowledge*, Oxford: Oxford University Press.

Popper, K. (1989[(1963]) *Conjectures and Refutation: The Growth of Scientific Knowledge*, London: Routledge.

Popper, K. (1991[1957]) *Poverty of Historicism*, London: Routledge.

Popper, K. (2002[1976]) *Unended Quest: An Intellectual Biography*, London: Routledge.

Putnam, H. (1981) *Reason, Truth, and History*, Cambridge: Cambridge University Press.

Putnam, H. (2002) *The Collapse of the Fact/Value Dichotomy and Other Essays*, Cambridge: Harvard University Press.

Sardoni, C. (1989) 'Chapter 18 of the General Theory: Its Methodological Importance', *Journal of Post Keynesian Economics*, 12(2), 293–307.

Torr, C. (1981) 'Microfoundations for Keynes's Point of Effective Demand', *South African Journal of Economics*, 49(4), 334–348.

Udehn, L. (2002) 'The Changing Face of Methodological Individualism', *Annual Review of Sociology*, 28, 479–507.

Weber, M. (1965) *Essais sur la théorie de la science*, Paris: Plon.

Weber, M. (1989[1919]) *Science as a Vocation*, London: Routledge.

Yildizoglu, M. (2003) *Introduction à la théorie des jeux*, Paris: Dunod.

5. A new methodological approach to economic theory: what I have learnt from 30 years of research on Keynes

Anna Carabelli

INTRODUCTION

As any scholar knows, 30 years are certainly not enough, in modern times, to acquire a complete understanding of a topic such as economics or even one of its branches. Now I am perfectly aware that they are insufficient even for claiming a mastery of one of the heroes of economics, or at least of one of its main heroes, namely John Maynard Keynes, to whom I have devoted so much of my academic life. But I also know, now, that this owes much to Keynes's peculiar vision of economics; and that learning from Keynes is, to a relevant extent, learning about economics itself. And I guess that if a true epistemologic revolution has not occurred in economic theory after Keynes, this is because Keynes had come to develop a complexity approach to economics, one which regards economics as essentially a method to cope with the complexity of the economic material, which cannot be even partially grasped if adopting the lens of the mainstream of the discipline. What follows is a bird's-eye view of Keynes's attempted methodological revolution in economics as I came to understand it throughout 30 years of research; of what I have learnt, in other words, working on the *Treatise on Probability* (hereafter: *TP*) as Keynes's 'essay on method' and focusing on the consistency between such methodological positions and Keynes's economic writings, notwithstanding varying circumstances and changing theories.

ECONOMIC THEORY AS A METHOD: A NEW WAY OF REASONING IN ECONOMICS

The first, and most important thing I have learnt from my research is that Keynes's economic theory is more precisely, and truly, a method, and a logic, a new way of reasoning in economics, wherein form and content are not independent entities (Carabelli 1988). Here is Keynes speaking of economics:

> It seems to me that economics is a branch of logic, a way of thinking; and that you do not repel sufficiently firmly attempts . . . to turn it into a pseudo-natural-science. (Letter to Harrod, July 4, 1938; *The Collected Writings of John Maynard Keynes* (hereafter: *CW*), Vol. 14: 296)

> The theory of economics does not furnish a body of settled conclusions immediately applicable to policy. It is a method rather than a doctrine, which helps its possessor to draw correct conclusions. (*CW* 12: 151)

> The object of our analysis is, not to provide a machine, or method of blind manipulation, which will furnish an infallible answer, but to provide ourselves with an organised and orderly method of thinking out particular problems. (*CW* 7: 297)

Keynes's method is best described as an apparatus of probable reasoning, where the term 'probable' refers to the logical conception of probability he exposed in *TP*. Probable reasoning is therefore a non-demonstrative organized way of thinking, which however cannot furnish infallible answers nor settled conclusions. Keynes's theory of economics is in fact non-positivistic: it consists in a method of analysis, which necessarily requires readers' involvement. Readers are also called upon to follow Keynes in his 'further analysis' of the economic material. Keynes's is in fact an open-end theory shaped by an open system of thought. In Keynes's economics, there are no theoretical limits to 'further analysis': all closures are provisional, and the list of probable repercussions is never complete.

The *General Theory* (*GT*) provides a perfect illustration of such an open-end theory produced by an equally open system of thought. Chapter 18 of Keynes's magnum opus is conceived by the author as a guide for its reading (see Carabelli and Cedrini 2011b). Having offered, in Chapters 1 to 17, provisional conclusions 'by isolating the complicating factors one by one' (that is using *ceteris paribus* and conditions of independence: see Chick 2004; Chick and Dow 2001; Jespersen 2008), Keynes makes explicit, in Chapter 18, the assumptions of independence he had tacitly introduced in the previous chapters, so as to open the way for the analysis, in Chapters 19 to 21, of the 'probable interactions of the factors amongst themselves', that is between (previously taken as) independent variables. He thereby shows that when using the concept of 'independence', he is in truth employing a notion of 'independence for knowledge': the causal relations he referred to in Chapter 18 while summarizing *GT* up to Chapter 17 are in truth to be regarded as logical connections between arguments rather than material connections between events. In Chapters 19 to 21, Keynes deals with roundabout repercussions and the consequences of removing simplifying assumptions. In Chapter 19, in particular, Keynes applies his own method of analysis to answering the following questions:

> Does a reduction in money-wages have a direct tendency, *cet. par.*, to increase employment, '*cet. par.*' being taken to mean that the propensity to consume, the schedule of the marginal efficiency of capital and the rate of interest are the same as before for the community as a whole? And does a reduction in money-wages have a certain or probable tendency to affect employment in a particular direction through its certain or probable repercussions on these three factors? (*CW* 7: 260)

He then lists seven 'probable' roundabout 'repercussions', showing that variables previously taken as independent for the analysis (e.g. the propensity to consume) may in effect alter the provisional conclusions he had reached before removing these assumptions:

> 1. reduction in money-wages may diminish the propensity to consume *via* reduction of prices and consequent redistribution of real income from wage-earners to other factors of the production, and from entrepreneurs to rentiers.
> 2.–3. reduction in money-wages may increase the propensity to consume *via* reduction of domestic money-wages relatively to money-wages abroad, worsening terms of trade, and consequent reduction in real incomes.
> 4.–5. reduction in money-wages may increase investment if it expected to be a reduction relatively to money wages in the future (while it will have the opposite effect if money wages are expected to further diminish in the future)
> 6.–7. reduction in money-wages may produce a general tone of optimism (or pessimism) on entrepreneurs, so that they 'may break through a vicious cycle of unduly pessimistic estimates of the marginal efficiency of capital and set things moving on a more normal basis of expectation'. (*CW* 7: 264)

Remarkably, Keynes had already adopted this methodological stance in *A Treatise on Money* (*TM*). In Chapter 18 of *TM*, when dealing with 'Changes due to investment factors', Keynes openly describes the open-ended character of his way of reasoning in economics:

> The possible varieties of the paths which a credit cycle can follow and its possible complications are so numerous that it is impracticable to outline all of them. One can describe the rules of chess and the nature of the game, work out the leading openings and play through a few characteristic end-games; but one cannot possibly catalogue all the games which can be played. So it is with the credit cycle. We will begin, therefore, by examining the three openings and then proceed to an analysis of the characteristic secondary phase. (*CW* 5: 253)

Chapter 20 of *TM* is explicitly conceived as 'An exercise in the pure theory of the credit cycle'.

> I propose in this chapter to take a particular type of credit cycle and to work it out in full detail. Owing to the simplifying assumptions which have to be introduced in order to rule out the various complexities which are usually present in actual life, the example taken is somewhat artificial . . . The method and ideas of the preceding chapters will, however, be better illustrated in this way than if I were to cover more ground less intensively. (*CW* 5: 274)

As evident from these quotes, Keynes recurs to simplifying assumptions to be removed later on: 'Let us begin by simplifying the problem so as to set out the essential mechanism . . . in a manner which is free from non-essential complications. Our initial assumptions, which will be removed later on, are as follows . . .' (*CW* 5: 274–5). His discussion is articulated on a 'standard case' (so that, for instance, current savings must equal net new investment) and introduces eight 'simplifying assumptions', in whose absence the credit cycle becomes a 'complex phenomenon' (*CW* 5: 249). As later, in the discussion of the theory of prices in Chapter 21 of *GT*, with the assumptions of equal proportionality in changes in effective demand with respect to the quantity of money and of remunerations of factors entering into marginal cost, of homogeneity and interchangeability of resources, and so on, the simplifying assumptions of the credit cycle in *TM* are not independent one from another: after removing the 'no-hoarding hypothesis' – simplifying assumption point 3 in the list – Keynes distinguishes between a situation of 'correct' and one of 'mistaken expectations', that is between a situation in which the eighth assumption ('all those concerned accurately forecast the subsequent course of the credit cycle', *CW* 5: 276) is met and one in which it is not.

The Epilogue of *An Exercise in the Pure Theory of the Credit Cycle* shows that readers' involvement is not a pure rhetoric device in Keynes's writings; rather, his new way of reasoning forcedly requires it:

> the possible ramifications and extensions of the foregoing argument are so numerous that one could continue for many more pages amplifying, qualifying and generalising it. Perhaps, however, it has been carried far enough to enable a reader, who has entered the general system of thought here exemplified, to apply it for himself to any further interesting cases which may occur to him. (*CW* 5: 292)

As Gotti (1994) writes, Keynes 'wished to stimulate the reader into a cooperative effort of interpretation of the book'. This is because an open-ended theory with infinite probable repercussions invites the reader to 'further analyse' the economic material on the lines established by the economist:

When an economist writes in a quasi-formal style, he is composing neither a document verbally complete and exact so as to be capable of a strict legal interpretation, nor a logically complete proof. Whilst it is his duty to make his premises and his use of terms as clear as he can, he never states all his premises and his definitions are not perfectly clear-cut. It is, I think, of the essential nature of economic exposition that it gives, not a complete statement, which, even if it were possible, would be prolix and complicated, to the point of obscurity, but a sample statement, so to speak, out of all the things which could be said, intended to suggest to the reader the whole bundle of associated ideas, so that, if he catches the bundle, he will not in the least be confused or impeded by the technical incompleteness of the mere words which the author has written down, taken by themselves. This means, on the one hand, that an economic writer requires from his reader much goodwill and intelligence and a large measure of co-operation; and, on the other hand, that there are a thousand futile, yet verbally legitimate, objections which an objector can raise. (*CW* 13: 469–70)

A CORRECT ECONOMIC THEORY, OR THE NEED TO AVOID LOGICAL FALLACIES IN REASONING. THE METHODOLOGY OF CRITICISM OF THE CLASSICAL THEORY

A second important thing I have learnt about Keynes is that it is a necessary requisite that economic theory must be correct: it is a duty of the economist, so to speak, to avoid logical fallacies in reasoning. As seen, economic theory is to Keynes, as he observed in the introduction to the Series of Cambridge Economic Handbooks, 1922–3, 'a method rather than a doctrine, which helps its possessor to draw correct conclusions' (*CW* 12: 151). The list of logical fallacies economics can incur in is quite long:

Fallacy of independence (when reductionism is applied to a complex economic material)

Fallacy of composition (when conclusions about a whole are arrived at by analysing parts of it in isolation; partial equilibrium analysis, in Keynes's view, suffers from this fallacy)

Fallacy of *ignoratio elenchi* (when introducing tacit assumptions – of independence, etc.)

Fallacy of homogeneity (when treating heterogeneous magnitudes as if they were homogeneous)

False analogies (such as those related to the use of statistical inference in econometrics, or the shaping of conventional expectations on the market – 'market idola').

To grasp what Keynes meant when referring to a correct economic theory, one can look at his methodology of criticism of the classical theory, and particularly to the criticisms he makes in Chapter 19 of *GT* against Pigou (see Carabelli 1991):

> I have called my theory a *general* theory ... I argue that important mistakes have been made through extending to the system as a whole conclusions which have been correctly arrived at in respect of a part of it taken in isolation. (*CW* 7: xxxii)

Common observation is [not!] enough to show that facts do not conform to the orthodox reasoning (*CW* 7: 489):

> If orthodox economics is at fault, the error is to be found not in the superstructure, which has been erected with great care for logical consistency, but in a lack of clearness and of generality in the premises. (*CW* 7: xxi)

In Keynes's view, the *real* problem with classical theory is its unwillingness to make explicit those *tacit* assumptions of independence introduced into the analysis to support the generality and validity of its arguments. Such tacit assumptions of independence relate to:

- real variables: they are assumed to be independent from changes in the value of money;
- the economic system, which classical theory believes to be always operating to its full capacity;
- the fallacy of composition between individual's demand and community income.

The continuity between Keynes's methodological criticism of classical theory in *GT* and the criticism he moved against the classical theory of probability in his *TP* in 1907, 1908 and 1921 is simply striking. In *TP*, Keynes concerns himself with the *general* application of mathematical probability: his discussion is centred on the limits of valid reasoning and the introduction of the tacit assumptions of independence and homogeneity. Discussing Bernoulli's principle, he maintains that '[these considerations] have only served to make explicit what was always implicit in the principle [of indifference]' (*CW* 8: 66). As to *GT*, Keynes's criticism of the classical theory is logical, not empirical, nor is it based upon presumed unrealistic assumptions. Rather, Keynes makes explicit the introduction of tacit assumptions of independence and homogeneity. In his view, a *General Theory* is a theory which does not introduce tacit assumptions of independence and homogeneity. Hence, having exposed the methodological structure of the book in Chapter 18, Keynes devotes Chapter 19 to the main logical fallacy of the classical theory, a fallacy of 'ignoratio elenchi' (i.e. fallacy of independence or composition; *CW* 7: 259). One of the 13 types of fallacy of argument listed by Aristotle in *Sophistical Refutations* (1928), *ignoratio elenchi* is regarded in logic as an informal fallacy of relevance occurring when the premises of an argument are irrelevant to, and incapable of, establishing the truth of the conclusion of the argument.

MAKING SCIENCE WITH A COMPLEX WORLD: THE *TREATISE ON PROBABILITY* AND KEYNES'S ECONOMICS

I have learnt that Keynes concerned himself with the difficulty of making science in a complex world, that is a world possessing the attributes of complexity, and that the *TP* is the locus where one should search for the solutions he offered to the problem. *TP* is really Keynes's 'essay on method' (see Carabelli 1988). There, he depicts probability, which he treats as logical rather than mathematical, as the *general* case of knowledge. And I have learnt that *TP* is also, and more generally, an essay on complexity, wherein Keynes discusses: 'the logical foundations of mathematics, analogy and inductive reasoning; the principle of 'limited independent variety' and the role of the 'atomic hypothesis'; the hypotheses of independence and homogeneity' (*CW* 8: 21–43, 92, 116, 150, 182–3, 241–304, 313)

Conceived as a branch of probable, non-demonstrative logic, Keynes's economics is strictly connected to his work on probability. In both realms, Keynes firmly stands against the application of the atomic hypothesis:

> The atomic hypothesis which had worked so splendidly in physics breaks down in psychics. We are faced at every turn with the problem of organic unity, of discreteness, of discontinuity – the whole is not equal to the sum of the parts, comparison of quantity fails us, small changes produce large effects, the assumptions of a uniform and homogeneous continuum are not satisfied. (*CW* 10: 262)

Keynes's economics opposes both theoretical approaches of general and partial equilibrium. His criticism of general equilibrium (and mathematical economics and econometrics) focuses on the blind application of mathematical methods and the requirement of strict independence. The application of mathematics to economics is legitimate only in those cases in which the economic material under consideration is characterized by strict independence. In Keynes's words:

It is a great fault of symbolic pseudo-mathematical methods of formalising a system of economic analysis . . . that they expressly assume strict independence between the factors involved and lose all their cogency and authority if this hypothesis is disallowed; whereas, in ordinary discourse, where we are not blindly manipulating but know all the time what we are doing and what the words mean, we can keep 'at the back of our heads' the necessary reserves and qualifications and the adjustments which we shall have to make later on . . . Too large a proportion of recent 'mathematical' economics are merely concoctions, as imprecise as the initial assumptions they rest on, which allow the author to lose sight of the complexities and interdependencies of the real world in a maze of pretentious and unhelpful symbols. (*CW* 7: 297–98)

But partial equilibrium analysis is inadequate as well, in Keynes's view, as a tool for understanding a complex world, due especially to the use it makes of the *ceteris paribus* condition (which consists in 'breaking up a complex question, studying one bit at a time, and at last combining . . . partial solutions into a more or less complete solution of the whole riddle', Marshall 1961: 366). In this regard, Keynes moves his criticisms against Marshall but also, and above all, Pigou. In so doing, Keynes moves *beyond* Marshall, with the proposal of a method of economic analysis which makes use of the *cet. par.* condition, but not as a means to obtain partial equilibrium:

> The object of our analysis is, not to provide a machine, or method of blind manipulation, which will furnish an infallible answer, but to provide ourselves with an organised and orderly method of thinking out particular problems; and, after we have reached a provisional conclusion by isolating the complicating factors one by one, we then have to go back on ourselves and allow, as well as we can, for the probable interactions of the factors amongst themselves. This is the nature of economic thinking. (*CW* 7: 297)

In Keynes's coping with complexity, a central role is played by the notions of cause, relevance and independence as he used them in the *General Theory* (see Carabelli 1985, 1988; Carabelli and Cedrini 2011b). But in truth, such notions directly come from *TP*, where Keynes dwells on a concept of cause as logical relevance or dependence. There, he distinguishes between 'causa essendi', that is 'the cause why a thing is what it is', and 'causa cognoscendi', 'the cause of our knowledge of the event' (*CW* 8: 308). The former concerns material connections, whereas the latter relates to the cognitive conditions of the connection. When Keynes defines the causal analysis of the *General Theory* as 'strictly logical' (*CW* 29: 73), therefore, the mind should immediately go to the *causa cognoscendi* concept of *TP*. In Chapter 14 of *GT*, he holds that the determinants of the system 'are, indeed, themselves complex and each is capable of being affected by prospective changes in the others. But they remain independent in the sense that their values cannot be inferred from one another' (*CW* 7: 183). Moreover, he clarifies in Chapter ·18, 'this does not mean that we assume these factors to be constant; but merely that, in this place and context, we are not considering or taking into account the effects and consequences of changes in them' (*CW* 7: 245). In truth, the whole discussion of independent variables in the *General Theory* bears on a notion of *causa cognoscendi*, to the extent that on introducing them, he points out what he had named, while restating *GT* in Chapter 18, independent variables 'would be capable of being subjected to further analysis, and are not, so to speak, our ultimate atomic independent elements' (*CW* 7: 247), and the distinctions made when constructing the taxonomy of variables of the *GT*, he remarks with regard to that between given factors and independent variables in particular, is 'quite arbitrary from any absolute standpoint' (*CW* 7: 247).

THEORY, COMPLEXITY AND INCOMMENSURABILITY: MULTIDIMENSIONAL, HETEROGENEOUS AND INTERDEPENDENT MAGNITUDES

I have also learnt that complexity and incommensurability (which Keynes often treats as synonymous) of magnitudes is absolutely crucial in Keynes's way of reasoning in economics and in his philosophy of measurement (see Carabelli 1992, 1994, 1995). His works are literally full of references to various complex and incommensurable magnitudes. The list includes, starting with the early writings in ethics, probability and aesthetics:

- probability ('Ethics in Relation to Conduct' 1904 ; *TP*, 1907–8, 1921)
- utility ('Essay on Index Numbers', 1909)
- goodness ('Virtue and Happiness' 1905)
- beauty ('On Beauty and Art', undated).

The same for Keynes's economics; the central magnitudes of his economics are complex or incommensurable. The list includes, starting with the early to mature economic writings:

- general price level ('Essay on Index Numbers', 1909; 'The Tract on Monetary Reform', 1923; 'A Treatise on Money', 1930),

- real capital (*GT*, 1936)
- aggregate income (*GT*, 1936).

In *A Treatise on Money* (*TM*), Keynes defines magnitudes of this kind as 'complex and manifold' (*CW* 5: 88). They are characterized by heterogeneity, variety and pluralism of attributes (there is therefore no common unit to reduce these attributes to measurability), and involve problems, as he stated in the *Essay on Edgeworth* (1926), of organic unity, discreteness, discontinuity. Referring to these magnitudes, Keynes writes of *intrinsic* incommensurability: difficulties of measurement are intrinsic and do not depend on our inability to measure them (as he stressed in the *Essay on Index Numbers*, *CW* 11: 52, 135). Here is how Keynes defines intrinsic incommensurability, in *TP*, with respect to probability:

> It is not the case here [probability] that the method of calculation, prescribed by theory, is beyond our powers or too laborious for actual application. No method of calculation, however impracticable, has been suggested. Nor have we any prima facie indications of the existence of a common unit to which the magnitudes of all probabilities are naturally referrable . . . probabilities do not all belong to a single set of magnitudes measurable in terms of a common unit. (*CW* 8: 32–3)

Keynes's interest in measurement and comparison of utility dates back to 1905 ('Virtue and Happiness') and his analysis of the issue runs through his 1909 'Essay on Index Numbers' down to the *TM* and mature economic writings. It covers problems such as the heterogeneity of utility, the non-interpersonal comparison of utility, the measure of the amount of utility which a given sum of money can purchase and the non-exact measurement of utility which derives from taking into consideration organic unities. In the 'Essay on Index Numbers', Keynes points out that:

> The measure of the amount of utility, which a given sum will purchase, is intrinsically and from the nature of the case beyond our reach. Since the total utility of a commodity is not proportional to its quantity, we have no means of comparison between two different total utilities which are part of differing wholes, and the total utility of a given amount of wealth depends upon its distribution . . . Even if we know the distribution of wealth, there is no *measure* of the aggregate of individual utilities. The aggregate exists and is perfectly determinate, but we must not infer from this that two such aggregates can be measured in terms of a common unit . . . There is an aggregate of utilities, we may say, but not a sum. (*CW* 9: 59–60)

As seen, these sorts of problem concern economic magnitudes as well. First, the general price level, since Keynes writes of a '*complex* relation of money to the commodities' (*CW* 9: 66); capital, which Keynes describes as a collection, an aggregate of highly heterogeneous objects ('the difficulties as to the definition of the physical unit of capital, which I believe to be both insoluble and unnecessary', *CW* 7: 138); and aggregate output ('the community's output of goods and services is a non homogeneous complex which cannot be measured, strictly speaking, except in certain special cases, as for example, when all the items of one output are included in the same proportions in another output', *CW* 7: 38). When writing of 'complex and manifold' magnitudes in the *TM*, Keynes explicitly refers to Chapter 3 of *TP*: these concepts, he observes, are to be understood 'in the sense that they are capable of variations of degree in more than one mutually incommensurable direction at the same time' (*CW* 5: 88). But the problem of incommensurability informs *GT* as well: in the volume's Chapter 4, the same point is re-stressed when discussing the unit of measure (another implicit reference to *TP*):

> To say that net output to-day is greater, but the price level lower, than ten years ago or one year ago, is a proposition of a similar character to the statement that Queen Victoria was a better queen but not a happier woman than Queen Elizabeth – a proposition not without meaning and not without interest, but unsuitable as material for differential calculus. Our precision will be a mock precision if we try to use such partly vague and non-quantitative concepts as the basis of a quantitative analysis. (*CW* 7: 40)

KEYNES'S UNCERTAINTY. TRAGIC AND RATIONAL DILEMMAS

I have learnt that complexity and incommensurability are crucial issues in Keynes's economics, and that uncertainty, in this framework, has much to do with them (see Carabelli 1998; 2002b). Uncertainty covers a variety of cognitive situations:

- no reasons (even partial), arguments or grounds supporting a probability argument (ignorance);
- very low weight of arguments (no confidence in reasonable belief);
- incommensurable reasons (reasons are heterogeneous and non comparable, there is no common unit of measure to weight opposite claims).

The last situation is both the most interesting of Keynes's economics and the least explored by his readers. Uncertainty is in this case related to 'tragic' choices and the moral and rational dilemmas they produce. In these situations, there is an irreducible conflict between heterogeneous and equally compelling reasons or values. The option of reducing such reasons and moral claims to a common or homogeneous unit of measure is simply not available; nor is it possible to overcome the conflict. Keynes's notion of radical uncertainty relates to tragic dilemmas, and is itself a heritage of his early interest in Greek tragic moral dilemmas (Agamemnon's and Hecuba's dilemmas in particular).

Keynes was equally interested in rational dilemma in logic. One of the best known rational dilemmas is that of Buridan's ass, which represents a typical situation of indecision. Keynes refers to this dilemma both in his early version of the *Principles of Probability* (Keynes 1907: 75) and in his 1938 letter to Townshend (*CW* 29: 294). In rational dilemmas, conflicting arguments lead to indecision, indeterminate action and uncertainty. No general rule of decision to solve the dilemma is available. (Keynes undated) In *TP*, Keynes exposed the so-called dilemma of the umbrella (high barometer and black clouds are conflicting reasons for deciding for or against the umbrella):

> I am prepared to argue that on some occasions none of these alternatives hold, and that it will be an arbitrary matter to decide for or against the umbrella. If the barometer is high, but the clouds are black, it is not always rational that one should prevail over the other in our minds, or even that we should balance them, – though it will rational to allow caprice to determine us and to waste no time on the debate. (*CW* 8: 32)

A NEW VIEW OF RATIONALITY: RATIONALITY AS REASONABLENESS. PROBABILITY VERSUS MARKET CONVENTIONS

I have also learnt that Keynes's discussion of rational and moral dilemmas acquires great importance when examining his view of rationality as 'reasonableness', a notion based upon that of logical probability *à la TP* (see Carabelli 2002a). In short, reasonableness is 'having some reasons' to believe or to act. It is a kind of contingent rationality, which varies according to cognitive circumstances. An Aristotelian legacy – human contingent reason (practical reason) against calculus – is evident in the use Keynes makes of the concept, which is further connected with common sense against scepticism (that is with Keynes's own interpretation of Hume as sceptic). Another evidence of *TP* as the methodological approach later applied by Keynes to his economics, reasonableness grounds economic expectations of individual agents. Both Keynes's liquidity preference and his characterization of speculators as those who succeed in anticipating market conventions, or 'what average opinion expects the average opinion to be' (*CW* 7: 156), are based upon this notion. To Keynes, reasonableness does not depend on the fulfillment of expectations, for mere luck does not turn foolish judgments into reasonable judgments (a point against Friedman's instrumentalism or positivism). Reasonableness is based on a non-demonstrative logic and on intuition versus psychology and behaviourism. But reasonableness must not be confused with following habits, rules and market conventions: Keynes defends partial knowledge against mere experience. This is why Keynes's suggestion differs from Marshall's and Hayek's 'follow rules, routines and conventions'. Only in a situation of uncertainty (radical ignorance, very low weight of argument or confidence) and of incommensurability of magnitudes, rules, routines and market conventions may play a role and be reasonably justified. Most importantly, Keynes believes reasonableness to ground public action.

> The world is not so governed . . . that private and social interest always coincide. It is not so managed here below that in practice they coincide. It is not a correct deduction from the principles of economics that enlightened self-interest always operates in the public interest. Nor is it true that self-interest generally is enlightened; more often individuals acting separately to promote their own ends are too ignorant or too weak to attain even these. Experience does not show that individuals, when they make up a social unit, are always less clear-sighted than when they act separately. (*CW* 9: 288)

Reasonableness supplies a reasonable (probable, *à la Keynes*) justification of economic policy, as against Hayek's non-interventionism, and legitimates the role of public and semi-public institutions (see Carabelli and De Vecchi 1999, 2000, 2001; Carabelli 2002a). These latter are concerned with long-term perspectives and capable of coping with uncertainty. Although endowed with only partial knowledge they have more partial knowledge at their disposal than single individuals. Grounded upon deliberate and reasonable judgment, their public actions are explicitly designed to favour the general welfare, which individuals tend to escape or simply do not pursue, nor can be demanded to pursue.

ECONOMICS AS A MORAL SCIENCE AND KEYNES'S HAPPINESS AS ARISTOTELIAN EUDAIMONIA

Public intervention is required, in Keynes's economics, to counteract the impasse created by fallacies of composition and conflicts between particular and general interests. When money is valued for money's sake – which is both the engine of capitalism and, to its extreme, the *raison d'être* of rentiers, but also the by-product of uncertainty – the resulting disposition to hoard has disastrous consequences for the economic system as a whole: enterprise is transformed into a speculative activity, while radical uncertainty favours the formation of conventional, rather than reasonable expectations. When 'love of money as a possession' substitutes for 'love of money as a means to the enjoyment and realities of life' (*CW* 9: 329), money becomes an end in itself. I have learnt the importance Keynes assigned to confining economics within the realm of means. Economics, in Keynes's anti-positivist view, is 'a moral science' which deals with 'introspection and with values . . . with motives, expectations, psychological uncertainties' (*CW* 14: 300). More, Keynes believes it to be at the service of ethics: in his anti-utilitarian and anti-materialist vision (see Carabelli 1998 and 2002b; Carabelli and Cedrini 2001a), securely based on Greek ethics of virtue, economics and politics belong to the ethics of means, or 'practical ethics' as he called it. Their task is to help men achieve the material preconditions to enjoy the good and happy life of Aristotelian flavour (eudaimonia) which gathers together the ultimate aim of 'speculative ethics', the ethics of ends men will be finally free to pursue after defeating the economic problem. Keynes was in fact heartily convinced that:

> the problem of want and poverty and the economic struggle between classes and nations, is nothing but a frightful muddle, a transitory and an unnecessary muddle. For the western world already has the resources and the technique, if we could create the organisation to use them, capable of reducing the economic problem, which now absorbs our moral and material energies, to a position of secondary importance. (*CW* 9: xvii)

He rather believed that:

> the day is not far off when the economic problem will take the back seat where it belongs, and that the arena of the heart and head will be occupied, or reoccupied, by our real problems – the problems of life and of human relations, of creation and behaviour and religion. (*CW* 9: xvii)

A main lesson to draw from the most innovative economist of all times, therefore, is that it is possible to conceive economics as a means rather than an end, and as a tool for supplying the material prerequisites for social progress and the attainment of increasingly higher levels of goodness, which only allow men the freedom to consider and choose between those not-material ends whose pursuit is indispensable to express authentic human qualities.

KEYNES'S INTERNATIONAL ECONOMICS AND DIPLOMACY: COMPLEXITY, INTERDEPENDENCE, ETHICS

I have finally learnt that Keynes's international economics and diplomacy provides clear continuity with his own methodological positions about the economic material and the discipline of economics itself. And I have also learnt that Keynes's approach to international economic relations is characterized by a high degree of coherence, notwithstanding changing times and circumstances (see Carabelli and Cedrini 2010c). As remarked by Vines (2003), Keynes's revolution in international economics seems to owe much to the 'focus and method' (Vines 2003: 358) of his analysis.

In the final page of *Indian Currency and Finance* (ICF), Keynes's first 'mature' work (he was only 31 years old), Keynes stresses that

> Every part of the system fits into some other part. It is impossible to say everything at once, and an author must need sacrifice from time to time the complexity and interdependence of fact in the interest of the clearness of his exposition. But the complexity and the coherence of the system require the constant attention of anyone who would criticize the parts. This is not a peculiarity of Indian Finance. It is the characteristic of all monetary problems. The difficulty of the subject is due to it. (*CW* 1: 181–2)

In effect, in all his writings, as well as in his diplomacy, he repeatedly insisted on the complexity and interdependence which characterize the international economic order and its dynamics. The gold exchange standard proposed in ICF should combine 'cheapness with stability', thereby ensuring in his view a harmony of interest between debtor and creditor countries (see Carabelli and Cedrini 2010–11): a rather natural goal, for an economist who thinks organically. Keynes himself, in the 1940s, came to identify the 'secular international problem' with the asymmetry of adjustment (in favour of creditors) characterising nearly every international monetary system in recent history, with the relevant exception of Britain during the gold standard. This model of 'reasonable creditor' (one who allows debtor countries, the beneficiaries of her foreign lending, to 'use' their exchange reserves – rather than simply 'show' them – for purpose of international adjustment and growth) acquires great importance in the *Economic Consequences of the Peace* (1919), where Keynes refers to Europe as a 'body' affected by a civil war, the European Allies 'being so deeply and inextricably intertwined with their victims by hidden psychic and economic bonds' that, by aiming at the destruction of Germany, they would 'invite their own destruction also' (*CW* 2: 2). Hence his call to the United States and Britain for debt forgiveness to solve the 'dilemma of reparations'; it would have been an act of 'farseeing statesmanship' (*CW* 2: 93) on the part of creditors disposed to act in a public-spirited manner, so as to induce European countries to recede from asking for impossible indemnities to Germany, and at the same time to promote a shared-responsibilities approach to the imbalances generated by the war (see Carabelli and Cedrini 2010a).

Keynes's moral remarks on the American view of World War I inter-allied debts as ordinary business debts match his later criticisms of the rentier-like attitude of creditors in the renewed post-war gold standard. Debtor countries fell victim of the 'dilemma of the international monetary system' Keynes had exposed in *A Treatise on Money* (1930), compelling them to an undesirable choice between the straitjacket of international discipline and an isolationist version of national autonomy. In the absence of a new 'responsible' leadership, Keynes devised a plan for the establishment of an institution, the International Clearing Union, with the task of ensuring equilibrium in a globally interdependent world, by bringing international rentiers to 'euthanasia'. The final rejection of Keynes's plans for Bretton Woods led him to turn back to his early call for a responsible international leadership: hence his request for an American gift to Britain at the end of World War II, in the same spirit of his 1919 proposals. International indebtedness (with Britain as the ultimate debtor, so to speak) was posing a dangerous threat on the desired post-war multilateralism. Using an extraordinarily modern approach to the complex concept of gift, Keynes saw in the principle of 'something for nothing' the only opportunity to achieve this result, American generous assistance being conceived as the ignition key to allow a spiral of magnanimity to spread along the chain of countries (the sterling area, and even Britain, if given the chance to advance toward the multilateral world she herself desired) disposed to participate in Keynes's shared-responsibilities plan (see Carabelli and Cedrini 2010b).

Paradoxically enough, Keynes's desired new order ends up by exalting international discipline as an instrument to promote, rather than repress, member countries' freedom to choose and policy space. But this is consistent with the social philosophy of the *General Theory*, where Keynes invokes 'central controls' as a means to attain full employment while safeguarding the 'traditional advantages of individualism', that is 'personal liberty', 'the variety of life' and 'the field for the exercise of personal choice' (*CW* 7: 380). More, it is perfectly in line with his general ethical positions, placing the autonomy of individual judgement among the most important ends of speculative ethics, and making it the real aim of human life after the end of the 'economic problem'. While, therefore, the unrestricted laissez faire of the late gold standard and interwar period had 'mistake[n] private licence for public liberty', Keynes's new order should have shown the highest respect for the 'diversity of national policy' (see Carabelli and Cedrini 2010d).

CONCLUSIONS

By bringing attention to the theoretical continuity between the early epistemological concern of Keynes's work on probability and the attention he posed in the *General Theory* on the method, theory and practice of economics, pioneering works on the methodological foundations of Keynes's economics in the 1980s have made it possible to advance an original interpretation of Keynes as a 'thinker of complexity' (see Marchionatti 2010). Yet much remains to be done. Dow (2010: 283) rightly observes that 'there has not been a Keynesian revolution at the level of methodology that is consistent with Keynes's approach to economics'. Itself an essay in complexity, this paper should induce regarding this as truly a missed opportunity. A bulwark erected against attempts by exponents of the so-called 'neo-classical synthesis' as well as of 'New Keynesians' to neutralize, willingly or not, the most revolutionary traits of Keynes's economics, the post-Keynesian strand should be less reluctant to investigate the potential of Keynes's economic method as a tool to develop a complexity approach to economics. What I have learnt from 30 years of research on Keynes is that his research line is still the most promising one: we are in desperate need not so much of 'settled conclusions immediately applicable to policy', but of 'a method rather than a doctrine', helping economists 'to draw correct conclusions' for today's world.

REFERENCES

Aristotle (1928) *Sophistical Refutations*, William D. Ross (ed.) Oxford: Clarendon Press.
Carabelli, Anna (1985) 'J.M. Keynes on Cause, Chance and Possibility', in T. Lawson and H. Pesaran (eds), *Keynes's Economics: Methodological Issues*. London: Croom Helm (reprinted Routledge and Kegan, London, 1989).
Carabelli, Anna (1988) *On Keynes's Method*, Macmillan, London.
Carabelli, Anna (1991) 'The Methodology of the Critique of the Classical Theory: Keynes on Organic Interdependence', in B. Bateman and J. Davis (eds), *Keynes and Philosophy*, Cheltenham UK and Northampton MA: Edward Elgar, 104–125.
Carabelli, Anna (1992) 'Organic Interdependence and Keynes's Choice of Units in the *General Theory*', in B. Gerrard and J. Hillard (eds), *The Philosophy and*

Economics of J.M.Keynes, Cheltenham UK and Northampton MA: Edward Elgar, 3–31.

Carabelli, Anna (1994) 'Keynes on Mensuration and Comparison', in K.Vaghn (ed.), *Perspectives in the History of Economic Thought Volume X. Method, Competition, Conflict and Measurement in the Twentieth Century*, Cheltenham UK and Northampton MA: Edward Elgar, 204–38.

Carabelli, Anna (1995) 'Uncertainty and Measurement in Keynes: Probability and Organicness', in J.Hillard and S. Dow (eds), *Keynes, Knowledge and Uncertainty*. Cheltenham UK and Northampton MA: Edward Elgar, 137–60.

Carabelli, Anna (2002a) 'Speculation and Reasonableness: a non-Bayesian Theory of Rationality', in S. Dow and J. Hillard (eds), *Keynes, Uncertainty and the Global Economy: Beyond Keynes* (Vol. 2), Cheltenham UK and Northampton MA: Edward Elgar, 165–85.

Carabelli, Anna (2002b) 'Keynes on Probability, Uncertainty and Tragic Choices', in S. Nisticò and D. Tosato (eds), *Competing Economic Theories. Essays in Memory of Giovanni Caravale*, London: Routledge, 249–79

Carabelli, Anna and Mario Cedrini (2010a) 'Keynes and the Complexity of International Economic Relations in the Aftermath of World War I', *Journal of Economic Issues*, 44(4): 1009–27.

Carabelli, Anna and Mario Cedrini (2010b) 'Current Global Imbalances: Might Keynes Be of Help?', in M.C. Marcuzzo, T. Hirai and B. Bateman (eds) *The Return to Keynes*. Cambridge, Mass: Harvard University Press, 257–74.

Carabelli, Anna and Mario Cedrini (2010c) 'Global Imbalances, Monetary Disorder, and Shrinking Policy Space: Keynes's Legacy for Our Troubled World', *Intervention. European Journal of Economics and Economic Policies*, 7(2), 303–23.

Carabelli, Anna and Mario Cedrini (2010d) 'Veiling the Controversies with Dubious Moral Attitudes? Creditors and Debtors in Keynes's Ethics of International Economic Relations'. *SEMeQ Working Paper* 127/2010.

Carabelli, Anna and Mario Cedrini (2010–11) 'Indian Currency and Beyond. The Legacy of the Early Economics of Keynes in the Times of Bretton Woods II', *Journal of Post Keynesian Economics*, 33(2): 255–80.

Carabelli, Anna and Mario Cedrini (2011a) 'The Economic Problem of Happiness: Keynes on Happiness and Economics', *Forum for Social Economics* , 40, 335–59.

Carabelli, Anna and Mario Cedrini (2011b) 'Chapter 18 of the General Theory "Further Analysed". The Theory of Economics as a Method', SEMeQ Working Paper 128/2011, presented at the Fifth 'Dijon' Post-Keynesian Conference, University of Roskilde, Denmark, 14 May 2011.

Carabelli, Anna and Niccolò De Vecchi (1999) '"Where to Draw the Line?" Hayek and Keynes on Knowledge, Ethics and Economics', *European Journal for the History of Economic Thought*, 6(2): 271–96.

Carabelli, Anna and Niccolò De Vecchi (2000) 'Individuals, Public Institutions and Knowledge: Hayek and Keynes', in P.L. Porta, R. Scazzieri and A. Skinner (eds) *Knowledge, Social Institutions and the Division of Labour*, Cheltenham UK and Northampton MA: Edward Elgar, 229–48.

Carabelli, Anna and Niccolò De Vecchi (2001) 'Hayek and Keynes: from a Common Critique of Economic Method to a Different Theory of Expectations', *Review of Political Economy*, 13(3): 269–85.

Chick, Victoria (2004) 'On Open Systems', *Brazilian Journal of Political Economy*, 24 (1): 3–16.

Chick, Victoria and Sheila C. Dow (2001) 'Formalism, Logic and Reality: A Keynesian Analysis', *Cambridge Journal of Economics*, 25(6): 705–22.

Dow, Sheila C. (2010) 'Was There a (Methodological) Keynesian Revolution?', in R.W. Dimand, R.A. Mundell and A.Vercelli (eds), *Keynes's General Theory After Seventy Years*. London: Palgrave Macmillan, 268–86.

Gotti, Maurizio (1994) '"*The General Theory*" as an Open-ended Work', in A. Marzola and F. Silva (eds), *John Maynard Keynes: Language and Method*, Cheltenham UK and Northampton MA: Edward Elgar, 155–91.

Keynes, John M. (undated) 'On Beauty and Art. On Art Criticism and the Appreciation of Beauty', King's College Archive Centre, Cambridge, The Papers of John Maynard Keynes.

Keynes, John M. (1904) 'Ethics in Relation to Conduct', King's College Archive Centre, Cambridge, The Papers of John Maynard Keynes.

Keynes, John M. (1905) 'Virtue and Happiness', King's College Archive Centre, Cambridge, The Papers of John Maynard Keynes.

Keynes, John M. (1907) 'The Principles of Probability', submitted as fellowship dissertation to King's College in December. King's College Archive Centre, Cambridge, The Papers of John Maynard Keynes.

Keynes, John M. (1971–1989) *The Collected Writings of John Maynard Keynes*, Donald E. Moggridge (ed.), London: Macmillan.

Jespersen, Jesper (2008) *Macroeconomic Methodology. A Post-Keynesian Perspective*, Cheltenham UK and Northampton MA: Edward Elgar.

Marchionatti, Roberto (2010) 'J. M. Keynes, Thinker of Economic Complexity', *Journal of Economic Ideas*, 18(2): 115–46.

Marshall, Alfred (1961[1920]) *Principles of Economics* (revised ed.), London: Macmillan.

Vines, David (2003) 'John Maynard Keynes 1937–1946: The Creation of International Macroeconomics', *The Economic Journal*, 113(488): 338–61.

6. Keynes's early cognition of the concept of time

Mogens Ove Madsen[1]

INTRODUCTION

John Maynard Keynes wanted to revolutionize the way world thinks about economic problems. In his ultimate masterpiece *The General Theory* he changed the focus in economics from efficiency to the fundamental quaesitum of determination of national income and the volume of employment. From this focus it became of vital importance for Keynes to find those factors that in practice exercised a dominant influence on this quaesitum and to select those variables which could be managed by central authority:

> But as soon as we pass to the problem of what determines output and employment as a whole, we require the complete theory of a monetary economy. Or, perhaps we might make our line of division between the theory of stationary equilibrium and the theory of shifting equilibrium – meaning by the latter the theory of a system in which changing views about the future are capable of influencing the present situation. 'For the importance of money essentially flows from its being a link between the present and the future' (Keynes 1936: 293).

Keynes took it upon himself to hammer out a new methodology for economic science which could legitimize theorizing about new relations in economic thinking. Justification for this assertion can be noted by referring to Keynes's almost forgotten *Treatise on Probability* (1921, drafts 1907/1908). Here we find part of an epistemological foundation for a new and different methodology. In this work Keynes recognized that there might well be quite different laws for wholes of different degrees of complexity, and laws of connection between complexes which could not be stated in terms of laws connecting individual parts. Consequently, an economic system is organic and each decision-making unit is related to the rest of the system. Such interdependency requires decision-making under uncertainty – a crucial point in many respects in Keynes's *General Theory*.[2]

As Joan Robinson much later stated regarding Keynes's work with economics:

> The General Theory broke through the unnatural barrier and brought history and theory together again. But for theorists the descent into time has not been easy. After twenty years the awakened Princess is still dazed and groggy. (Robinson 1962: 75)

Robinson indicates a very crucial point. Time is of the essence in Keynes's work. Already in 1903, Keynes had read a philosophical paper entitled 'Time' for one of the countless undergraduate societies in Cambridge called *The Parrhesiasts Society*.[3]

KEYNES'S FIRST REFLECTIONS ON TIME

Of particular interest is that Keynes actually wrote this paper before having completed his participation in the lectures of two philosophers, both of whom were intrigued by notions of time, G.E. Moore and J.M.E. McTaggart, two outstanding representatives of the 'Discussion Society'. In addition to these great philosophers to whom he had direct access, Keynes was also inspired by articles on time that had been published in *Mind*.

According to his notes, Keynes was primarily concerned with the essential relativity of all time measurement, especially the essential interconnection of the ideas of time and change.

It is important to remember that Keynes was studying mathematics at the time, not economics. Obviously, however, as soon as time is recognized as a methodological and substantive assumption in the theory of a scientific theory, it will have rather far-reaching consequences for making progress in knowledge and even progress in knowledge regarding economics. Time is often the forgotten or hidden dimension, for it is usually treated in such a way which violates its real nature.[4] Winston explains this as follows:

> Careless attention to time can mislead economic and social analysis when the temporal perspective of an analyst-observer is confused with that of the actor as the subject of analysis; careless attention to time can lead to the use of inappropriate methodology when difference between repetitive and unique behaviour is ignored; and careless attention to time will hide important economic relationships when too crude a time unit is used. (Winston 1988: 32)

Keynes's interest in the concept of time undoubtedly occurred in a very stimulating environment in Cambridge around the turn of the century. Keynes's own inclinations drew him towards philosophy, and numerous observers have noted how Keynes was especially inspired by Moore. This was to some extent true,[5] but the question becomes whether Moore shadows for other important sources of inspiration from other philosophers, McTaggart in particular.

The latter philosopher especially brings to Keynes a vital introduction to an ontological difference between two theories of time. The same fundamental difference is known from contemporary philosophical discussions:

> Firstly, there is the dynamical approach (the A-theory) according to which the essential notions are past, present and future. In this view, time is seen 'from the inside'. Secondly, there is the static view of time (the B-theory) according to which time is understood as a set of instants (or durations) ordered by the before-after relation. Here time is seen 'from the outside'. (Øhrstrøm 2011: 48)

This tack will be pursued in the following. This cannot be done without demonstrating what is asserted about the relationship between Keynes and McTaggart, however, and it is also necessary to briefly digress back to the originally inspiring philosophical sources, their handling of the concept of time in particular, especially Kant and Hegel. Having done so, it is possible to characterize more accurately the debate on time between Moore and McTaggart and the subsequent impact of this debate. Against this background, the main thrusts of Keynes's own paper are presented.

KEYNES'S RELATIONSHIP WITH MCTAGGART

Some observers have characterized Keynes's relationship with McTaggart as sporadic. Keynes first biographer, Roy Harrod, wrote in his major opus and tribute, *The Life of John Maynard Keynes* (1951), that Maynard would have known of McTaggart's eminence from his father, John Neville Keynes. Furthermore, Keynes was invited to McTaggart's social arrangements, the *Wednesday Evenings*. Maynard was actually even encouraging his friends to attend McTaggart's lectures. In the description of the 'Essay on Time' (Keynes 1903), Harrod points out that Keynes could not accept Kant's view of time and, furthermore, that the paper posed problems without claiming to solve them.

Later, in *Hopes Betrayed*, Skidelsky (1983) describes how McTaggart congratulated Keynes in 1903 for having become a member of the Apostles, and McTaggart further invited Keynes to join a society called Eranus in 1911. Skidelsky clarifies that McTaggart always said about philosophy that it was valuable for the comfort it provided, and he covered the metaphysical aspects of time in his lectures in relation to Keynes in particular. Skidelsky also describes how Moore was skeptical concerning McTaggart's Hegel-inspired idealism and McTaggart was later defeated, according to Skidlesky, but unrepentant and certain that Moore was wrong.

Felix (1999), in his book *Keynes's Philosophical Development*, stresses that McTaggart merely had a passing effect on Keynes, although McTaggart's exposure to philosophy led to an extended metaphysical *jeu d'esprit* – the *Time* paper. Felix describes the essay as a game with other persons' ideas – characterized by dexterity rather than originality.

In *The Philosophy of Keynes's Economics*, Runde and Mizuhara (2003) proclaim that, in his early philosophical thinking, Keynes was largely influenced by the fundamental disagreement between Moore and Russel, on the one hand, and the neo-Hegelians such as Bradley, Bosanquet, Green and McTaggart on the other. In the optic of Runde and Mizuhara, Keynes adopted Moore's way of philosophical thinking, for example in an Apostle paper from 1904, *Ethics in relation to conduct*.

Davidson (2007) estimates that Keynes's own home was a residence in which the most famous economists and philosophers of the day socialized and where moral science was a daily event. According to Davidson's assessment, Moore's *Principia Ethica* was to become The Manifesto of Modernism (Keynes 1938, in Davidson 2007: 5), and Keynes made further use of Moore's method when revolutionizing economic thought.

Dostaler's 2007 book *Keynes and his Battles* makes clear that McTaggart's lectures challenged Keynes's intellect. Particularly at stake is Kant's vision of time. In contrast to Harrod, Dostaler claims that Keynes is closer to Kant than Hegel on the grounds that Kant conceived of time as a formal a priori condition of phenomena – a category of understanding.

Against this background, the connection between Keynes and McTaggart is best characterized as sporadic and temporary. Closer scrutiny of Keynes's recognition and use of the concept of time will reveal whether this is indeed the case. At first, as already mentioned, it means that it is necessary to present two very classical philosophers, Kant and Hegel, who are frequently referred to in the philosophical debate that Keynes participated in as a student. Subsequently, the plan is to pursue two of their heirs: Moore and McTaggart.

KANT AND HEGEL

The mission of this section is solely to clarify how Kant and Hegel, respectively, dealt with the concept of time. Kant (1724–1804) was the founder of critical philosophy and defends the classical science to the skepticism that was made from empiricism and which claimed that recognition continues to be reliable only if established on proven experience. Hegel (1770–1831), in turn, is a more speculative philosopher and idealist – *Das Wahre ist das Ganze*[6] is Hegel's hallmark: it is first when we know the whole truth and the whole world that we have 'absolute knowledge'. Hegel was also responsible for putting the dialectic into system and suggested it as a driving force in both the logical and historical development.

Kant defeated the apodictic cognition as it existed in mathematics and physics. By means of the transcendental method, he believed to have found a way of explaining how synthetic judgments were possible in mathematics and science.

Kant distinguishes between the pages of our recognition that come from our selves (a priori), and the pages arising from our sensory experience (a posteriori). He defines our concepts of space and time as a formal a priori condition of phenomena, and they are a precondition for any experience. Intuition is also introspection. This applies to the outer position that is available both in space and time, whereas the inner belief only exists in time. Kant recognizes a single reality which alone makes itself known in time, but not in space. Time thus constitutes the formal condition of all existence.

Modes of perception are transcendental conditions of our experience that go beyond the experience itself. They are not a part of the experience, but rather the order and structure of our experience, without which it would simply be a confused mass of sensations. In other words, it is a necessary condition for the realization and notions of space and time that it is not derived from sense experience.

The form which Kant uses to argue the transcendental deduction is derived from his conception of time. He perceives time as something consecutive – he assumed that time could be comprehended as something uniform, something that could be set as a sequence. Space is three-dimensional, whereas time has only one dimension. The structure of the a priori condition for these categories is different, because the space is structured geometrically, while time is structured arithmetically, as in the difference between contours and numbers.

It is important to notice that events occur in time. Without this form of time, it would not be possible to recognize events in progress, and Kant saw temporal moments succeed one another. Event E1 comes before E2, and time is a prerequisite for this sequence in structuring the appearance of nature.

But Kant's approach deemphasizes the difficulties concerning the dynamic aspect of time – the temporal becoming of the internal dynamism of these moments.

Hegel owed much to Kant but nevertheless refuted many of Kant's arguments using logic. Hegel believed that Kant studied knowledge through a purely subject-object relationship. Because time and space were part of humanity, he held that a full understanding of life and knowledge required the presence of both.

Hegel moves from an ontological way of thinking towards a more historically oriented thought. According to Hegel, the history of thought is identical to real history – real is the rational and the rational is real! He therefore agrees both on the principle of empiricism and idealism. The idea is central in both thinking and in real history.

The problem of history is that the reality of the past is not independent of the science of it. A distinction must therefore be drawn between the events as they occurred and the science which took place.

Hegel is concerned that the realization is equal to a commemorative. Knowledge can only be related to the past history, and the future is without form and therefore cannot be thematized. The present unifies the past and the future negatively – time is the contradiction in and ceaseless motion of finite beings. Time forms the boundary conditions of phenomena as the limit of the phenomenal world. In *Phänomenologie des Geistes*, Hegel presented this alternative concept of time – an irreversible historical concept of time as opposed to the mathematical, natural science concept of time.

Hegel's understanding of time is distinct from that of Kant, as described in the first part of his *Kritik der reinen Vernuft*. For Hegel, time and space are not subjective forms or conditions of sensory experience, but ontological. Time is the formative process of consciousness without which history is unthinkable. One could also argue that since all of the categories in Hegel's logic are ontological and not epistemological and time is one of them, then time is ontological and has its own reality outside the domain of thought. Temporality of consciousness draws a line of demarcation between human beings and the given objects. Consciousness, in this view, is temporality, and unlike a given object it is therefore not identical to itself. In other words, consciousness is what it is not, because it is incomplete and dynamic and in a state of constant flux, striving to fulfil itself. This movement of consciousness is also self-determined, as the 'other' is nothing more than the externalization of consciousness. For this reason, there is no distinction between external and internal consciousness.

This significant characteristic of consciousness provides the grounds for freedom and is essential for understanding the meaning of the 'True Infinite' category in dialectical logic.

MOORE AND MCTAGGART

According to the 1903 lecture notes (JMK/UA/1/), Keynes attended both Moore's lectures on ethics and McTaggart's lectures on metaphysics.

During Moore's lectures on ethics, Keynes read Kant's *Theory of Ethics*[7] and Sidgwick's *Methods of Ethics* (1907[1874]). This was certainly supplemented with *The Philosophical Notes of* John Neville Keynes (JMK/UA/2A), consisting of several volumes containing notes on modern ethics, metaphysics, Kant, Descartes, Locke and Hume.

According to Keynes's own notes, Moore's lectures introduced him to the fundamental question: what is good in itself? This was then highlighted, inter alia, through discussion of the distinction between ethics and politics and an examination of four schools of ethics: hedonism, intuitionism, evolutionary ethics and metaphysical ethics.

Moore was not a representative of the neo-Kantian school, which tended to emphasize scientific readings of Kant in the late 18th century, often downplaying the role of intuition in favor of conceptual clarity.

He was instead a founder and representative of the analytic programme in philosophy in the early 20th century. In analytic philosophy, the search for conceptual clarity has been very important. One of the central points in analytic philosophy is that the problems of philosophy can be solved by showing the simple constituents of complex notions. Moore, and with him Bertrand Russell, began developing a new sort of conceptual analysis based on new developments in logic.

One of the most important parts of Moore's philosophical development was his break from a Hegelian-oriented idealism that dominated British philosophy. This becomes very clear in his *A Defence of Common Sense*. The main achievement in Moore's early period is his book, *Principia Ethica*. Published in 1903, it was the culmination of the reflections which Moore started in his 1897 dissertation on *The Metaphysical Basis of Ethics*, meaning that Keynes would be familiar with his philosophical leanings.

In 1897, Moore also commented on the question, in what sense, if any, do past and future time exist? There is really not much doubt in his answer to this question of time:

> I would say that neither Past, Present, nor Future exists, if by existence we are to mean the ascription of full Reality and not merely existence as Appearance. On the other hand I think we may say that there is more Reality in the Present than in Past and Future, because, though it is greatly inferior to them in extent of content, it has that coordinate element of immediacy which they entirely lack. Again, and lastly, I think we may distinguish in this respect between Past and Future. The Past seems to be more real than the Future, because its content is more fully constituent of the Present, whereas the Future could only claim

a superiority over the Past, if it could be shown that in it Appearance would become more and more at one with Reality. (Moore, 1897)

In the words of Moore, this proves the unreality of time. The present is not real, because it can only be thought of as infinitely small; and past and future cannot be real, not only because they also must be thought of as infinitely divisible, but also because they wholly lack that immediacy, which according to the neo-Hegelian Bradley is a necessary constituent in reality. If neither present, past, nor future is real, however, there is nothing real left in time as such (Moore, 1897).[8]

Just as Moore is not a real neo-Kantian, neither is McTaggart a full-blown representative of the neo-Hegelian school, although he is referred to as a dedicated interpreter and champion of Hegel; however, it is interesting that Moore and McTaggart share the same view on the unreality of time.

As a matter of fact, McTaggart's research and teaching of Hegel were also very important in the development of philosophers such as Moore and Russell. McTaggart himself was inspired by the already mentioned neo-Hegelian, F.H. Bradley.

McTaggart characterizes metaphysics as the systematic study of the ultimate nature of reality, and he argues that the empirical sciences, such as physics, cannot replace metaphysical inquiry. He claims that the rationality of using induction in general is questionable.

Early in his studies, McTaggart had the idea of the elimination of time. In *Studies in the Hegelian Dialectic* (1896), he introduced arguments for the unreality of time. McTaggart describes his denial of the reality of time as Hegelian rather than Kantian, since although both thinkers denied the reality of time, only Hegel thought that there was an underlying reality to which the apparent reality of time corresponds.

Even if McTaggart thinks that time is unreal, temporal judgements can be made on how things are because temporal ordering captures real facts about the underlying reality that gives rise to the appearance of time.

In 1908, McTaggart summarized his arguments for why time is unreal, arguments unlike the arguments of Spinoza, Kant, Hegel or Schopenhauer:

> Positions in time, as time appears to us *primâ facie,* are distinguished in two ways. Each position is Earlier than some, and Later than some, of the other positions. And each position is either Past, Present, or Future. The distinctions of the former class are permanent, while those of the latter are not. If M is ever earlier than N, it is always earlier. But an event, which is now present, was future and will be past. (McTaggart 1908: 458)

The earlier/later distinction is called a B series and the past, present and future distinction is called an A series. McTaggart sees the A series as more essential to time than the B series, which is also why he regards time as unreal. Why so?

> We perceive events in time as being present, and those are the only events which we perceive directly. And all other events in time which, by memory or inference, we believe to be real, are regarded as past or future – those earlier than the present being past, and those later than the present being future. Thus the events of time, as observed by us, form an A series as well as a B series. (McTaggart 1908: 458)

But the two series are not equally fundamental: 'The distinctions of the A series are ultimate. We cannot explain what is meant by past, present and future. We can to some extent, describe them, but they cannot be defined. We can only show their meaning be examples.' (McTaggart 1908: 463)

McTaggart states that the relations forming the A series must then be relations of events and moments to something not itself in the time series and which might be difficult to say something about:

> Past, present, and future are incompatible determinations. Every event must be one or the other, but no event can be more than one. This is essential to the meaning of the terms . . . For time, as we have seen involves change, and the only change we can get is from future to present, and from present to past. (McTaggart: 1908: 468)

According to McTaggart, the characteristics are therefore incompatible. But every event has them all, and all of the three incompatible terms are predictable of each event, which is obviously inconsistent with their being incompatible and inconsistent with their producing change.

There can be no time without an A series, but the A series cannot exist due to this inconsistency; and therefore time cannot exist.

KEYNES'S ESSAY ON TIME

Keynes undoubtedly found metaphysics very difficult but also very stimulating. From his *Essay on Time*, he is inspired both by Kant and Hegel and, of course, the more recent interpreters thereof.[9] In one of his notes to the reading to the Parrhesiast's Society, he explains:

> When I have attended Dr McTaggart's lectures, I have felt the plunge from ordinary life into metaphysics a very violent one; it usually takes me an appreciable time to gather my wits for a sustained dialectical outlook upon the Universe, despite the lecturer's efforts to relieve the tension by the introduction

of so unmetaphysical a thing as laughter – I mean therefore to approach the subject gently. (Keynes (1903),[10] JMK/UA/17: Essay on Time)

The way he approached the subject of time was gentle by way of the mathematical aspects of time and especially of measurement. It is important to remember that Keynes had studied mathematics, not economics, which obviously characterizes his reflection.

He knows that he is introducing 'one of the greatest stumbling blocks in every metaphysical system', but on the other hand he states that '[m]easure of time is no more than a measure of change' and it is his belief that it is 'impossible to arrive at any conception of time which should be independent of the conception of change', because '[a] changeless state is, of necessity, a timeless state' (Keynes (1903), JMK/UA/17: Essay on Time).

It is important to note that Keynes wants to make a distinction between a consistent definition of time and then the familiar common-sense approaches:

> . . . our perception of time means, therefore, simply our awareness of change, and it has no further raison d'être whatever this is, of course, entirely opposed to the common-sense view of time, and as our common sense views of time and space considerably colour our metaphysical views, it is important to get these conceptions of time and as consistent as is possible for us (JMK/UA/17).

He provides a few examples of common sense views of time such as time as a stream, the flight of time or as a line indefinitely stretched in both directions.[11]

In Keynes's optic, one must regard the world either as working towards an end at a time – like the Christians – or as a perpetual cycle of continuality like others. So if we suppose that the purpose and end of the universe is already achieved, then all change is a delusion. By world or universe, Keynes meant the aggregation of everything, including God and the devil.

In the McTaggart lectures on metaphysics that Keynes attended while writing the essay on time, a lot of time in these lectures was clearly devoted to the question of the purpose of God and the devil in the universe (JMK/UA/1/2, 41–65).

Not much is said in the McTaggart lecture notes about the concept of time, except

> Perhaps time is a reality not so independent of the content as is generally supposed. That there is some difference between past and future is indispensible. Perhaps this difference has in the fact that time is progressive, that the whole is progressively and ever more perfectly manifested in time. (JMK/UA/1/2, 62).

For Keynes, this last sentence represents a problem of considerable difficulty. He circles back on it in his essay: '. . . the most important question that I have omitted all together is that of past, present and future', although he states: 'Yet it is difficult to see in what sense if time exists, the past and future can exist'. This is a statement not very unlike McTaggart's.

Two other topics remain unsolved in his essay – the subjects of free will and the possibility of progress. Somehow, all of the knowledge we seek and all of the generalizations we make, we suppose to be in some way permanent and out of time, he says. 'Not only do we think of truth as out of time but we conceive our own personality to be existent independently of it' (JMK/UA/17: 20).

Keynes notes that there are different kinds of symptoms of belief in the timeless:

> Whether, as Kant said, time is a form of perception, a *conditio cognoscendi*, whether it is an inexplicable delusion on our past, or whether it is an element of experience which in some higher state we shall be to comprehend as compatible with timeless perfection. (JMK/UA/17: 20)

Nevertheless, Keynes admits that philosophy cannot see its way to a doctrine of a timeless reality without some kind of experience.

In the final lecture that Keynes attended on metaphysics, the philosophical positions of the day were on the agenda. It was stated that Kant has an influence of a different kind – it is not his methods that have been accepted (JMK/UA/1/2, 66). On the other hand, Hegel has not been amended and repealed – people do not believe in Hegel because they have lost their philosophic nerve (JMK/UA/1/2, 68). Few would accept every detail of the dialectic, but many would accept an idea of the absolute (JMK/UA/1/2, 68).

Keynes's final remark in his lecture notes is and might be a direct citation from McTaggart – that the attempt of the day is to steer the line between the Hegelian and Agnostic approaches.

CONCLUSION

Keynes's early reflection on metaphysics and time is primarily inspired by McTaggart, and his thoughts about ethics and politics stem from Moore. His paper on time increases his awareness to avoid common sense notions of time. On the other hand, the writing reflects the contemporary deeper philosophical considerations about the existence of time.

Kant perceives time as something consecutive – he assumed that time could be comprehended as something uniform, something that could be set as a sequence, but this approach deemphasizes like the B-theory the difficulties concerning the dynamic aspect of time. According to Hegel knowledge can only be related to the past history, and the future is without form and therefore cannot be thematized. The present unifies the past and the future negatively – time is the contradiction in and ceaseless motion of finite beings like it is in the A-theory.

Moore and McTaggart share the same view on the unreality of time. The present is not real, because it can only be thought of as infinitely small; and past and future cannot be real, not only because they also must be thought of as infinitely divisible, but also because they wholly lack that immediacy, which is a necessary constituent in reality.

In Keynes's paper, time is about the awareness of change and change requires that at least one aspect differs with respect to what is happening, i.e. whether the event is future, present or past – in McTaggart's theory, its A characteristics. On the contrary, B series alone cannot account for change, because 'earlier than' or 'later than' cannot differ in its characteristics – a changeless state is a timeless state.

In other words, static time interprets the indivisible aspect of being, so to speak, and dynamic time interprets the unreal aspect of becoming. That there is some difference between past and future is indispensible, as Keynes said.

In this way, his paper on time became a breaking point for Keynes, where the dynamic concept of time appeared. An important stone is being laid for the later Keynesian revolution in economics.

NOTES

1. I owe much gratitude to the librarian at King's College Library, Cambridge for access to the unpublished writings of J.M. Keynes: The Provost and Scholars of King's College Cambridge 2012©.
2. See Chick (2004) for an interesting introduction to the concept of time and open systems.
3. The paper is available at the King's College Archive in a handwritten form, Cambridge, UK: JMK/UA/17: Essay on Time. At a conference in Denmark, Roy Rotheim informed me of his transcription of Keynes's paper on time. I am very grateful to him for subsequently sending me a copy.
4. Andrada (2009: 2), and he continues: 'It is a fact of human affairs in general, and economic conduct in particular, that the passage of time pervades circumstances affecting agent's actions. This is an essential aspect of existence, for human beings do not exist outside time: history exists, and does not repeat itself.'
5. Davis (1991) raises interesting questions concerning the development of Keynes's philosophical thinking. Keynes could not follow his teacher Moore in all the latter's views.
6. For an elaboration of the theme, see Hegel, G.W.F. (1807) System der Wissenschaft, Erster Theil, Phänomenologie des Geistes.

7. Kant's ethical theory is often cited as the paradigm of a deontological theory. Although the theory certainly can be seriously criticized, it remains probably the finest analysis of the bases of the concepts of moral principle and moral obligation.
8. Moore's Prize-Fellowship dissertation from 1897 on 'The Metaphysical Basis of Ethics'.
9. Cited as references in Keynes's paper: Sidgwick (1894), Schiller (1895), McIntyre (1895), Hyslop (1898) and Calkins (1899).
10. Keynes, J.M. (1903) 'Essay on Time', unpublished.
11. According to Calkins (1899: 218–219), however, even everyday experiences can be interesting: 'Everyday reflexions has always, indeed, identified time with succession, and has sharply emphasized its opposition to duration or permanence; the "flight of time", "the elusiveness of the moment, the stream of time, are all expressions of our ordinary consciousness".'

REFERENCES

King's College Archive, Cambridge, UK

JMK/UA/1/1: Lecture notes on Moore.
JMK/UA/1/2: Lecture notes on McTaggart.
JMK/UA/2A: Philosophical notes of John Neville Keynes.
JMK/UA/16: Essay on P. Abelard.
JMK/UA/17: Essay on Time.
JMK/UA/19: Three papers for the Society of Apostles.
PP/45/168: John Neville Keynes and Florence Ada correspondence.
PP/45/316: Lytton Strachey.
REF/13/25: Photographs of portraits by Roger Eliot Fry.

Others

Andrada, Rogerio, P. (2009) 'History, crucial choices and equilibrium', Discussion paper, IE/UNICAMP, University of Campinas, Brazil, 170.
Backhouse, R.E. and Batemann, B.W. (2006) 'John Maynard Keynes: Artist, Philosopher, Economist', *Atlantic Economic Journal*, 34(2), 149–159.
Baldwin, T. (1996) 'G E Moore', *Cambridge Philosophers V. Philosophy*, 71, 275–285.
Bosanquet, B., Hodgson, S. and Moore, G.E. (1897) 'In What Sense, If Any, Do Past and Future Time Exist?', *Mind*, 6(22), 228–240.
Calkins, Mary W. (1899) 'Time as Related to Causality and to Space', *Mind*, 8(30), 216–232.
Carabelli, Anne M. (1988) *On Keynes's Method*, London: Macmillan.
Chick, Victoria (1983) *Macroeconomics after Keynes*, Oxford: Philip Allan.
Chick, Victoria (2004) 'On Open Systems', *Brazilian Journal of Political Economy*, 24(1), 3–16.
Davidson, P. (2007) *John Maynard Keynes*, Palgrave Macmillan: New York.
Davis, J.B. (1991) 'Keynes's critiques of Moore: Philosophical foundations of Keynes's economics', *Cambridge Journal of Economics*, 15, 61–77.
Dostaler, Gilles (2007) *Keynes and his Battles*, Cheltenham UK and Northampton MA: Edward Elgar.

Felix, David (1999) 'Keynes's Philosophical Development', in R. Backhouse (ed.) *The Cambridge Companion to Keynes*, Cambridge: Cambridge University Press.

Harrod, Roy (1951) *The Life of John Maynard Keynes*, New York: The New York Times Book Review.

Hegel, Georg Wilhelm Friedrich (2009) *Phänomenologie des Geistes*, Munich: GRIN Verlag.

Hyslop, James H. (1898) 'Kant's Doctrine of Time and Space', *Mind*, 7(25), 71–84.

Jaques, Elliott (1982) *The Form of Time*, London: Heinemann Educational Books.

Kant, Immanuel (1900) *Kritik der reinen Vernunft*, Nebraska, USA: The Colonial Press.

Keynes, J.M. (1904) 'Ethics in Relation to Conduct', Keynes Papers, MSS, King's College, Cambridge, UK.

Keynes, J.M. (1921) *A Treatise on Probability*, London: Macmillan.

Keynes, J.M. (1973[1936]) *The General Theory of Employment Interest and Money. The Collected Writings of John Maynard Keynes*, Volume VII, The Royal Economic Society, London: Macmillan.

Madsen, Mogens Ove (1994) 'Økonomi og tid. Repræsentation af tid', Peter Øhrstrøm (ed.), *Topics in Cognitive Science and HCI 3*, Centre for Cognitive Informatics, Roskilde.

McIntyre, J.L. (1895) 'Time and the Succession of Events', *Mind*, 4(15), 334–349.

McTaggart, J. (1896) *Studies in the Hegelian Dialectic*, Cambridge: Cambridge University Press.

McTaggart, J. (1897) 'Hegel's Treatment of the Categories of the Subjective Notion', *Mind*, 7, 164–181, 342–358.

McTaggart, J. (1900) 'Hegel's Treatment of the Categories of the Idea', *Mind*, 9, 145–183.

McTaggart, J. (1908) 'The Unreality of Time', *Mind*, 17(68), 457–474.

Moore, G.E. (2002[1903]) *Principia Ethica*, Cambridge: Cambridge University Press.

Moore, G.E. (1903) 'The Refutation of Idealism', *Mind*, 12(48), 433–453.

Moore, G.E. (1925) *A Defence of Common Sense*, London: Allen & Unwin.

Øhrstrøm, Peter (2011) 'Towards a Common Language for the Discussion of Time Based on Prior's Tense Logic', in Vatakis, A. Esposito, M. Giagkou, F. Cummins and G. Papadelis (eds) *Time and Time Perceptions*, Berlin Heidelberg: Springer-Verlag, 46–57,

Robinson, Joan (1962) *Economic Philosophy*, Middlesex, England: Penguin.

Robinson, Joan (1971) *Economics Heresies*, London: Macmillan.

Runde, J. and Mizuhara, S. (2003) *The Philosophy of Keynes's Economics*, Routledge: London.

Schiller, F.C.S. (1895) 'The Metaphysics of the Time-Process', *Mind*, 4(13), 36–46.

Sidgwick, H. (1907[1874]) *The Methods of Ethics*, London: Macmillan.

Sidgwick, H. (1894) 'A Dialogue on Time and Common Sense', *Mind*, 3(12), 441–448.

Skidelsky, Robert (1983) *Hopes Betrayed*, London: Macmillan.

Turetzky, Philip (1998) *Time*, London: Routledge.

Wegener, Mogens (1992) *Glimt af tidsbegrebets idehistorie*, Højbjerg, Denmark: MW-forlag.

Winston, Gordon C. (1988) 'Three problems with the treatment of time in

economics: perspectives, repetitiveness, and time units', in Winston, Gordon
C. and Richard Teichgraeber (eds), *The Boundaries of Economics*, Cambridge:
Cambridge University Press, 30–52.
Yourgrau, Palle (1991) *The Disappearance of Time: Kurt Gödel and the Idealistic
Tradition in Philosophy*, Cambridge: Cambridge University Press.

7. When Keynes and Minsky meet Mandelbrot . . .

Stefan Voss

WHY SHOULD ECONOMIC MODELS CONSIDER UNCERTAINTY?

Since the Financial Crisis (2007/09) the relevance of 'uncertainty' has increased significantly. *The Black Swan* (Taleb 2010) became synonymous with 'uncertainty' in economic discussion. Uncertainty is a fact in our economic life. And some managers also argue that uncertainty has become more important in terms of making decisions for a company. 'We have to anticipate that more uncertainty will occur and this will happen permanently . . . The world economy has become more complex and more unclear; there are to consider more risks . . . Everything is interconnected, especially financial flows . . . Reason and effect are not so easy to disentangle.'[1]

However, mainstream economics still denies the role of uncertainty even though it is an obvious fact. New-Keynesians describe uncertainty just as 'asymmetric information' but do not agree that uncertainty plays an autonomous role in economy. If these asymmetries were to be reduced or abolished, uncertainty would be minimized and would have no impact on the economy. Only minor economic theories, the Austrian School and the post-Keynesian School have implemented uncertainty in their models. Uncertainty plays a significant role in these theories; even though it leads to quite different views and consequences.

WHAT IS UNCERTAINTY?

To find a clear definition for uncertainty is very difficult. Everyone has experienced uncertainty as a feeling, but it is difficult to define this rationally. Jespersen defines uncertainty as a lack of information (Jespersen 2009: 3). What is information? Shannon (1948) defines information as 'deletion of uncertainty' (Shannon 1948: 22). So, when we compare both definitions we are running into a logic circle. The problem is that no generally accepted definition for 'information' exists. When we go along the path to find a definition of 'information' or 'uncertainty' it looks like we are searching for a black cat in a dark room and we do not even know whether or not the black cat is really in the room.

WHAT SOLUTIONS CAN BE FOUND?

Even though it is difficult to find a clear definition for 'uncertainty', we are not helpless. Knight, the founder of the School of Chicago, defined 'uncertainty' for economic thinking. Knight defined uncertainty in his book 'Risk, Uncertainty and Profit', published in 1921, while Keynes was working on *Treatise on Probability* (Keynes 2008) in 1908/09. At first there is no difference in between both definitions, but when you take a closer look at both definitions, you will find a big difference. We will first evaluate Knight's definition of uncertainty, then we will examine Keynes's definition and then we will compare both definitions. The 'small difference' between both definitions of uncertainty leads to quite different views of economic models and policy.

KNIGHT'S DEFINITION OF UNCERTAINTY

In the first chapter of his book 'Risk, Uncertainty and Profit' (1921) Knight clearly outlines the difference between 'risk' and 'uncertainty'. The essential fact is that 'risk' means in some cases a quantity susceptible of measurement, while at other times it is something distinctly not of this character; and there are far reaching and crucial differences in the bearings of the phenomenon depending on which of the two is really present and operating. We shall accordingly restrict the term 'uncertainty' to cases of the non-quantitative type. It is the 'true uncertainty', and not risk, as has been argued, which forms the basis of a valid theory of profit and accounts for the divergence between actual and theoretical competition (Knight 2006: 19–20).

Knight clearly defines 'uncertainty' as a risk that is not measurable. The question that has to follow is how uncertainty is related to knowledge or information.

'The practical limitation of knowledge, however, rests upon very different grounds. The universe may not be ultimately knowable . . . but it is certainly knowable to a degree so far beyond our actual powers of dealing with it . . .' (Knight 2006: 210).

In other words the information exists, but we do not have access to all the information due to our own limitations.

Knight also gives an example: 'We know as little why we expect certain things to happen as we do the mechanism by which we recall a forgotten name.' (Knight 2006: 230) This example clearly underlines Knight's idea that uncertainty is a lack of information in the sense there is no access to the existing information. Knight proceeds:

> As we have repeatedly pointed out, an uncertainty which can by any method be reduced to an objective, quantitatively determinate probability can be reduced to complete certainty by grouping cases . . . with the result that when the technique of business organization is fairly developed, measurable uncertainties do not introduce into business any uncertainty whatever. (Knight 2006: 231–232)

In conclusion, for Knight uncertainty can be reduced to a quantifiable risk by just finding the right 'technique' to get access to the missing information. He also argues it could be completely eliminated. Knight also argues that 'It is this *true uncertainty* which by preventing the theoretically perfect outworking of the tendencies of competition gives the characteristic form of "enterprise" to economic organization as a whole and accounts for the peculiar income of the entrepreneur.' (Knight 2006: 232)

By defining 'uncertainty' Knight reaches much more extensive conclusions. He identifies uncertainty in a process of competition and the right management to reduce the uncertainties to quantifiable risks or by deleting them completely. The reward of an enterprise is not taking risks in general but reducing them as much as possible related to other competitors. The income of an entrepreneur is the reward of reducing these risks and transferring them to a quantifiable result, a profit!

KEYNES'S DEFINITION OF UNCERTAINTY

Comparing *A Treatise on Probability* (*TP*) with 'Risk, Uncertainty and Profit' (*RUP*), we have to consider that *RUP* was already linked to economic theory. *TP* has set its focus less on economics.

> In '*A Treatise on Probability*', Keynes uses the expression 'rational belief' to cover the individual assessment of the partially unknown probability that, for example, it will rain tomorrow. The 'rational belief' is based in principle on all accessible information, which is not always quantifiable; however . . . in '*Treatise on Probability*' Keynes offered a logical justification for a personal attitude to 'good conduct'. But precisely because many qualitative assessments had to be included, the relevant decision model could not be presented as a rational calculation of optimal behaviour . . . '*A Treatise on Probability*' is not a

textbook of economic theory. It is a moral-philosophical treatise that discusses which beliefs the individual ought to base his actions on, if he wishes to be rational in a broader (human) sense. (Jespersen 2009: 126–127)

So, to make a closer comparison of Keynes's sense of uncertainty with Knight's definition, it is more useful to compare *RUP* with the *General Theory* (*GT*).

In '*A Treatise on Probability*', it was the behaviour of the individual actor that was discussed. In '*The General Theory*', it is the understanding of which causal mechanisms co-determine the development of the macroeconomic system that is the subject of the investigation . . . The outstanding fact is the extreme precariousness of the basis of knowledge on which our estimates of prospective yield have to be made. Our knowledge of the factors which will govern the yield of an investment some years hence is usually very slight and often negligible. If we speak frankly, we have to admit that our basis of knowledge for estimating the yield ten years hence of a railway, a copper mine, a textile factory, the goodwill of a patent medicine, an Atlantic liner, a building in the City of London amounts to little and sometimes to nothing; or even five years hence. In fact those who seriously attempt to make any such estimate are often so much in a minority that their behavior does not govern the market. (*GT*: 97)

Keynes describes uncertainty as a fundamental uncertainty which cannot be calculated.

For it can be easily shown that the assumptions of arithmetically equal probabilities based on a state of ignorance leads to absurdities. We are assuming, in effect, that the existing market valuation, however arrived at, is uniquely *correct* in relation to our existing knowledge of the facts which will influence the yield of the investment, and that will only change in proportion to changes in this knowledge; though, philosophically speaking it cannot be uniquely correct, since our existing knowledge does not provide a sufficient basis for a calculated mathematical expectation. In point of fact, all sorts of considerations enter into the market valuations which are in no way relevant to the prospective yield. (*GT*: 99)

Hereby, Keynes confirms uncertainty as a risk that cannot be calculated by any mathematical methodology.

In Chapter 13 ('The General Theory of the Rate of Interest') uncertainty gets a major role in the context of liquidity-preference.

The necessary condition is the existence of uncertainty as the future of the rate of interest, i.e. as to the complex of rates of interest for varying maturities which will rule at future dates. For if the rates of interest ruling at all future times could be foreseen with certainty, all future rates of interest could be inferred from the present rates of interest for debts of different maturities, which could be adjusted to the knowledge of the future rates . . . If, on the contrary, the rate of interest is uncertain we cannot safely infer . . . the rate of interest. (Jespersen 2009: 162)

. . . there is a risk of loss being incurred in purchasing a long-term debt and subsequently turning into cash, as compared with holding cash. The actuarial profit or mathematical expectation of gain calculated in accordance with the existing probabilities – if it can be so calculated, which is doubtful – must be sufficient to compensate for the risk of disappointment. There is, moreover, a further ground for liquidity-preference which results from the existence of uncertainty as to the future of the rate of interest, provided that there is an organised market for dealing in debts. (Jespersen 2009: 163)

MINSKY'S CONTRIBUTION TO THE INTERPRETATION OF 'UNCERTAINTY' IN THE KEYNESIAN SENSE

In the book *John Maynard Keynes*, written by Hyman Minsky, first published in 1975, Minsky compares the standard versions and the neoclassical synthesis of the *GT* to the original Keynesian sense. Minsky describes in detail that these interpretations are not in line with Keynes's original meaning.

The most important document for this investigation is Keynes's rebuttal to Viner. In Chapter 3 of this book ('Fundamental Perspectives', Minsky also writes a whole section about 'uncertainty' in this chapter): 'To understand Keynes it is necessary to understand his sophisticated view about uncertainty, and the importance of uncertainty in his vision of the economic process. Keynes without uncertainty is something like *Hamlet* without the Prince.' (Minsky 2008)

In the rebuttal to Viner, Keynes characterizes the meaning of uncertainty:

at any given time facts and expectations were assumed to be given in a definite and calculable form; and risks, of which, to admitted, not much notice was taken, were supposed to be capable of an exact actuarial computation. The calculus of probability, to mention of it was kept in the background, was supposed to be capable of reducing uncertainty to the same calculable status as that of certainty itself. (*Quarterly Journal of Economics* 1937: 212–213)

Furthermore Keynes explains what he means by 'uncertain knowledge':

By 'uncertain' knowledge, let me explain, I do not mean merely to distinguish what is known for certain from what is only probable. The game of roulette is not subject, in this sense, to uncertainty; nor is the prospect of a Victory bond being drawn. Or again, the expectation of life is only slightly uncertain. Even the weather is only moderately uncertain. The sense in which I am using the term is that, in which the prospect of a European war is uncertain, or the price of copper and the rate of interest twenty years hence, or the obsolescence of a new invention or the position of private wealth owners in the social system in 1970. About these matters there is no scientific basis on which to form any calculable probability whatever. We simply do not know. (*QJE* 1937: 213–214)

Considering the rebuttal to Viner it is clear what Keynes really means by uncertainty: a non-quantifiable risk. In analogy we can conclude that Keynes defines quantifiable risks as 'risks' in *GT*. It is also important to note that Keynes does not believe one could reduce uncertainty to a quantifiable risk by any methods or techniques.

This definition stands in contrast to Knight who believed it would be possible to reduce uncertainty to quantifiable risks or certainty just by finding the right methods or techniques. This is a fundamental difference of the definition of uncertainty between Keynes and Knight.

HAYEK, KNIGHT AND KEYNES ARE DEALING WITH UNCERTAINTY BUT THE OUTCOME OF UNCERTAINTY FOR THEIR ECONOMIC MODELS IS QUITE DIFFERENT

'Uncertainty' and 'risk' have the same meaning for Hayek and Keynes in the sense that uncertainty cannot be reduced to a quantifiable risk by any method. In Knight's sense the systematic reduction of uncertainty to a quantified risk or a certainty is possible and leads to a profit for a single business unit. So it is a microeconomic view that the reduction of risk and uncertainty leads to profitability. Knight was a founder of the School of Chicago, which developed quantifiable risk models later.

In the Keynesian sense the macroeconomic future is uncertain. The 'liquidity-preference' is not distinguishable without uncertainty. One motive for keeping liquidity is the uncertain macroeconomic future. Also investors in the stock market can diminish the uncertainty by the liquidity of the markets. Every day investors can switch from one investment to another, when sentiment or estimates regarding the 'marginal efficiency of capital' have changed. Liquidity of the markets keeps the investors certain in the sense that they can change their investment permanently if an event happened which might change their subjective future perspectives for a capital investment or if they simply change their personal preferences.

The Austrian School does not explain liquidity in the Keynesian sense. According to the Austrian School markets *tend* to efficiency and there is no need for holding cash permanently as a precautionary motive as in the Keynesian sense. Keeping cash is more or less inefficient because markets *tend* to the optimal allocation of capital assets. In the original Keynesian sense there is only a temporary equilibrium of supply and demand. Even when both factors are equalized by the market, the process of investment in an uncertain environment *tends* to disequilibrium permanently.

Hayek believes that the knowledge of the common people is much brighter than the knowledge of specialists and economists, market processes would diminish uncertainty to a sufficient level necessary for an efficient economy. In contradiction Keynes believes in interventions led by the knowledge of institutions such as governments and central banks.

PAUL DAVIDSON: UNCERTAINTY IN AN ERGODIC OR A NON-ERGODIC SYSTEM

Paul Davidson interpreted Keynes in the way that he defined uncertainty in a non-ergodic system. Davidson clearly points out that Keynes never used this formulation, but this interpretation could be in line with Keynes's view.

> Keynes never knew of this ergodic terminology and hence did not use the expression 'ergodic axiom' in his emphasis on the importance of uncertainty and the demand for liquidity in his 1936 book or any other writings. Nevertheless, the idea of the inapplicability of the ergodic axiom to the economic system in which we live is embedded not only in Keynes's writings on uncertainty, but also in his famous criticism of Professor Tinbergen's econometric methodology. (Davidson 2009: 33)

Ergodicity is defined as a character of dynamic systems, which is related to the medium behavior of the system. Such a system is defined by a function that describes the development of a system depending on its current condition. There are only two ways to average the system: one is to observe the development of the system in the long run (time average); another is to observe all possible conditions in one moment (space average). In an ergodic system the result in both cases must be the same.

Example: the average result of flipping a die a thousand times leads to the same result in terms of a stochastic distribution as if one flips a thousand dice once.

In an ergodic system every outcome is quantifiable. Every move is independent of the move before and all future moves flow into a distinguishable stationary probability distribution. So, in this case the future is only a shadow of the past. Time is a linear and reversible function. If you flip a coin the probability of the result is always 1:1 and every toss is independent of the toss before.

In a non-ergodic system the future is not predictable in statistical terms. The distribution of probabilities is unknown and unstable. The future probability is not independent of the past. Time is not a linear function; it is historic time which is irreversible. The flow of events is not homogenous and not stable. So, there is a big difference between the two systems and it can be explained by the appearance of the *Black Swan* for example.

THE 'BLACK SWAN' – AN EXPLANATION FOR UNCERTAINTY?

Taleb's book *The Black Swan* became a bestseller during the financial crisis, because many people believed that Taleb had found the essential truth for the disaster. For Taleb the 'Black Swan' was a unique event, an event with a very low probability that was not considered. Taleb argues that the risk models of the financial institutions did not cover events with such a low probability, so that the appearance of this very low probability led to a significant outcome that simply was not calculated in these models. 'In an ergodic universe, any single event will appear to be unique to the observer only if she does not have a sufficient *a priori* or statistical knowledge of reality to properly classify this event with a group of similar conditional events.' (Davidson 2010: 567–570)

Does the appearance of the 'Black Swan' in an ergodic or a non-ergodic system really mean anything ? In the second edition of his book, Taleb tries to confuse the issue of epistemological uncertainty in an ergodic system from ontological uncertainty in a non-ergodic world. Taleb states: 'I believe the distinction between epistemic uncertainty and ontic (i.e., ontological) uncertainty is important philosophically but entirely irrelevant in the real world . . . [It] is the case of a "distinction" without difference.' (Taleb 2010: 53)

In Taleb's view the difference is only significant for philosophers but not for practical men in the business world. This argument is not profound and it is not scientific, it is just conventional wisdom which ignores fundamental aspects. It is the 'skepticism' in the sense that philosophers are out of reality and are living in their own world, which is not related to the 'real world'.

The truth is that philosophers create a reality. This reality might be wrong or true, but it does not matter if it is right or wrong. It only matters if the majority 'accepts' it as reality. The generally accepted philosophy creates a reality, independently from whether it is a right or wrong reality.

However, if the 'inner reality' does not match the reality, divergences will appear and there will be contradictions. The 'inner reality' also leads to different views in the sense of which actions should be taken, if divergence or contradictions appear.

Marx said that philosophers only interpreted the world in different ways, but it would be more important to change the world. Marx did not consider that these 'interpretations' created a world and that other 'interpretations' of the world would change the world, if a new interpretation were to be generally accepted. So, the only question is which reality currently is in power. But if a 'reality' is in power the next question is, if this 'reality' is consistent and mapping the reality or not. If this 'reality' is inconsistent it can be denied or ignored, but it cannot be ignored in the long run, if this inconsistency leads to contradictions within the created system of reality which is set to fail by its own contradictions or insufficient relations to reality.

In an ergodic model, the future is considered as pre-determined. To the contrary in a non-ergodic model, the outcome is uncertain, because the future is assumed to be partly unknowable for decision makers. So, the first step to be made is to draw a sharp line between whether the world of business, the world of free markets, is an ergodic or a non-ergodic system.

THE IDEA-HISTORIC PREDECESSORS OF MODERN FINANCIAL THEORY: BACHELIER AND BRONZIN

In 1900 a young mathematician, Louis Bachelier, was in the oral examination of his dissertation 'Théorie de la Spéculation' (Bachelier 1900). His theme was speculation with government bonds, which were traded on the Bourse de Paris. Such a theme was not very common at the time. One of his judges was Henri Poincaré, one of the most famous mathematicians.

> But it was not the kind of paper that won the highest honors: The grade was a respectable 'mention honorable', not the 'trés honorable' that would have assured Bachelier a first-class ticket to an august mathematical career. And so he spent the next 27 years battling for recognition and tenure from the French academic establishment . . . Fortunately for him the thesis appeared in a major journal and was not lost to history . . . His thesis laid the foundations of financial theory and, far more generally, of the theory of all forms of probabilistic change in continuous time. (Mandelbrot 2008: 45)

The essence of his dissertation is that price movements under market conditions flow into a normal distribution, while changes in price are series of independent moves. This theory is also related to the Brownian movement.

In addition, independently from Bachelier, the Italian mathematician Vinzenz Bronzin (Bronzin 1908) developed a model of valuation for option contracts. It was quite similar to Bachelier's thesis. His paper was published in 1908. It did not attract attention in the academic world and was widely ignored.

The poor reception of the fundamental work of both mathematicians was probably due to the fact that speculation and financial business was not a theme for academics in those days.

THE SCHOOL OF CHICAGO DID NOT INVENT SOMETHING REALLY NEW

Later the School of Chicago, Markowitz, Black-Scholes, Sharpe, Fama and others, designed the Modern Financial Theory, which does not differ substantially from the works of Bachelier and Bronzin. Most of the 'new' works of these scientists were honoured with the Nobel Prize.

All models of the modern financial theory are based on similar assumptions:

- The existence of a complete and sufficient capital market without transaction costs. No limits for short sales and the possibility of arbitrage.
- The returns of the underlying values, i.e. the relative changes of price movements, are distributed identically and the movements are completely independent of each other. That means that volatility of returns is constant.
- There is a constant interest rate to which in every period someone can borrow or lend money.

The extension of these models i.e. dividend payments, stochastic interest rates or stochastic volatilities are also considered.

In addition in their theory it is also obvious that people are rational and only want to get rich as all investors are the same. It is the world of the rational 'homo oeconomicus' where everyone is targeting the same thing.

In conclusion, the fundamental works of Bachelier and Bronzin and the further developments by the School of Chicago are all based on the same assumptions and the same techniques. They reduce uncertainty to quantifiable risks. These tools were developed for decision-makers in single business units in order to quantify the risk of entrepreneurial decisions and to estimate the risk of the business unit itself. Banks use similar models to calculate their credit risks (for example 'Value at Risk-profile'). Insurance companies have to hold high amounts of assets and make their portfolio decisions (asset allocation) usually according the portfolio theory of Markowitz.

The shadow banks also define their risk-profile according to the models of the School of Chicago. This microeconomic approach is linked with Knight's idea, who imagined that uncertainty could be reduced to a quantifiable risk just by using the right method or technique to get access to the hidden information. To reach this information in a competitive environment gives single companies the opportunity to make a profit, when they are just better than their competitors.

So, it has taken more than 100 years of scientific work for all significant companies in the world of today to use the same methods for calculating their risk-profiles.

The core sense of these ideas is based upon the fundamental works of Knight. In consequence it is the utopia in the sense of creating a world, where everything can be made possible by using the correct methods. These techniques are the 'deus ex machina' which provides every participant in the market with complete information. In the last sense the market is the correct decision-maker in terms of shifting the economy into a stage of equilibrium.

The theory as a whole can be qualified as an ergodic system. In contradiction, uncertainty in the Keynesian sense is related to macroeconomics and it cannot be reduced to a quantifiable risk. Uncertainty is not as productive as in Knight's sense; it is a hurdle for the whole economy, which cannot succeed in overcoming the difficulties by mathematical calculations. Uncertainty related to *GT* is a non-quantifiable risk in a non-ergodic system.

THE EMPIRICAL TESTS OF MANDELBROT RELATED TO THE QUESTION HOW MARKETS REALLY BEHAVE

To answer the question whether markets are ergodic or non-ergodic I consult the empirical tests and conclusions of the scientific works of Mandelbrot related to market processes. Were Bachelier's theses right or wrong?

> Thus it was not until 1962 . . . I analyzed more than a century of data on U.S. cotton prices and studied the way they had varied daily, monthly, and yearly. The results were clear and irrefutable. Far away from being well-behaved and normal as the standard theory then predicted, cotton prices jumped wildly around. Their variance, rather than holding steady as expected, gyrated a

hundred-fold and never settled down to a constant value. In the world of financial theory that was a bombshell . . . (Mandelbrot 2008: 55).

Mandelbrot extended his research on stocks and currencies and found the same results (Mandelbrot 2008: 96–97). So, it is of empirical evidence that market processes do not follow any normal distribution and they are non-ergodic. However one could argue again, that this would not really matter. The models that are used in the financial world of today are just approximations to reality and they are useful. Only the results are important. However, the results of these models are wrong and misleading in many cases. The defenders of the Modern Financial Theory define these effects as 'anomalies', even these 'anomalies' appear more often than the 'normal' outcomes. 'Finally, an especially lively pastime for economists these days is to try poking holes in the grand unified theory of modern finance, the Efficient Market Hypothesis that markets are rational, prices reflect all available information, and you cannot beat the market.' (Mandelbrot 2008: 102–103)

One of the most famous examples which confirms that these models are wrong is the failure of the Long Term Capital Management (LP) in 1998, which was – among others – also founded by the Nobel Prize winners Merton and Scholes. The fund temporarily had 25 bearers of a PhD on its payroll.

The next question is why financial institutions still work with models based on wrong assumptions and leading to wrong results. Mandelbrot argues that it is 'Habit and convenience' (Mandelbrot 2008: 105). In my own view this is just half of the story. In the beginning the School of Chicago had to find ways to reach the world of business for their theory. Their idea was that if they could win over the business sector they would be generally accepted and could conquer the economic theory. While Keynesians were only discussing macroeconomic models without getting real access to the business people, the School of Chicago was able to integrate macro- and microeconomics. They could offer tools for business people for reducing risks. They also made non-quantifiable risks – uncertainty – to quantifiable risks, because these models suggest the possibility of reaching information, which could not be reached before. These models also suggested being 'scientific' and 'objective'. They might be consistent in terms of statistics and mathematics, but they are not scientific in terms of empirical evidence. The target of the School of Chicago was not to integrate macro and micro only, the main target was to integrate the business sector to the theory of the School of Chicago. Many School of Chicago professors were awarded the Nobel Prize. So, if these models were abolished due to the fact that markets are not efficient and these models were based on false assumptions it would also mean that the School of Chicago was wrong; fundamentally and in general. The whole aura of this School would simply disappear. To avoid these insights, wrong signals from these models were defined as 'external shocks', 'anomalies' and so on. It is not scientific; it is just a rhetoric strategy to defend a theory which is based on false assumptions and leads to wrong information.

SYSTEMIC RISK OR SYSTEMIC ERROR?

Deregulation of financial markets and the belief that risk and uncertainty could be exactly calculated by models of the financial theory related to the School of Chicago led to a sharp increase of multiple financial products. The shift was backed by international regulations.

> In 1996, large banks sought more favorable capital treatment for their trading and the Basel Committee on Bank Supervision adopted at the Market Risk Amendment to Basel I. This provided that if banks hedged their credit or market risks using derivatives, they could hold less capital against their exposures from trading and other activities. (The Financial Crisis Inquiry Report 2011: 49)

According to the FCIR these regulations led to the creation of financial institutions with high risk profiles:

> . . . AIG; the largest U.S. insurance company, would accumulate a one-half trillion dollar position in credit risk through the OTC market without being required to post one dollar's worth of initial collateral or making any other provisions for loss. AIG was not alone. The value of the underlying assets for CDS outstanding worldwide grew from 6.4 trillion dollars at the end of 2004 to a peak of 58.2 trillion dollars at the end of 2007. A significant portion was apparently speculative or naked credit default swaps . . . Market participants and regulators would find themselves straining to understand an unknown battlefield shaped by unseen exposures and interconnections as they fought to keep the financial system from collapsing. (The Financial Crisis Inquiry Report 2011: 50–51)

Basel I created the fundamentals of the financial crisis. An unregulated market of derivatives and dysfunctional risk models led to the situation that major financial institutions underestimated their risk profiles and the risk of squeezing the company's liquidity.

'The Commission concludes that some large investment banks . . . experienced massive losses . . . because of significant failures of corporate governance, including risk management. Executive and employee compensation systems at these institutions disproportionally rewarded short-term risk taking.' (The Financial Crisis Inquiry Report 2011: 279)

In August 2007 markets for short term borrowings like interbank rates and repo markets ran out of liquidity due to a lack of confidence. IKB was the first bank where problems with securitized mortgage lending became visible. Concerns spread over the markets that many other institutions could follow in the same way.

Liquidity preference from the precautionary motive in the Keynesian sense played no role for these companies. In their theory all risks were calculable and keeping money for unknown risks was not necessary, because all risks were supervised. If they needed liquidity they could lend it overnight on the interbank or repo markets. In their view markets were efficient and could not collapse. Uncertainty and liquidity preference in the Keynesian sense, if they ever heard something about it, was only a footnote of academic literature without any link to their reality of efficient markets.

CAN THE FINANCIAL INSTABILITY HYPOTHESIS (FIH) OF MINSKY EXPLAIN THE FINANCIAL CRISIS?

The FIH of Minsky is based on the fundamental works of Keynes's *General Theory*. Minsky's method is to concentrate the FIH on the Wall Street paradigm and the meaning of uncertainty for the macroeconomic system according to *GT*. In the book *John Maynard Keynes* (1975) Minsky rejects the standard versions of GT:

> ... such Keynesian models are either trivial (the consumption-function models), incomplete (the IS-LM models without a labor market), inconsistent (the IS-LM models with a labor market but no real-balance effect), or indistinguishable in their results from those of the older quantity-theory models (the neoclassical synthesis). (Minsky 2008: 50–51)

Keynes's fundamental perspectives are composed, among others, of private portfolios, real-capital assets, speculative financial assets and banks. The 'Wall Street-Paradigm' of Keynes was lost to standard versions as it evolved into the neo-classical synthesis.

Minsky also outlines some fundamental aspects of the *General Theory* such as business cycles, uncertainty and investments in disequilibrium. 'Uncertainty' is the major part of the rule in so far as it cannot be quantified. 'Risks' can be quantified, but uncertainty cannot be quantified by mathematical calculations.

The fundamental perspectives show that uncertainty determines portfolio decisions of households, firms and financial institutions. In the investment theory of cycles, consumption only plays a passive role as an amplifier; aggregate fluctuations are determined by investment fluctuations. 'As a result of the effect on behavior of the need to make decisions under conditions of imperfect knowledge, investment by business can be volatile even though production relations are stable.' (Minsky 2008: 66)

The publication of the book *John Maynard Keynes* in 1975, is also the basis of the FIH which Minsky established in 'Stabilizing an unstable Economy' in 1986.

Hedge finance, speculative finance and Ponzi-Finance are the key elements of the FIH, which explain the current economy as endogenously unstable due to its financial structure. The FIH is based on fundamental views of *GT* by Hyman Minsky and was widely ignored by mainstream economists until the biggest financial crisis since 1929. The FIH today has a much better reputation, but a severe worldwide financial crisis was necessary to decline this theory as 'obscure'.

Related to the last financial crisis there are other details that Minsky could not foresee in 1986, when 'Stabilizing an Unstable Economy' was published. While Minsky postulated 'Big Government' for the financial system, which means stricter regulations of financial markets, the opposite happened. Markets became more and more deregulated and derivatives increased sharply in terms of volume and complexity. Big financial institutions hedged their positions also with derivatives in over-the-counter markets. Basel I opened the possibility of hedging risks positions with derivatives instead of underlying these with equity. AIG mutated from a traditional insurer to a complex system of derivatives. Uncertainty was reduced to a calculable risk by dysfunctional risk models. Liquidity-preference from the precautionary motive in the Keynesian sense no longer played any role for 'modern' companies. Liquidity could be lent on spot markets overnight, if necessary. Modern Financial Theory created an illusion of security. In addition, in 1986, Minsky had no idea of securitization for example in the form of 'subprime loans' which split risk and return for the lender. The lender issued credit contracts to borrowers, and then formed a package of contracts which he sold for a provision to other financiers, who bought these contracts financed by short-term borrowings. So, there was build up of a pyramid of debts where every market participant believed he would be a hedge financier based upon misleading valuation and risk models of the School of Chicago. In the end it was a global Ponzi-Finance. The irony is that it is not necessary that companies increase their risks consciously due to a favourable economic environment as Minsky suggested, it is also possible that companies increase their risks due to misleading risk models while believing their risk-profile would be conservative.[2] The financial system collapsed like a house of cards in September 2008.

Minsky clearly defined the basic structure of an endogenous unstable economy due to its financial system. He had no influence on economic policy-makers, who acted promptly in the opposite direction. The dogs were barking but the caravan of the blind was still moving on until the biggest financial crisis since 1929.

CONCLUSION

In the end financial institutions did not learn very much from the financial crisis. For the valuation of assets and the estimation of risks or uncertainty they still use misleading models of the School of Chicago. The Obama administration wanted to regulate the financial markets more, but Republicans are torpedoing these initiatives intensively. The belief of self-regulating and efficient markets of the libertarian Austrians still dominates the legislation. A post-Keynesian perspective to the financial crisis according to the FIH in connection with Big Government is not on the agenda.

Shadow banks are the main problem. Banks are currently transferring their risks and toxic assets to non-regulated financial institutions. In the USA the credit volume of shadow banks amounts to US$16 trillion – more than the official banking sector amounting to around US$13trillion.[3] Banks are funding 'Dark Pools', unregulated dealing platforms where banks can make their deals strictly confidential. The sector has developed new instruments such as 'Regulatory Capital Relief Trades' (Reg Caps), where regulatory capital can be set free.[4] Many banks save equity by transferring credit risks to other institutions located in exotic parts of the world. *Manager Magazin* estimates that only a third of all credit risks are positions held by the official banking sector in reality.[5]

Stress tests for banks and financial institutions are a complete farce, because their biggest risks are transferred to the shadow banking system and they are not visible. The tests also consist of risk models that are insufficient and misleading.

There are many contradictions, frictions and hidden risks in the financial system. However, it is impossible that policy-makers and central banks can compensate these dysfunctions in the long run. Neither the Federal Reserve Bank nor other central banks nor the taxpayer will be able to pay for credit defaults and entrepreneurial failures to an unlimited extent. The limits of the financial system are still being tested.

To quote Hamlet: 'Though this be madness, yet there is method in it.'

NOTES

1. Wolfgang Reitzle, CEO of Linde AG, in an interview with *Manager Magazin*, 4/11: 53 (translated by the author).
2. 'Bounded Rationality' as the idea that in decision-making, rationality of individuals is limited by the information they receive, the cognitive limitations of their minds and the finite amount of time they have to make a decision does not really get the point. The risk-models themselves are completely irrational due to the lack of empirical evidence. So, the source of information individuals receive is not rational but irrational. The idea of 'Bounded Rationality' deviates from the real fact of wrong decisions: the pseudo-rational models of the 'Modern Financial Theory'.
3. *Manager Magazin*, 4/11: 32.
4. *Manager Magazin*, 4/11: 36.
5. *Manager Magazin*, 4/11: 38.

REFERENCES

Bachelier, Louis (1900) *Théorie de la Spéculation, Annales scientifiques de l'École Normale Supérieure*, 3(1), 21–86.
Bibow, Jörg (2009) *Keynes on Monetary Policy, Finance and Uncertainty*, London, New York: Routledge.
Bronzin, Vinzenz (1908) *Theorie der Prämiengeschäfte*, Leipzig, Wien: Franz-Deuticke-Verlag.
Davidson, Paul (2009) *John Maynard Keynes*, Hampshire: Palgrave Macmillan.
Davidson, Paul (2010) 'Black Swans and Knight's Epistemological Uncertainty', *Journal of Post-Keynesian Economics*, 32, Summer.
Fleck, Ludwig (1980) *Entstehung und Entwicklung einer wissenschaftlichen Tatsache*, Frankfurt am Main: Suhrkamp.
Jespersen, Jesper (2009) *Macroeconomic Methodology*, Cheltenham UK and Northampton MA: Edward Elgar.
Jespersen, Jesper (2009) 'Effective Demand: Uncertain Expectations, Profitability and Financial Circuit', Paper presented at the Dijon-conference, Dijon, 10–12 December 2009, Roskilde.
Kessler, Oliver (2008) *Die internationale politische Ökonomie des Risikos*, Wiesbaden: VS Verlag.
Keynes, John Maynard (2008[1936]) *The General Theory of Employment, Interest and Money*, Breinigsville: BN Publishing.
Keynes, John Maynard (2008[1921]) *A Treatise on Probability*, Breinigsville: Rough Draft Printers.
Knight, Frank H. (1921) *Risk, Uncertainty, and Profit*, Hart, Schaffner, and Marx Prize Essays, No. 31. Boston and New York: Houghton Mifflin.
Knight, Frank H. (2006[1921]) *Risk Uncertainty and Profit*, Mineola, New York: Dover Publications.
Mandelbrot, Benoit (2008) *The (Mis) Behavior of Markets*, London: Profile Books.
Minsky, Hyman P. (2008[1975]) *John Maynard Keynes*, New York: McGraw-Hill.
Minsky, Hyman P. (2008[1986]) *Stabilizing an unstable Economy*, New York: McCraw-Hill.

Rubinstein, Ariel (1998) *Modelling Bounded Rationality*, Cambridge, Mass., London: The MIT Press.
Runde, Jochen and Mizuhara, Sohei (2003) *The Philosophy of Keynes's Economics*, London, New York: Routledge.
Shannon, C.E. (1948) 'A Mathematical Theory of Communication', reprint from *The Bell System Technical Journal*.
Taleb, Nassim (2010) *The Black Swan*, New York: Random House.
Terzi, A. (2010) 'Keynes's Uncertainty Is Not About White or Black Swans', *Journal of Post-Keynesian Economics*, 32, Summer.
The Financial Crisis Inquiry Report (2011) 'Final Report of the National Commission on the Causes of the Financial and Economic Crisis in the United States', New York.

8.   Keynes's *General Theory* after 75 years: time to re-read and reflect[1,2]

Jesper Jespersen

I believe myself to be writing a book on economic theory which will largely revolutionise – not, I suppose, at once but in the course of the next ten years – the way the world thinks about economic problems . . . (Keynes in a letter to George Bernard Shaw, 1935; Keynes 1973a: 492).

INTRODUCTION

No doubt, Keynesian unemployment and even *The General Theory* are still referred to in mainstream textbooks of macroeconomics. But if you have happened to read *The General Theory* you may be wondering if the textbook author has read the same book as you. In most textbooks so-called Keynesian economics is analysed within a general equilibrium model, where the special Keynes feature is an assumption of real-wage inflexibility which may cause involuntary unemployment in the short run. There might also be a reference to a 'Keynesian' consumption function, which is derived from the microeconomic theory of an optimizing household with rational expectations. On the other hand you will hardly find any reference to phenomena like uncertainty, effective demand and liquidity preference, which are some of the distinct novelties explained in *The General Theory* and emphasized by Keynes in the preface and the very first pages of the book.

This book is chiefly addressed to my fellow economists . . . its main purpose is to deal with difficult questions of theory . . . I myself held with conviction for many years the theories which I now attack . . . (Keynes 1936: v).

For if orthodox economics is at fault, the error is to be found not in the super-structure, which has been erected with great care for logical consistency, but in a lack of clearness and of generality in the premises. (Keynes 1936: v)

Those, who are strongly wedded to what I shall call 'the classical theory', will fluctuate, I expect, between a belief that I am quite wrong and a belief that I am saying nothing new . . . (Keynes 1936: v).

This book . . . is primarily a study of the forces which determine changes in the scale of output and employment as a whole . . . (Keynes 1936: vii).

I have called this book the General Theory of Employment, Interest and Money, placing the emphasis on the prefix **general** . . . (Keynes 1936: 3).

There is, however, a necessary condition failing which the existence of a liquidity-preference for money as a means of holding wealth could not exist.

This necessary condition is the existence of uncertainty as to the future of the rate of interest . . . (Keynes 1936: 168).

Keynes is stating from the very beginning that within macroeconomics one should be aware of the distinction between 'Them and me'. My fellow economists use the same language, but the meaning is different, because the premises, i.e. analytical model and the methodology, are fundamentally different and add up to a fundamentally different methodology. The recognition of this different world-view is a precondition for understanding the theoretical implications of the 'principle of effective demand'. Keynes claimed that the genuine theoretical novelty was this theoretical concept, which he would demonstrate within the book, is deductively indispensable for an analysis of 'the economic society in which we actually live'. If one does not see this link from methodology to real world economics, one will, as Keynes predicted, 'fluctuate between a belief that [either The General Theory] is quite wrong [or it is] saying nothing new', (Keynes 1936: v). In fact, this is a rather precise description of the perception of *The General Theory* by the neoclassical economists.

TOWARDS *THE GENERAL THEORY*[3]

The General Theory was published on 4 February. Expectations were high, because Keynes was definitely Mr Somebody, in both the academic world and in the public eye.

It had been long in preparation. The case can be made that Keynes intellectually started on *The General Theory* the day after the publication of *A Treatise on Money* (1930). He was not satisfied with the outcome. He was disappointed by himself, because he had not within the *TM* been able to give a theoretically convincing argument of the persistent unemployment which had characterized the British economy for more than 10 years. At the best he had only managed to give an elaborate account of a thorny adjustment process to full employment equilibrium: 'The relation between this book and my "Treatise on Money" . . . is probably clearer to myself than it will be to others . . . [But] I failed to deal thoroughly with the effects of changes in the level of output . . . (Keynes 1936: vi–vii).

The theoretical problem for any economist in those days was the lack of a theoretical macroeconomic model which could support public investments as a measure against unemployment. Keynes himself had experience during the campaign up to the general election of 1929, when he supported Lloyd George's proposal for more public investment, of being caught by the question, 'where should savings come from?' The American president, Franklin D. Roosevelt, had the very same problem, when he initiated his New Deal programme in 1933 against the advice of a majority of the established economists. The neoclassical argument against public investment was very simple: that they would take up a part of the limited savings available for private and public investment. Savings were considered as being of a given magnitude.

These experiences were an important part of the theoretical challenge, because he could see that public investment (and house building) did increase employment – but how? Keynes wrote a long essay in support of Roosevelt's policy: *The means to prosperity*, where we can see today that he was halfway in his sloughing off the general equilibrium analytical framework and embracing the open-system framework. Here the method of shifting equilibrium is employed and even more important the analytical meaning of equilibrium deviates from market clearing. In this essay he presented the multiplier theory, which only makes theoretical sense if the amount of savings is variable.

The amount of savings might change during the adjustment process to full employment; only when full employment is assumed will public investment crowd private investment out in the proportion of one-to-one.

But this answer to the question of, 'where should the extra saving come from?' could not be given convincingly, until the theory of the 'principle of effective demand' was established, and that waited for a new analytical framework to be developed.

The most pressing methodological question in that context was addressed in Keynes's radio talk delivered on 19 November 1934 'Poverty in Plenty: Is the Economic System Self-adjusting?' (*CWK* XIII: 485–92). During this rather informal talk he took the role of the little boy in the fairytale of Hans Christian Andersen called *The Emperor's New Clothes*, because after asking the audience the rhetorical question, 'what do we know about the stability of the market-economic system?', he gave the empirically indisputable answer *very little*, because substantial and persistent unemployment had lasted, at that time for nearly 15 years, without any significant tendency to disappear on its own.

He continued the radio talk by characterizing the society of fellow economists, i.e. the economic profession, as divided into two distinct groups separated by an analytical gulf:

> On the one side are those who believe that the existing economic system is, in the long run, a self-adjusting system, though with creaks and groans and jerks and interrupted by time lags, outside interference and mistakes. (*CWK* XIII 1934: 486)

> On the other side of the gulf are those that reject the idea that the existing economic system is, in any significant sense, self-adjusting . . . (*CWK* XIII 1934: 487).

> The gulf between these two schools of thought is deeper, I believe, than most of those on either side of it are aware of. On which side does the essential truth lie? That is the vital question for us to solve. (*CWK* XIII 1934: 488)

The neoclassical economists used a general equilibrium model when macroeconomics questions were to be analysed. If market prices and money wage were made perfect flexible – within the model – this market system was by assumption made self-adjusting. Keynes gave this analytical prejudice the following comment: 'This is, however, pure assumption. There is no theoretical reason for believing it to be true. A very moderate amount of observation of the facts, unclouded by preconceptions, is sufficient to show that they do not bear it out . . . ' (*CWK* XIII: 490).

On the other side of the gulf is a much smaller group of macroeconomists (those whom Keynes called the heretics; today, we would rather call this group the 'heterodox' economists), which persistently claims that supply and demand also have to be present in macroeconomic analyses. Unfortunately, Keynes was not yet ready to give a full explanation of why it had to be so; but he was on the track of an explanation which fundamentally broke with the axioms of individual rationality, market clearing and full information in macroeconomics due to the methodological implications of taking uncertainty seriously. Hence, he concluded his position in 1934 the following way:

> Now I range myself with the heretics. There is, I am convinced, a fatal flaw in that part of the orthodox reasoning which deals with the theory of what determines the level of effective demand and the volume of aggregate employment (*CWK* XIII 1934: 489).

NOVELTIES IN *THE GENERAL THEORY*[4]

Keynes focused on the 'principle of effective demand' as the main theoretical novelty of *The General Theory*. He was astonished to realize that within traditional neoclassical macroeconomics there was no room to consider an independent role of aggregate demand. Output as a whole was determined by the supply of factors of production and technology. On brief form one could conclude the neoclassical macro-model by stating that 'supply creates its own demand'.

Keynes was puzzled, how could it be that the fathers of neoclassical microeconomics (especially Marshall) who had emphasized the role of supply *and* demand in the partial market analysis, seemed entirely to disregard the impact of aggregate demand at the macro-level? A number of 'open-minded' neoclassical scholars accepted also at that time the argument that due to rigidities and transaction costs there could in the short run, but only in the short run, be arguments for a limited (in size and space) role in macroeconomics to be played by the demand curve.[5] Those economists who accepted this interpretation of *The General Theory* fell into the category of basically claiming 'nothing new'. Hicks's ISLM-model was one of the first attempts to box the principle of effective demand into a general equilibrium framework 'with sand in the wheels' and to demonstrate that it was just a matter of how the explanatory variables were chosen, which determined the adjustment process to full employment.[6] In this view there was no 'gulf' between Keynes and the Classics. The ISLM-model became the first stepping stone on a slippery road leading to the so-called neoclassical synthesis, where only wage and price rigidities were left to explain involuntary unemployment.

On the other hand the (although hesitant) acceptance by John Hicks (1937) of aggregate demand as one of the driving factors in the short run model was a vindication of one of Keynes's major theoretical achievements to put aggregate demand on even terms with aggregate supply, at least in the short run.

But the second distinct conclusion of *GT*, that involuntary unemployment can be persistent and even be characterized as an equilibrium position, caused an outcry among the orthodox economists. According to neoclassical economics represented by the Walrasian equilibrium model a non-clearing market cannot be in a competitive equilibrium. In that respect Keynes's conclusion was doomed 'quite wrong'. If he had used the expression 'persistent disequilibrium' the outcry would, probably, have been less expressive.

The quite different reception of the two most significant conclusions of *The General Theory* is telling of the dilemma which Keynes had to face after publication.

He could join forces with those colleagues who accepted the importance of aggregate demand, without abandoning the general equilibrium model as the basic analytical framework. Or he could have rejected the ISLM presentation of 'Mr Keynes and the Classics', because it did not incorporate uncertainty and open-system analytical reasoning. (In fairness to

Keynes, I think that it has to be added, that this dilemma is probably easier to identify in the light of 75 years of hindsight.)

Anyhow, one year after the publication Keynes had the opportunity to sum up what he considered as his main achievements. This summary was presented under the title of 'The General Theory of Employment' and had the form of a reaction to four of his (numerous) critics, who had taken a constructive although critical judgment of the book.

> I sum up, therefore, the main grounds for my departure as follows:
>
> (1) The orthodox theory assumes that we have a knowledge of the future of a kind quite different from that which we actually possess. (*CWK* XIV: 122)
>
> (2) The orthodox theory would by now have discovered the above defect, if it had not ignored the need for a theory of the supply and demand for output as a whole . . . (*CWK* XIV: 123).

It seems without doubt that Keynes put the main emphasis on the lack of knowledge, i.e. uncertainty, which cannot methodologically be made compatible with the general equilibrium model. The problem was that, after having realized the methodological consequences of open-system analysis, a new world of possible models of demonstrating how the macroeconomic system works opens up. In the perspective of aggregate behaviour reflecting individual decision making partly based on uncertain expectations, a rich menu of theoretical models can be presented. The real challenge became to develop a method to choose a relevant model for the macroeconomic issue under consideration:

> Economics is a science of thinking in terms of models joined to the art of choosing models which are relevant to the contemporary world. It is compelled to be this, because, unlike the typical natural science, the material to which it is applied is, in too many respects, not homogeneous through time. (*CWK* XIV: 296).

TIME TO RE-READ AND REFLECT

> Keynes's perception was that economies did not behave in the way economists said they did, that something vital had been left out of their accounts, and it was this missing element which explained their malfunctioning; Keynes accused economists of his day of abstracting from the existence of uncertainty. (Skidelsky 1992: 538–9)

I will bring to the fore three important macroeconomic phenomena which are entailed in *GT* and could be very useful for a richer understanding of how the economic crises develop and perhaps give inspiration to proposing ways out:

1. Microfoundation based on the assumption of individual rationality and interdependent behaviour with explicit consideration of 'uncertain knowledge';
2. Principle of effective demand as a macroeconomic theory explaining 'output as a whole';
3. How to avoid making an analytical 'fallacy of composition' or 'fallacy of equilibrium'.

Microeconomic Uncertainty with Macroeconomic Implications

It is often emphasized in mainstream economics that macroeconomics need a firm microeconomic foundation. In this it is striking that within the usually applied microeconomic foundation no consideration of uncertainty is demonstrated. Keynes took the reverse position that the macroeconomic changes are, if not solely then to a large extent, caused by economic actors' changing perception of uncertainty, state of confidence and lack of information often summarized under the heading of 'animal spirits'. Households and firms have to make decisions every day with consequences ranging far into the future. It does not make sense in reality to sit and wait for full information that will never turn up, in that case investment opportunities will pass by. The rather loosely defined concept of 'state of confidence' might change through time for many reasons, which might all be rational from an individual point of view given the (lack of) information. Except for very rare cases all economic activities are characterized by some uncertainty, because one cannot know or estimate the exact outcome. Individual expectations are by nature uncertain due to the inherent lack of information (which is further enforced by a constantly changing environment).

Risk is analytically different. It is defined as individual uncertain events which have such a social structure and stability that an insurance company can apply the law of large numbers to the total outcome. For instance, if an identical, but random event is experienced by a large number of people who act independently of each other, e.g. natural death, then an exact number with a small variance can be calculated with regard to the 'macro-death rate' of the entire population. In these cases a private insurance company or some other institution could transform the individual uncertainty with regard to the specific outcome into risk for the group as a whole. In the society in which we live, one can take out an insurance against the narrow economic consequences of, e.g., theft, fire, sickness and death. Buying an insurance policy implies that individual uncertainty, with regard to the money aspects of such incidents, is removed. But, as we know, most activities have also unforeseeable consequences. Therefore, even a well-designed insurance contract can only transform individual uncertainty into calculable risk in cases where all possible outcomes are known.

One important conclusion is that due to the lack of knowledge macroeconomic phenomena can rarely be described by a stable (and known) probability function. Hence there is no exact, calculable risk function. In that perspective only the government, if any, has the capacity of taking parts of the responsibility of macroeconomic uncertainty on its shoulders. For instance, the real value of financial savings is uncertain. No one can predict future inflation, and the distribution of outcomes is not known. Even the average life expectancy of human beings is increasingly unpredictable, which a number of pension funds regretfully seem to have realized.

Hence, at the individual level there are at least three obvious appearances of uncertainty, when an individual activity is undertaken:

1. there is imperfect information about the institutional environment;
2. the macroeconomic context and other decisive parameters for decisions (e.g. economic policies) are not fully known;
3. we do not have full knowledge about the consequences of our actions.

We are all, as individuals, acting without knowing the exact consequences, and we also act without having full information about the external factors which make an impact on the outcome. Furthermore, we simply cannot know the future, because the macroeconomic reality is (partly) hidden (Jespersen 2009a: Chapter 2). Hence, it would be misleading and pretentious to assume that agents have full knowledge about the future – so-called 'rational expectations'. In fact, to assume rational expectations in macroeconomics is not in any real analytical sense rational – one may rather say that 'it is to assume our difficulties away' (Keynes 1936: 34).

Keynes's main research question was how to avoid undertaking unrealistic assumptions in macroeconomic analysis. In fact, his ambition was to preserve the very realistic assumption that people do behave rationally, but under condition of uncertainty, illustrated in Figure 8.1. Collective behaviour characterized by, for instance, conventions and group-related behaviour or organized according to formal institutions can also be individually rational, if this behaviour reduces the unpredictable consequences of limited information and unknowable external events. Decisions cannot

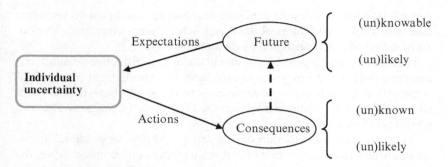

Source: Jespersen (2009): Chapter 4.

Figure 8.1   The anatomy of individual uncertainty

be postponed until uncertainty has been cleared away. If we ask for certainty as a precondition for rational actions – then we cannot act, which,
of course, in some way is an act by itself. Hence, we have to act one way or
the other against the backdrop of uncertainty. The really intriguing question is how to make a proper macroeconomic analysis, where uncertainty
is given the epistemological role which it deserves.

Keynes's *Principle of Effective Demand* developed in *The General
Theory* is an example of an open-system analysis which incorporates
uncertain expectations at the individual/business level and transforms
them into a consistent macroeconomic theory of output and employment
as a whole, see Setterfield (2003).

The Principle of Effective Demand

> As I now think, the volume of employment is fixed by the entrepreneur under
> the motive of seeking to maximise his present and prospective profits; whilst the
> volume of employment which will maximise his profit depends on the aggregate
> demand function given by his expectations of the sum of the proceeds. (Keynes
> 1936: 77)

Effective demand is one of the distinctive analytical concepts that Keynes
developed in *The General Theory*. Demand and demand management have
thereby come to represent one of the distinct trademarks of Keynesian
macroeconomic theory and policy. It is not without reason that the central
position of this concept has left the impression that Keynes's macroeconomic model predominantly consists of theories for determining demand,
while the supply side is neglected. From here it is a short step within a

superficial interpretation to conclude that Keynes (and post-Keynesians) had ended up in a theoretical dead end, where macroeconomic development is exclusively determined by demand factors.

Fortunately, a rich post-Keynesian literature on 'Effective demand' has emerged during the last years overcoming the above mentioned misinterpretation and adding more arguments to the subtle analytical concept than in fact can be found in *The General Theory*, see for instance Hartwig (2007) and Gnos (2009).

As mentioned, the intention of this paper is to give an example of how an important macroeconomic causal relationship can be modelled on the basis of both supply and demand factors with the inclusion of specific institutional conditions such as different forms of competition and the working of the financial sector. The choice of the analytical method plays a determining role for the macroeconomic 'behaviour' that can be deduced on the basis of an aggregate model structure based on the assumption of rational microeconomic behaviour under condition of uncertainty within a relevant institutional context and supported by empirical observations. Obviously, this methodological procedure is contrary to methodological individualism, where representative agents within a given market structure optimize with full information about the general market clearing equilibrium.

In any case, it is the behaviour of profit-seeking firms acting under the ontological condition of uncertainty that is at the centre of the post-Keynesian concept of effective demand. It is entrepreneurs' *expectations* with regard to proceeds from demand compared to the factor costs that determine output as a whole and by that the *effective demand* for labour.

Therefore, it was somewhat unfortunate that Keynes called his new analytical concept 'effective *demand*', which may have contributed to misleading generations of open minded macroeconomists to concluding that it was exclusively realized *demand* for consumer and investment goods that drives the macroeconomic development. Hereby a gateway for the IS/LM-model interpretation of effective demand was opened, where demand could create its own supply in the short run.

On the contrary, it is the interaction between the sum of the individual firms' sales expectations (aggregate demand) and their estimated production costs (aggregate supply) that together with a number of institutional conditions (bank credit, labour market organization, global competition and technology) determine the business sector decisions on output as a whole and employment.[7]

Thus, it is my intention with this chapter to eradicate the often presented point of view that Keynes's macroeconomic theory does not

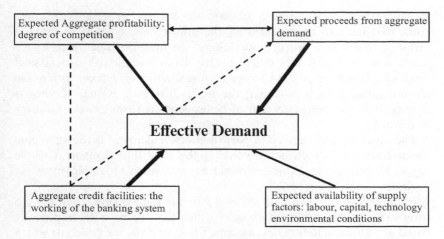

Explanation of the figure: effective demand determines how much output and employment the business sector as a whole plan to undertake in the next 'production period'. It consists of (at least) four analytical components:

1. Expected (by the business sector) aggregate demand in money terms
2. Expected (by the business sector) costs and likely profitability in money terms, dependent on the degree of competition
3. Bank credit facilities and costs (rate of interest etc.)
4. Availability of factors of production.

Figure 8.2   Outlines for the macroeconomic principle of effective demand

have microeconomic foundation or supply side considerations. In fact, 'Keynes's economics is a theory of rational choice under uncertainty' (Skidelsky 1992).

Firms' Production Plans Determine 'Effective Demand'

The supply side in the goods market is an aggregate presentation of firms' cost functions considered as a whole. It shows a relation between what Keynes called 'supply price', i.e. the sales proceeds that, given the production function and cost structures, is needed to 'just make it worth the while of the entrepreneurs to give that employment' (Keynes 1936: 24). This means that behind the supply curve there is a combination of variable costs plus an expected profit at different levels of employment. At each level firms try to maximize their profit; if they succeed there is no (further) incentive for firms to change production or employment.

These assumptions entail that the *aggregate supply function* (what

Keynes called the Z-curve) is upward sloping and represents the proceeds that have to be expected by the industry as a whole to make a certain employment 'worth undertaking'. In fact, this *aggregate supply function* looks like it was taken directly from a standard, neoclassical textbook, where *decreasing marginal productivity of labour* within the representative firm is assumed; the main difference is that Keynes is dealing with the aggregate sum of heterogeneous firms *i.e.* the industry as a whole.[8]

The other equally important part of effective demand is the *aggregate demand function*, which is the value of the sales that firms as a whole *expect* at different levels of *macro*-activity measured by employment (as a whole).

In order for firms to act on the best information available they have to form expectations about future sales which have to be both empirically based and forward looking at the same time: 'let D be the proceeds which entrepreneurs *expect* to receive from the employment of N men, the relationship between D and N being written D = f(N), which can be called the Aggregate Demand Function' (Keynes 1936: 25, my emphasis).

It is a definition of few words that opens the possibility for a number of hypotheses with regard to how the entrepreneurs' total expectations of proceeds are formed. But to me it seems undeniable that Keynes is speaking about a macroeconomic relationship. How much money will be spent in society as a whole on consumption and investment at different levels of activity (measured by employment)?

The concept of aggregate demand can perhaps be best understood with reference to the far newer statistical concept of a 'business sentiment index'. The business sentiment index is based on a survey among a cross-section of firms of their expectations about sales in the nearer future. This published index helps to form expectations of sales proceed for the industry as a whole and even for the entire macroeconomy. It is assumed that on this information firms make a kind of survey-based expectation with regard to the most likely development in sales and proceeds in the nearer future.[9] This expectation of aggregate demand (as a whole) is a useful point of departure for the *individual* firms when they have to form their specific expectation of future proceeds. This sales expectation[10] will therefore centre around the future *macro*economic demand (and on the intensity of international competition).

Accordingly, Keynes's *macro*-theory has a microeconomic foundation of firms trying to maximise profit, but differs from neoclassical theory by introducing uncertainty related to the future, which makes an explicit introduction of *aggregate demand* relevant i.e. the *expected sales proceeds by business as a whole.*

The implication of this behaviour under uncertainty by the individual firms is that it is not reasonable to expect the individual demand curve to be infinitely price-elastic at the ruling market price (see Hartwig 2007). In the short run firms have to behave under the constraint of a somewhat constant market share and a fixed stock of real capital. In this case it would not be rational for individual firms to plan their future production as though they operated under the condition of a horizontal demand curve and should not expect the market price to be solely given 'from outside', not to speak about being constant. This means that the neoclassical assumption of firms exclusively adjusting the production on the basis of a given price (and cost) structures leaving demand neglected can be discharged, when uncertainty prevails. In the short run firms know that the aggregate demand at the macro-level is confined. On the other hand market prices will be somewhat flexible. Both aspects have to be included in the individual firm's production plans.

This semi-closed analysis of firms operating under the constraint of a bounded market share makes it relevant to assume firms (as a whole) will behave like a monopolistic competitor who has to react on a change in aggregate demand. In addition, the aggregate macro-behaviour is not in dissonance with the assumption that individual firms try to maximize profit given the available, but uncertain knowledge about the future: costs, sales proceeds, market share and competitive conditions (domestic and foreign).

In this case it has been explained why post-Keynesian economics has dismissed the neoclassical abstraction that the macro-supply curve can be presented by the behavioural relationship of one representative micro-firm. In post-Keynesian theory firms are assumed to behave with respect to their uncertain knowledge about aggregate demand (demand as a whole), knowing that they can only achieve an uncertain share of this aggregate demand.

Finally, it was important for Keynes to make clear that aggregate supply and aggregate demand are two clearly separate analytical entities; but they are not entirely independent of each other. Keynes's main objection to 'classical' theory is exactly that it equates the macro-supply and macro-demand functions in such a way 'that supply always creates its own demand'. On the other hand, the conclusion that demand always creates its own supply is equally misleading. It depends.

> Essentially, what Keynes did in The General Theory was to devise a method of addressing the question he posed by extending the supply-side/demand-side analysis of the Marshallian tradition from commodities and factors of production to output as a whole. (Fanning and Mahony 2000:10)[11]

A METHODOLOGICAL REFLECTION – OPEN SYSTEM ANALYSIS, THE FALLACY OF COMPOSITION AND OF EQUILIBRIUM[12]

> Though an individual whose transactions are small in relation to the market can safely neglect the fact that demand is not a one-sided transaction, it makes nonsense to neglect it when we come to aggregate demand. This is the vital difference between the theory of the economic behaviour of the aggregate and the theory of the behaviour of the individual unit . . . (Keynes 1936: 85).

The fallacy of composition is committed when a single (macro) market is analysed in isolation from the 'economy as a whole'. That might happen if the *ceteris paribus* assumption is employed in macroeconomics and the analytical outcome is presented without explicit reference to the limitations which are caused by assuming all other markets in unchanged equilibrium. In such cases the error would be that results are achieved from a partial market analysis and not from an analysis of *the economy as a whole*.

The neoclassical textbook treatment of the labour market is also illustrative for this fallacy of composition.

An 'Isolated' Labour Market

I will demonstrate the consequences of making a fallacy of composition by isolating the labour market from the economy as a whole. I have discussed above a number of difficulties that are connected with giving an empirically relevant representation of supply and demand in the labour market by using the method of representative microeconomic agents. Here I put this discussion aside and look only at the adjustment in the labour market from a neoclassical point of view, where an analysis based on representative agents is considered both consistent and relevant.

> Keynesian or demand-deficient unemployment . . . arises when wages have not yet adjusted to restore labour market equilibrium . . . without a boost to demand, involuntary unemployment will slowly bid wages down, moving the economy from A down to E. (Begg *et al.* 2001: 203–04)

Assuming general equilibrium (*ceteris paribus*) in all other macro markets, the analysis is reduced to the labour market. Hence, 'supply creates its own demand' and the analysis boils down to a matter of (real) wage adjustment. Lower nominal wage levels lead by assumption to lower real wages and higher employment in this isolated macroeconomic analysis. If, however, there are significant spill-over effects from the labour market adjustment or expectations are not rational (in the new classical meaning), then 'all other things' will not stay unchanged and the

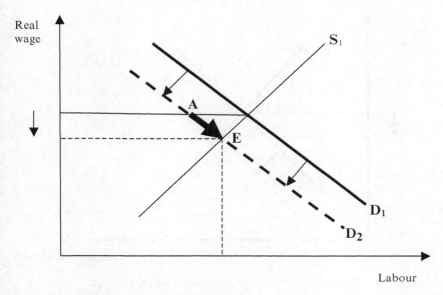

Figure 8.3   The new-Keynesian textbook representation of labour market adjustment

assumption about unchanged equilibrium values cannot be maintained. In that case a reduced real wage might cause the purchasing power of wage earners to fall, which would more likely than not reduce consumption. On the other hand an increased profit margin could have a positive effect on the export of goods and services. Therefore, in the end wage adjustments might have rather complicated spill-over effects on effective demand for goods and services (i.e. output) and thereby on demand for labour.

The analytical point made above is to emphasize that when there is a mutual interdependency between macro-markets (in reality this is the most likely case) macroeconomic consequences cannot be analysed within an isolated macro-market model without running the risk of committing a fallacy of composition.

An Increased Propensity to Save – The Fallacy of Equilibrium

Another, almost as 'classic', example of a fallacy of composition, is the analysis of an increased individual propensity to save within an isolated loanable funds model. The argument is persuasive, if everybody increases his or her propensity to save, then the aggregate amount of savings will increase. In a neoclassical loanable funds market equilibrium (where the

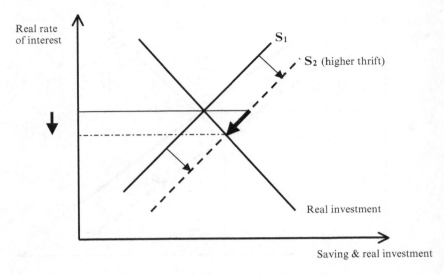

Figure 8.4   A neoclassical isolated saving-investment analysis

real rate of interest clears the market for real investment and savings) this conclusion is confirmed. When the propensity to save is increased the rate of interest will fall (see Figure 8.4; see also Mankiw (2000: 62)). A lower rate of interest ensures that the increased propensity to save is transformed into an equivalent amount of increased real investments, whereby the total output and total employment remain unchanged.

A changed saving behaviour has no spill-over effect on output as a whole or employment. The assumption of *ceteris paribus* isolates the 'market' for saving and real investment and the (real) interest rate from the other markets of the economy ensures that the market clears. However, if this assumed isolation is analytically illegitimate because of significant spill-over effects between the market for saving and investment and other macro markets, then the model is not relevant from a realistic point view, i.e. out of general equilibrium analysis.

There is no magic here, no mystery; but a reliable scientific prediction.
Why should this method of approach appear to so many people to be novel and odd and paradoxical? I can only find the answer in the fact that all our ideas about economics, instilled into us by education and atmosphere and tradition are, whether we are conscious of it or not, soaked with theoretical presuppositions which are only properly applicable to a society which is in equilibrium, with all its productive resources already employed. Many people

are trying to solve the problem of unemployment with a theory which is based on the assumption of no unemployment. (*CWK* IX: 349–50).

CONCLUSION WITH RELEVANCE FOR TODAY

> The outstanding faults of the economic society in which we live are its failure to provide for full employment and its arbitrary and inequitable distribution of wealth and incomes. The bearing of the foregoing on the first of these is obvious. But there are also two important respects in which it is relevant to the second. (Keynes 1936: 372)

In a highly specialized market economic system uncertainty prevails. This is even truer when the markets are extended worldwide through the process of globalization. In that case it is an illusion to imagine the market forces by themselves can 'create their own demand'. If one gives up the analytical pre-condition of assuming that the underlying framework is a stable general equilibrium system, then it becomes obvious – by logic – that 'we do not know what the future will bring'. This is true for the individual and for the government. But, and this is an important 'but': the individual has no power to change this overall situation. In fact, following the argument of 'the fallacy of composition' there is a risk that the rational response of many individuals to increased uncertainty undertaken at the same time might aggravate the macroeconomic imbalances – known as the paradox of savings (or the paradox of reducing wages).

Governments, on the other hand, in most countries still have the power to influence effective demand significantly – for good, and some sceptical neoliberals would probably say for bad. This implies that the *General Theory* is not only relevant for understanding a depression economy. The Chinese government could also benefit from reading it in its attempt to control the rampant growth.

However, Keynes did put forward in his concluding chapter one more politically controversial argument that the outcome of unregulated market processes may cause an arbitrarily and inequitable distribution of wealth and income. Existing inequalities are not helpful in creating the saving needed for the real investment. To the contrary, Keynes had demonstrated that saving is an automatic outcome from the undertaking of real investment either in the private or public sector. Hence, wealth inequalities could be reduced without doing any harm to real investment. In fact, increased financial saving could easily reduce effective demand and make real resources underutilized. Especially in cases with abundant supply of labour, an increased tax rate could make society fairer without obstructing the growth process.

But Keynes did not take a definite stand on what government ought to do. In fact, there is rather little in *The General Theory* on specific policy recommendations. If anything, Keynes expressed a preference for monetary policy rather than fiscal policy, when effective demand is deficient. He considered himself all way through mainly as a theorist, especially when he addressed his fellow-economists by giving a toast to: '. . . economics and economists, who are the trustees, not of civilisation, but of the possibility of civilisation' (Keynes 1945, when he gave up his editorship of *Economic Journal*, quoted in Harrod (1951: 194)).

NOTES

1. Sections of this chapter have previously been presented at the 4th Post Keynesian Conference at Université de Bourgogne, Dijon, December 2009 and at a meeting organized by Nordic History of Economic Doctrines, Copenhagen, August 2010. In addition, I have drawn on my *Macroeconomic Methodology* (Jespersen 2009a), which has benefited from intensive conversation with Victoria Chick.
2. Any re-read of *The General Theory* could take advantage of starting with a consultation of *A 'Second Edition' of the General Theory*, which is a scholarly collection of reflexions on current macroeconomic issues looked upon through the prism of *The General Theory*. In fact, Keynes had made some plans for a second book with the tentative title 'footnotes to the General Theory'; but he went hardly further than setting up a possible table of content, cf. *CWK*, XIV.
3. The story of how Keynes matured from *A Treatise on Money* to *The General Theory* is commonplace for Keynes scholars. Except for my own reading I have benefited from several contributions. Space only allows me to mention a few: Harrod (1951), Skidelsky (1992), Clarke (1988, 2009).
4. If telling the story of Keynes's transition from *TM* to *GT* is a crowded road then the 'genuine' content of *GT* is even more crowded among scholars of post-Keynesian economics. Here, John King, *A History of Post Keynesian Economics since 1936* gives a superb overview (King 2002). Skidelsky has chosen a very telling title for the chapter discussing the different interpretations of the *GT*, *Whose General Theory?* (Skidelsky 1992).
5. But Keynes ridiculed Pigou in the appendix to Chapter 19 for assuming that *a shift* in aggregate demand could be used as a short run explanation of changes in (un)employment. Keynes accused Pigou of 'forgetting' that in the neoclassical macro model the demand curve for labour is derived from the production function, which is primarily determined by technology; see Jespersen 2009, appendix to Chapter 8.
6. In fairness to John Hicks it has to be said that within his seminal paper on 'A suggested interpretation' the adjustment process was left open. And perhaps in even more fairness to Hicks, he got second thoughts on the ISLM model as a relevant interpretation of the *General Theory*, Hicks 1981.
7. Within a modern interpretation of 'effective demand' one has to add the role of credit, see Graziani (2003) and Lavoie (2006). The financial crisis exposed the importance of bank credit as the necessary, but not sufficient, vehicle to realize production plans. In a broader (and longer) perspective institutional conditions in the labour market, the availability of natural resources and impact on environmental issues have to be integrated within a macroeconomic analysis.
8. Firms do not have to undertake profit maximizing behaviour, and there might not be decreasing marginal labour productivity.

9. 'Nearer future' means an analytical period that corresponds to the time it takes to implement decisions related to hiring and firing in the labour market.
10. How the total sales would be distributed among the individual firms within the branch would be of lesser importance from a macroeconomic perspective.
11. A conclusion which could also be extracted from the reading of Chick (1983).
12. This section owes a heavy intellectual debt to Chick (2003), Dow (2001,2003).

REFERENCES

Begg, D., S. Fischer,and R. Dornbusch (2001) *Foundations of Economics*, 2nd ed., New York: McGraw-Hill Education.

Chick, V. (1983) *Macroeconomics after Keynes: A Reconsideration of the General Theory*, Oxford: Philip Allan and Cambridge, MA: MIT Press.

Chick, V. (2003) 'On Open Systems', *Brazilian Journal of Political Economy*, 24 (1), 3–16.

Clarke, P. (1988) *The Keynesian Revolution in the Making, 1924–36*, Oxford: Oxford University Press.

Clarke, P. (2009) *Keynes – the Twentieth Century's Most Influential Economist*, London: Bloomsbury.

Dow, S. (2001) 'Post Keynesian Methodology', in Holt, R.P.F. and S. Pressman (eds) (2001) *A New Guide to Post Keynesian Economics,* London: Routledge.

Dow, S. (2003) 'Probability, Uncertainty and Convention: Economists' Knowledge and the Knowledge of Economic Actors', in Runde, J. and S. Mizuhara (eds).

Fanning, C. and D. O. Mahoney (2000) *The General Theory of Profit Equilibrium: Keynes and the Entrepreneur Economy*, Basingstoke: Macmillan Press.

Gnos, C. (2009) 'Circuit Theory Supplementing Keynes's Genuine Analysis of the Monetary Economy of Production', in Ponsot, J.-F. and S. Rossi (eds) *The Political Economy of Monetary Circuits: Tradition and Change in Post-Keynesian Economics*, Basingstoke and New York: Palgrave Macmillan, 1–20.

Graziani, A. (2003) *The Monetary Theory of Production*, Cambridge: Cambridge University Press.

Harcourt, G.C. and P.A. Riach (eds) (1997) *A 'Second Edition' of the General Theory*, two vols, London: Routledge.

Harrod, R. (1960[1951]) *John Maynard Keynes*, London: Penguin.

Hartwig, J. (2007) 'Keynes vs. the Post Keynesians on the Principle of Effective Demand', *The European Journal of the History of Economic Thought*, 14(4), December, 725–739.

Hicks, J. (1937) 'Mr Keynes and the "Classics": A Suggested Interpretation', *Econometrica*, 5, April, 147–59.

Hicks, John (1980–1981) 'IS-LM: An Explanation', *Journal of Post Keynesian Economics*, 3: 139–55.

Hicks, J. (1989) *A Monetary Theory of Markets*, Oxford: Clarendon Press.

Holt, R.P.F. and S. Pressman (eds) (2001) *A New Guide to Post Keynesian Economics,* London: Routledge.

Jespersen, J. (2004) 'Macroeconomic Stability: Sustainable Development and Full Employment', in Reisch, L.A. and I. Røpke (eds), *The Ecological Economics of Consumption*, Cheltenham UK and Northampton MA: Edward Elgar, 233–250.

Jespersen, J. (2009a) *Macroeconomic Methodology – a Post-Keynesian Perspective*, Cheltenham UK and Northampton MA: Edward Elgar.

Jespersen, J. (2009b) 'Bridging the Gap between Monetary Circuit Theory and Post-Keynesian Monetary Theory', in Ponsot, J.-F. and S. Rossi (eds) *The Political Economy of Monetary Circuits: Tradition and Change in Post-Keynesian Economics*, Basingstoke and New York: Palgrave Macmillan, 21–35.

Jespersen, J. (2010) 'Keynes's lost distinction between industrial and financial circulation', *European Journal of Economic and Social Systems*, 23(1), 119–134.

Keynes, J.M. (1972–1989) *The Collected Writings*, vols. I–XXX, Donald Moggridge (ed.), Macmillan & Cambridge University Press for The Royal Economic Society (references in the text are *CWK* followed by the volume number).

Keynes, J.M. (1931) *Essays in Persuasion*, *CWK*, IX.

Keynes, J.M. (1936) *The General Theory of Employment, Interest and Money*, *CWK*, VII.

Keynes, J.M. (1973a) *The General Theory and After: Part I, Preparation*, *CWK*, XIII.

Keynes, J.M. (1973b) *The General Theory and After: Part II, Defences and Development*, *CWK*, XIV.

King, J. (2002) *A History of Post Keynesian Economics since 1936*, Cheltenham UK and Northampton MA: Edward Elgar.

King, J. (ed.) (2003) *The Elgar Companion to Post Keynesian Economics*, Cheltenham UK and Northampton MA: Edward Elgar.

Lavoie, M. (2006) *Post Keynesian Economics*, Reading: Palgrave Macmillan.

Lawson, T. (1997) *Economics and Reality*, London: Routledge.

Mankiw, G. (2000) *Macroeconomics*, 4th ed., New York: Worth Publishers.

Ponsot, J.-F. and S. Rossi (eds) (2009) *The Political Economy of Monetary Circuits: Tradition and Change in Post-Keynesian Economics*, Basingstoke and New York: Palgrave Macmillan.

Rochon, L.-P. and S. Rossi (eds) (2003) *Modern Theories of Money: The Nature and Role of Money in Capitalist Economies*, Cheltenham UK and Northampton MA: Edward Elgar.

Runde, J. and S. Mizuhara (eds) (2003) *The Philosophy of Keynes's Economics – Probability, Uncertainty and Convention*, London: Routledge.

Setterfield, M. (2003) 'Effective Demand', in King, J. (ed.) *The Elgar Companion to Post Keynesian Economics*, Cheltenham UK and Northampton MA: Edward Elgar.

Skidelsky, R. (1992) *John Maynard Keynes: Hopes Betrayed, 1883–1920*, London: Macmillan Press.

Skidelsky, R. (1992) *John Maynard Keynes: The Economist as Saviour, 1920–1937*, London: Macmillan Press.

9. *The General Theory* after the sub-prime crisis: a Minskyan perspective

Elisabetta De Antoni

INTRODUCTION

Opposing the mainstream's blind faith in the efficiency of the free market, throughout his life H.P. Minsky constantly warned 'that the capitalist market mechanism is flawed, in the sense that it does not lead to a stable price-full employment equilibrium and that the basis of the flaw resides in the financial system' (1974: 267). In Minsky's view, the economy follows a cyclical path that involves recurrent financial crises. Historical evidence in fact testifies that financial crises are systemic and not idiosyncratic (Minsky 1991).

Minsky's central question – the title of Minsky (1963, 1982a) – thus becomes: can 'It' happen again?. 'It' is the Great Depression and Minsky's answer is affirmative. If this is true, however, the return to laissez faire actively promoted by the profession in recent decades represents 'a prescription for economic disaster' (Minsky and Whalen, 1996–97: 161). That foretold disaster is now before our eyes. The world economy is experiencing one of the most devastating financial crises within human memory.

This chapter re-reads *The General Theory* through Minsky's eyes. Specifically, Sections 2 and 3 analyze the relationship between Minsky and Keynes. This will lead to a focus on Chapter 12 of *The General Theory,* where Keynes brings the Stock Exchange into the analysis. This market is not conceived as a source of funds for investing firms. It is instead considered as a secondary market in which existing capital assets can be bought and sold. According to Keynes, this possibility has two major drawbacks for capital accumulation (analyzed, respectively, in Sections 4 and 5). Firstly, it allows the predominance of speculation over entrepreneurship. Secondly, it introduces the revocability of investment decisions: investments which are fixed for the community become liquid for the individual. In Keynes's view, however, this is only a dangerous mirage.

If Keynes's observations are extended to the unprecedented development experienced by secondary financial markets in past decades, the recent financial turmoil becomes easily understandable. The seeds of the ongoing financial crisis can thus be found in Chapter 12 of *The General Theory*. Section 6 of this chapter concludes by wondering what Keynes would advise us to do.

THE CYCLICAL PERSPECTIVE: MINSKY AND KEYNES'S CHAPTER 22

Minsky's 'financial instability hypothesis' was presented (and is often acknowledged) as an authentic interpretation of Keynes's thought.[1] In Minsky's re-reading, Keynes lived through the experience of the Great Depression. He thus dwelled upon the particular case of an economy which – as a consequence of a financial crisis followed by a debt deflation – fell into a deep depression. According to Minsky, however, Keynes considered the Great Depression to be only an extreme case. Despite not developing it, he had in mind a cyclical perspective: 'References to cyclical phenomena occur not only in chapter 22 of *The General Theory*, "Notes on the Trade Cycle", which explicitly deals with business cycles, and in the rebuttal to Viner in *The Quarterly Journal of Economics* of February 1937, but throughout his book.'(Minsky 1975: 58)

From a cyclical perspective, recessions may be traced back to the preceding boom. This is precisely what Minsky does:

> In some important sense, what was lost from the insights of the 1920s and 1930s is more significant than what has been retained . . . The spectacular panics, debt deflations, and deep depressions that historically followed a speculative boom as well the recovery from depressions are of lesser importance in the analysis of instability than the developments over a period characterized by sustained growth that lead to the emergence of fragile and unstable financial structures. (Minsky 1986: 173)

On these bases, Minsky devotes almost all of his writings to the expansionary phase of the cycle.[2]

We thus come to an important point: Minsky's fundamental instability is upward (Minsky 1975: 165, Minsky 1980: 518). His 'financial instability hypothesis' applies the economics of Keynes to a vibrant and euphoric economy. The Keynesian tendency towards the exhaustion of investment opportunities and stagnation is replaced by the Minskyan tendency towards over-investment and over-indebtedness. As well known, whilst Keynes experienced the tragedy of the Great Depression, Minsky was formed by the post-war political and economic renaissance. In the light of the different historical experience of the two authors, the change in the subject of the analysis is understandable. It led, however, to a different conception of the business cycle. To show this, we shall compare the 'financial instability hypothesis' with Chapter 22 of *The General Theory*, which Keynes devotes to the trade cycle.

Let us start with the upswing. In Minsky, the excess of planned investment over saving (even more so, over firm's saving) is so great that it inevitably requires business indebtedness.[3] Finance is at the centre of Minsky's architecture. Keynes's Chapter 22, by contrast, does not even mention firms' indebtedness. Given the smaller excess of planned investment, producers may have sufficient liquidity to finance it. The different role of finance engenders disparate concerns about growth. In the euphoria of Minsky's boom, external financing grows proportionally more than internal financing. As a result, debt commitments eventually rise above profits. At this point, they are honoured out of borrowing (speculative and ultra-speculative or Ponzi finance) rather than out of profits (hedge finance).[4] As Minsky puts it, the initially robust financial system turns fragile. It is precisely financial fragility that threatens Minsky's boom.[5] As we shall see, in Keynes's stagnant economy the problem is not over-indebtedness but the over-optimistic profit expectations fuelled by the boom.

This brings us to the peak. In Minsky's case, expansion leads to an endogenous rise in the interest rate.[6] In the regime of financial fragility (of speculative and ultra-speculative finance) inherited from the boom, this triggers the financial crisis.[7] Keynes expressly rejects any such diagnosis.[8] In his view, it is the inevitable disappointment of the over-optimistic profit expectations and the consequent collapse in the propensity to invest that triggers the crisis. In short, the crisis is financial in Minsky and real in Keynes. The corresponding income levels are also different. Minsky's upswing may attain or even surpass full employment.[9] According to Keynes (1936: 322), by contrast, income growth tends to stop before that point: the marginal efficiency of capital is generally insufficient to ensure full-employment.[10]

With Minsky's financial crisis, the fulfillment of debt commitments by the ordinary sources of financing (profits and borrowing) turns out to be no longer possible. The primary activity of firms becomes selling assets in order to reduce debt and debt service. The fall in the asset prices reduces the net wealth of firms and financial intermediaries, decreasing the availability to lend and to borrow. This reinforces the need to squeeze indebtedness by selling assets. The expectation of further falls in prices further fuels sales. Asset prices fall cumulatively. The debt deflation ends by making the fulfillment of debt commitments impossible. Insolvency triggers a wave of bankruptcies. The goods market experiences a collapse in investment and income. Despite its drama, however, Minsky's downswing ultimately performs a somehow cathartic role. It restores the robustness of the financial system, paving the way for the ensuing recovery.[11] In Keynes's economy, the crisis turns the boom's over-optimistic profit expectations into a contrary 'error of pessimisms'.[12] Investment and income thus collapse again. This time, however, there is no cathartic or beneficial effect. By sweeping away even sound and promising economic activities, recessions and depressions belong 'to the species of remedy which cures the disease by killing the patient' (Keynes 1936: 323).

A last important difference between the two authors concerns the weakest turning point, the one at which the interruption of the cycle is most likely. According to Minsky's 'upward instability proposition',[13] 'stability – or tranquillity – is destabilising' and 'the fundamental instability is upward'.[14] A period of tranquillity (in which profits are systematically greater than inherited debt commitments) fosters greater confidence in the future, giving rise to a wealth re-allocation from money to non-monetary assets.[15] The result is an externally financed increase in investment that stimulates the economy. In short, Minsky's lower turning point is not open to question. After the storm comes the calm, and tranquillity inevitably leads to recovery. Minsky's 'obsession' is the upper turning point. Why does his vibrant economy turn downwards, instead of entering on a steady growth path?[16] As we have seen, Minsky finds his answer in the financial sphere of the economy.

Keynes's Chapter 22 takes the opposite tack. Here, it is the upper turning point that is unquestionable: the over-optimism of the boom is bound to clash with reality. Keynes's perplexities concern the lower turning point.[17] He admits that the decline in the capital stock tends to stimulate investment and thus the economy, but he worries that this stimulus may be too weak to spark recovery.[18] Not by chance, the main message of the first 21 chapters of *The General Theory* is that the persistence of the slump is perfectly possible.

In line with *The General Theory*, the 'financial instability hypothesis' reaffirms the crucial role of uncertainty, the volatility of expectations, the centrality of investment in the determination of income. As we have seen, however, it applies Keynes's economics to a system whose fundamental instability is upward. With this, Minsky banished many important issues raised in *The General Theory*: the persistent damage of depression, the precariousness of recovery, the endemic nature of unemployment. He had, however, the indisputable and remarkable merit of highlighting the crucial role of finance. Rereading Minsky in a Keynesian perspective, he warned that finance – whilst initially sustaining growth – may end up by making growth itself unsustainable, thus fuelling capitalism's tendency towards stagnation.

CAPITALISM' FINANCIAL EVOLUTION: MINSKY AND KEYNES'S CHAPTER 12

According to Minsky, 'Capitalism is a dynamic, evolving system that comes in many forms. Nowhere is this dynamism more evident than in its financial structure' (Minsky and Whalen 1996: 3). Focusing on the US financial system, Minsky identifies the following phases of capitalism's financial development.[19]

(i)   *Commercial capitalism.* This was the phase preceding the industrial revolution. At that time, the modest dimension (and the modest cost) of investments allowed entrepreneurs to purchase them out of their own funds. External finance essentially satisfied the transactions requirements associated with manufacturing and trade.[20]

(ii) *Industrial capitalism.* This phase covered the first decades of the twentieth century. The industrial revolution had inaugurated a new era requiring large long-term capital assets. Investment now became too expensive for individual entrepreneurs. Its financing required the issue of shares and bonds. As a result, the corporate form emerged (introducing the distinction between the management and the ownership of capital assets). Capital accumulation also implied increasing recourse by firms to borrowing. The consequent growth of financial markets was associated with the development of financial intermediation.[21] Indebtedness, however, is a source of financial fragility as well as of growth. An internally-financed bad investment impoverishes its owners without necessarily jeopardizing their existence. An externally-financed bad investment entails a risk of insolvency that threatens not only the investors' existence but also the viability of their financiers. The great crash of 1929–1933 brought this second stage to an end.

(iii) *Paternalistic capitalism.* The New Deal restructuring ushered in a paternalistic era based on a countercyclical fiscal policy oriented to the support and the stabilization of profits and on the low interest rates determined by a Federal Reserve unconstrained by gold-standard considerations. In this period the government took over responsibility for the adequacy of profits. As a result, internal cash flows of firms could finance their investments. Firms (rather than bankers) were the masters of the private economy. Government support, however, spread optimism boosting speculative behaviours.

(iv) *Money-manager capitalism.* This is the current stage of capitalism, characterized by the development of a new layer of financial intermediaries. These are the money managers (mutual funds, pension funds, money market funds, bank trusts, insurance companies and so on) which have currently come to dominate the scene. In recent decades, savers have allocated an increasing share of their wealth holdings to the liabilities of these new intermediaries, allowing them to purchase an increasing share of the liabilities of corporations. The main target of money-managers is the maximization of the value of the investments made by the fund holders, i.e. of the total return on assets (dividends and interest received plus – and above all – the appreciation in per share value). Most of their activity consists in buying assets in order to sell them at higher prices and vice versa. Minsky's conclusion is that today the financial system does not conform with Schumpeter's (1934) vision of financial institutions as the 'ephors of capitalism',[22] which carefully select what can be financed with a view to promoting the economy's capital development. Today's financial structure is more akin to Keynes's (1936) characterization of advanced financial capitalism as a casino in which speculative behaviours prevail.

With this, Minsky again converges with Keynes. This time, the reference is to the specific chapter of *The General Theory* (Chapter 12, entitled 'The state of long-term expectations') where the concept of 'casino capitalism' is introduced. From the outset, Keynes warns that this chapter is different from the rest of the book:

> There is, however, not much to be said about the state of confidence *a priori*. Our conclusions must mainly depend upon the actual observation of markets and business psychology. This is the reason why the ensuing digression is on a different level of abstraction from most of this book. (Keynes 1936: 149)

The peculiarity of Chapter 12 was confirmed by Richard Kahn, who pointed out that – contrarily to the others– this chapter was not subject to the scrutiny of the group of the younger colleagues assembled by Keynes to help him.[23] The aforementioned reference to the 'actual observation of markets and business psychology' may reflect Keynes's more than 10-year intense activity on the stock market, an individual experience the success of which had already been widely confirmed by facts.[24]

In Chapter 12, Keynes's problem is to clarify the determinants of the prospective yield of capital assets. To this end, he brings the Stock Exchange into the analysis. The noteworthy aspect is that this market is not conceived as a source of funds for investing firms. It is instead considered as a secondary market in which existing capital assets can be bought and sold. As such, the Stock Exchange crucially affects the accumulation process. To show this, Keynes focuses on two of its functions: the evaluation of assets, and the introduction of the revocability of investment decisions. These functions will be the subject of the next two sections.

THE STOCK MARKET EVALUATION OF ASSETS

It may be useful to start with Minsky's (1972, 1975, 1986) reformulation of Keynes's investment theory. In Minsky's view, the basic characteristic of a capitalist economy is the existence of two prices: the (volatile and uncertain) price of capital assets and the price of current production.[25] Belonging to both categories, investment has the function of aligning the two prices. By doing so, however, it attracts uncertainty, passing it on to the rest of the economy. The two prices at the basis of Minsky's analysis are shown in Figure 9.1. The demand price of capital assets is equal to the present value of their expected profits, PV. By analogy, it also represents the demand price for investment goods.[26] The supply price of investment goods is given by the marginal cost MC, and coincides with the general price level. The intersection between the demand and the supply price gives the profitable investment level I^p.

Thus far, Minsky's framework essentially coincides with Tobin's famous 'q theory'.[27] The point is that Minsky's equality between the demand and the supply price of investment goods also reflects Keynes's equality between the marginal efficiency of capital and the interest rate.[28] A Minskyan excess of the demand over the supply price implies a Keynesian

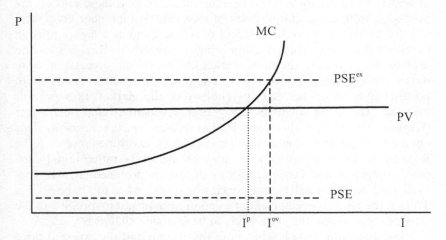

Figure 9.1   The determination of the investment level

excess of the marginal efficiency of capital over the interest rate (and vice versa). From this viewpoint, Minsky's 'two price theory' is perfectly in line with Chapter 11 of *The General Theory*. In Chapter 12, however, things radically change: the evaluations of the Stock Exchange forcefully enter the scene. To quote Keynes, these evaluations:

> inevitably exert a decisive influence on the rate of current investment. For there is no sense in building up a new enterprise at a cost greater than that at which a similar enterprise can be purchased; whilst there is an inducement to spend on a new project what may seem an extravagant sum if it can be floated off on the Stock Exchange at an immediate profit. (Keynes 1936: 151)[29]

Chapter 12 thus introduces two additional prices: the current and the expected price of shares. As we shall see, if these two prices fall outside the area included between MC and PV in Figure 9.1, the investment level will generally differ from the profitable one I^p. Specifically, if the current price of shares (PSE in Figure 9.1) is lower than the marginal cost of investment goods, MC, the entrepreneur will prefer to buy the cheaper existing capital assets. The demand for new capital goods will consequently fall from I^p to zero. Investments projects that would have been profitable from a productive point of view will not be undertaken.[30] The economy will experience an under-investment situation.

By contrast, if the expected price of shares (PSE^{ex} in Figure 9.1) is higher than the present value, PV, the demand for new capital goods will rise from I^p to I^{ov}. The economy will experience an over-investment situation: investments projects that are not profitable from a productive point of view ($I^p I^{ov}$ in Figure 9.1) will be undertaken. In fact, these projects are profitable from a speculative point of view: the entrepreneur buys them not 'for keeps' but with the prospect of selling them at a higher price in the Stock Exchange. This situation brings us directly to Keynes's 'casino capitalism'. Thanks to the stock market, the short-run forecasts of share prices (PSE^{ex}) replace investment long-term prospective yields (with present value PV). The 'mass psychology of the market' thus prevails over the 'dark forces of time and ignorance which envelop our future' (Keynes 1936: 155): in short, speculation replaces entrepreneurship. This obviously jeopardizes the accumulation process. Investment comes to be ruled by the short-sighted views of 'ignorant investors' rather than by the more competent and farsighted views of 'expert professionals' (Keynes 1936: 154). Keynes's well known conclusion is that, when this happens, i.e. '[W]hen the capital development of a country becomes a by-product of the activities of a casino, the job is likely to be ill-done' (1936: 159).

A last interesting case is when both the current and the expected price of shares fall outside the area included between MC and PV, i.e. when

PSE and PSE^{ex} coexist in Figure 9.1. In this case, Keynes's 'casino capitalism' reaches its climax. The Stock Exchange promises profits that are remarkably higher than those associated with the investment activity. Entrepreneurs will stop investing, transforming themselves into speculators. Given the high expected capital gains, all their energies will be devoted to buying and selling shares. This situation is obviously unbalanced and unsustainable. According to the textbooks, the traditional task of the financial system is to redistribute prospective returns on investment between firms and their financiers. If this is the case, however, financial yields should not exceed the real ones. The financial system should not promise more than what the real sector will be able to produce. Sooner or later, some promises will inevitably not be kept. As a result, some expectations are bound to be disappointed. In situations of indebtedness, disappointment will entail the risk of insolvency for firms and for their financiers.

However, 'Keynesian economics ... is the economics of permanent disequilibrium' (Minsky 1986: 68). Insofar as everybody thinks that the times are not yet ready or that they are cleverer than the others, there is no incentive to change strategy renouncing the generous attractions of Wall Street. In the meantime, however, the situation continues to deteriorate. The postponement of the adjustment makes it increasingly painful. Possible attempts to restore financial sustainability will further unbalance the real sector. All of this is unfortunately before our eyes.[31]

THE REVOCABILITY OF INVESTMENT DECISIONS

Let us now analyze the second function of the Stock Exchange. In Keynes's view, this market adds an additional degree of freedom: it enables entrepreneurs to sell investment goods to others instead of holding them for all their lives. As a consequence, the investment decision becomes revocable. As known, Keynes's presupposition is that – as we look further ahead into the future – our knowledge decreases and consequently our forecasts become less reliable. Under these circumstances, the shortening of the time horizon increases the liquidity and decreases the riskiness of investment, stimulating capital accumulation.

These beneficial effects, however, are only a mirage. Investment actually is the same as before; it is the Stock Exchange which makes it look more liquid and less risky. The perception error induced by the stock market jeopardizes the capital development of the country, leading to less liquid and more risky investments. Keynes's lapidary comment is: 'Of the maxims of orthodox finance none, surely, is more anti-social than the fetish of liquidity . . . It forgets that there is not such thing as liquidity of investment for the community as a whole' (1936: 155).

Keynes's 'fetish of liquidity' may be re-read in the light of a sort of 'fallacy of decomposition' in decision-making. The 'decomposition' refers to the distinction between the decision to buy and the decision to hold investment goods (between managers and owners of capital assets). In the presence of the stock market, as we have seen, the two kinds of decisions do not necessarily coincide any more. The 'fallacy' consists in the fact that 'investments which are 'fixed' for the community are . . . made "liquid" for the individual' (Keynes 1936: 153) with the consequence of becoming even less liquid and more risky for society as a whole.

The financial evolution of capitalism outlined by Minsky subtends an increasing decomposition in decision making. Firms' recourse to direct external financing introduces the distinction between the purchase of investment goods and their financing (between firms and savers). Financial intermediation introduces the further distinction between the lenders/creditors and the ultimate financiers (between financial intermediaries and savers). According to Minsky, however, these 'decompositions' in decision making do not necessarily imply any fallacy.[32] After all, the success of the financier depends on the success of the borrower. Insofar as savers and/or financial intermediaries contribute to the assessment of investment profitability, they actually perform the Schumpeterian function as 'ephors of capitalism'.

The 'fallacy of decomposition' reappears, however, with the increasing intervention of financial intermediaries in the secondary financial markets. We refer to the growth of 'market oriented' investment banks (Wray 2010) and, recently, of money managers (Minsky and Whalen 1996 and 1996–97; Wray 2010). These institutions buy financial assets mainly with the purpose of selling them at a higher price. Thanks to secondary financial markets, their decision to buy securities does not necessarily imply the decision to hold them. As a result, expected capital gains replace the evaluation of prospective yields up to maturity and this misleads capital accumulation. In addition, securities turn out to be more liquid and safer for their individual owners, becoming by contrast more illiquid and riskier for the economy as a whole. This means that the financial system becomes more fragile.

Analogous considerations hold for the recent development of the secondary credit market associated with the securitization processes. This market introduces the distinction between the lender (the originator of the loan) and the ultimate creditor (to whom debt commitments are due). This has misleading effects on the accumulation process. If the financial institution that originates the loan can transform it into securities and sell it to others, '. . . the selection and supervisory function of the lenders and underwriters are not as well done as they might be when the fortunes of the originators are at hazard over the longer term' (Minsky 1992: 23). In addition, the financial system becomes more fragile. Whilst turning out to be more liquid and safer for individual lenders, credit becomes less liquid and riskier for the economy as a whole.

In the specific case of sub-prime loans, the secondary house market (with the associated distinction between the decision to buy and the decision to hold houses) was an additional source of financial fragility. The credit worthiness of American households was evaluated on the basis of the expected capital gains on houses instead than on their expected cash inflows. After all, it did not matter whether the borrower could actually make the mortgage payments. Given the rising trend of house prices, troubled borrowers could always either refinance or pay off the mortgage by selling the house. But the rising trend of house prices could not last for ever: the solvency of sub-prime borrowers turned out to be only a mirage. To conclude, Keynes's perplexities about the role of secondary markets can help us to understand the spreading of junk assets and loans which led to the ongoing crisis.

CONCLUSION

The re-reading of *The General Theory* through Minsky's eyes leads to focus on Keynes's Chapter 12, where Keynes brings the Stock Exchange into the analysis. This market is not conceived as a source of funds for investing firms. It is instead considered as a secondary market in which existing capital assets can be bought and sold.

In Keynes's view, this possibility has two dramatic drawbacks for capital accumulation. Firstly, it allows the predominance of speculation over entrepreneurship. Secondly, it introduces the revocability of investment decisions: investments which are fixed for the community become liquid for the individual. This, however, is only a dangerous mirage which leads to even less liquid and riskier investments for the economy as a whole. Given the unprecedented development experienced by secondary financial markets in past decades, Keynes's perplexities can help us to understand the spreading of junk assets and loans which led to the ongoing crisis.

What is to be done? What suggestions can we draw from *The General Theory*? In Keynes's view, 'To make the purchase of an investment permanent and indissoluble, like marriage . . . might be a useful remedy for our contemporary evils'. Unfortunately, however, 'if individual

purchases were rendered illiquid, this might seriously impede new investment' (1936: 160). Realistically speaking, secondary markets cannot be
closed. However, they should at least be made 'inaccessible and expensive'.[33] Specifically, 'The introduction of a substantial Government ...
transfer tax on all transactions might prove the most serviceable reform
available, with a view to mitigating the predominance of speculation
over enterprise in the US' (Keynes 1936: 160). If it is true that secondary markets are the main source of problems, however, this tax should
mainly concern them.

NOTES

1. Not by chance, Minsky's famous 1975 book is entitled 'John Maynard Keynes'.
2. One of the rare exceptions is Minsky (1982b), which deals with debt-deflation.
3. Minsky's writings explicitly refer to advanced capitalist economies with large and costly long-term investment that is debt financed.
4. Minsky takes the expected profitability of ongoing investment for granted. His famous distinction among hedge, speculative and ultra-speculative (or Ponzi) finance concerns the synchronization between expected cash inflows and outflows. In the case of hedge finance, creditors and debtors foresee cash receipts greater than debt commitments in every single period of the life of the loan. In the case of non-hedge finance, this holds only for the distant future. Given the expectation of a future bonanza, the plan concern-ing the present and the near future is to cover commitments by borrowing: principal in the case of speculative units, and interest as well in the case of ultra-speculative or Ponzi units. Thus, initially, the debt of speculative units is rolled over while that of ultra-speculative units automatically grows with interest payments.
5. The dependency on credit makes speculative and ultra-speculative units financially fragile. An unfavourable unexpected event would jeopardize the fulfillment of their debt commitments by the ordinary sources of financing (profits and borrowing). Their only alternative would be to reduce debt and debt service by liquidating non-monetary assets. But the resulting fall in asset prices would imply the risk of selling them off and of becoming insolvent. See Minsky (1964).
6. 'For a variety of reasons – the limited equity base of banks, internal and foreign drains of bank reserves, and, in modern times, central bank (Federal Reserve) actions to restrain the money supply – the supply of finance from banks eventually becomes less than infinitely elastic.' (Minsky 1986: 195)
7. As the interest rate rises, speculative and ultra-speculative firms have insufficient profits and borrowing capacity to discharge the higher debt commitments: the ordinary sources of financing dry up. This situation corresponds to Minsky's (1982b) definition of the financial crisis.
8. 'Now, we have been accustomed in explaining the 'crisis' to lay stress on the rising tendency of the rate of interest under the influence of the increased demand for money both for trade and for speculative purposes. At times this factor may certainly play an aggravating and, occasionally perhaps, an initiating part. But I suggest that a more typical, and often the predominant, explanation of the crisis is, not primarily a rise in the rate of interest, but a sudden collapse in the marginal efficiency of capital.' (Keynes 1936: 315)
9. Minsky (1986: 177), for instance, explicitly refers to 'a more than full-employment speculative boom'.
10. 'It is a particular characteristic of the system in which we live that, whilst it is subject

to severe fluctuations in respect of output and employment, it is not violently unstable. Indeed it seems capable of remaining in a chronic condition of sub-normal activity for a considerable period without any marked tendency either towards recovery or towards complete collapse. Moreover, the evidence indicates that the full, or even approximately full, employment is of rare and short-lived occurrence.' (Keynes 1936: 249)

11. 'However, it is worth noting that during the liquidation phase of a deep depression the financial 'stage' is set for a long-wave expansion as debts are reduced, equity assets decline in value, and the stock of ultimate liquidity increases.' (Minsky 1964: 325)

12. 'But over and above this it is an essential characteristic of the boom that investments which will in fact yield, say, 2 per cent. in conditions of full employment are made in the expectation of a yield of, say, 6 per cent., and are valued accordingly. When the disillusion comes, this expectation is replaced by a contrary "error of pessimism", with the result that investments, which would in fact yield 2 per cent. in conditions of full employment, are expected to yield less than nothing; and the resulting collapse of new investment then leads to a state of unemployment in which the investments, which would have yielded 2 per cent. in conditions of full employment, in fact yield less than nothing.' (Keynes 1936: 321, 322)

13. Minsky applied this proposition to every 'coherent' situation, be it under-employment equilibrium (1975: 61, 127, 165; 1978: 36, 37), full-employment equilibrium (1974: 268; 1980: 26; 1986: 177, 183) or steady growth (1974: 267).

14. For the two quotations see, respectively, Minsky (1975: 127; 1978: 37) and Minsky (1974: 272; 1975: 165). Analogously, in Minsky (1986: 219) we read: 'Any transitory tranquillity is transformed into an expansion.' A similar concept is repeated many times in Minsky (1980).

15. As Minsky puts it (1986: 183): '[B]ut tranquility diminishes the value of the insurance (liquidity) embodied in the dollar, so that a rise in the absolute and relative prices of capital and financial assets that are valued mainly for income will take place'.

16. Thus, we read: '[T]he main emphasis will be on the upper turning point and the possibility of generating steady growth' (Minsky 1957: 859) '. . . in this paper the lower turning point is essentially unexplained' (Minsky 1957: 867). Analogous considerations can be found in Minsky (1965).

17. '[T]he substitution of a downward for an upper tendency often takes place suddenly and violently, whereas there is, as a rule, no such sharp turning-point when an upward is substituted for a downward tendency.' (Keynes 1936: 314)

18. We read: '[I]t is not so easy to revive the marginal efficiency of capital, determined, as it is, by the uncontrollable and disobedient psychology of the business world. It is the return of confidence, to speak in ordinary language, which is so insusceptible to control in an economy of individualistic capitalism.' (Keynes 1936: 317)

19. See Minsky and Whalen (1996 and 1996–97) and Minsky (1993a, 1993b and 1996). For an interesting and updated extension of Minsky's analysis of capitalism's financial evolution, see Wray (2010).

20. According to Wray (2010), in this phase the financial system was characterized by the predominance of commercial banks that granted short-run credit and issued short-run liabilities. Bank credit in turn financed advance payments for wage bills, raw materials, intermediate and final goods, and it was paid back as soon as borrowers (firms or traders) sold their products. The success of the banker would depend on the success of the borrower.

21. According to Wray (2010), this development implied a change in the structure of financial intermediation. The diffusion of the corporate form led to the increasing importance of investment banks, which issued liabilities in order to purchase firms' equities and bonds. These banks in turn gradually abandoned the 'bank model' in favour of the 'market model'. According to the 'banks model', the investment bank holds the corporate shares and bonds purchased from firms in its portfolio. The success of the banker still depends on the success of the borrower. According to the 'markets model', by contrast, the investment bank places the equities and shares purchased from firms

into wealth holders' portfolios. With this, the quality of the assets over their whole lives stops being important. What matters is the opportunity of selling them at a 'better' price. The result is a relaxation in underwriting and in credit standards which makes the financial system more fragile.

22. In ancient Sparta, the 'ephor' was a magistrate who controlled the kings' powers and activity.
23. See Matthews (1984).
24. When he became bursar of King's in 1924, Keynes decided to concentrate the college's resources into a fund called the Chest. By the time Keynes died in 1946, the fund had grown from £3,000 to £380,000, an annual compounding rate of over 12 percent. In the same period, the British stock market had fallen by 15 percent.
25. Among other things, Minsky's 'two price theory' has the merit of highlighting that money supply directly affects asset prices and interest rates, not goods prices as maintained by the Quantity Theory.
26. Minsky is assuming a high substitutability between old and new capital assets.
27. We are omitting Minsky's considerations about investment financing (borrower's and lender's risk, safety margins and so on). The reason is that in Keynes's Chapter 12 the Stock Exchange is not considered as a source of funds, but as a determinant of the marginal efficiency of capital.
28. By imposing equality between the interest rate and the marginal efficiency of capital, we get $r=MEC=Q/MC$, where r is the interest rate, Q is the (by assumption perpetual) expected profit from investment, MC is the marginal cost of investment, Q/MC is the marginal efficiency of capital MEC. The same relationship can be written as $MC=Q/r$, where MC and Q/r represent – respectively – Minsky's supply and demand price.
29. As Minsky, Keynes is assuming a high substitutability between old and new capital assets.
30. Analogous considerations hold if the expected price of shares is lower than the marginal cost. In this case, the purchase of existing capital assets is simply postponed. To quote Keynes: 'For it is not sensible to pay 25 for an investment of which you believe the prospective yield to justify a value of 30, if you also believe that the market will value it at 20 three months hence.' (1936: 155)
31. The dominant theory would obviously reject Figure 9.1 and all that follows. It would object that the rationality of agents and the efficiency of markets align the price of assets to their fundamental values. In Keynes's view, however, both individual and collective rationality are notoriously limited. The individual knowledge of the factors governing the future is so 'slight and . . . negligible' (1936: 149) that rational calculation becomes impossible. Market mechanisms and incentives in turn are often distorted. Managers and expert professionals generally 'possess judgement and knowledge beyond that of the average private investor' (1936: 154). However, they are 'often so much in the minority that their behaviour does not govern the market' (1936:150). Above all – as we have seen – in the interest of their firms (1936:155) managers themselves will adopt the speculative behaviours of the crowd.
32. In defining his hedge, speculative and Ponzi finance, for instance, Minsky (1986: 206–207) considers firms and their financiers as a single entity.
33. To quote Keynes: 'it is usually agreed that casinos should, in the public interest, be inaccessible and expensive' (1936: 159).

REFERENCES

Arestis, P. and Skouras, T. (eds) (1985) *Post Keynesian Economic Theory: A Challenge to Neoclassical Economics*, Armonk, N.Y.: M.E. Sharpe, 24–55.

Keynes, J.M. (1936) *The General Theory of Employment, Interest and Money*, London: Macmillan.
Matthews, R.C.O. (1984) 'Animal spirits', *Proceedings of the British Academy*, 70, 209–29.
Minsky, H.P. (1957) 'Monetary systems and accelerator models', *American Economic Review*, 47(6), 859–83.
Minsky, H.P. (1963) 'Can 'It' happen again?', in Carson, D. (ed.) *Banking and Monetary Studies*, Homewood, Illinois: R.D. Irwin, 101–11.
Minsky, H.P. (1964) 'Longer waves in financial relations: financial factors in the more severe depressions', *The American Economic Review*, 54(3), 325–35.
Minsky H.P. (1965) 'The integration of simple growth and cycle models', in Brennan, M. (ed), *Patterns of Market Behaviour*, Providence: Brown University Press, 175–91.
Minsky, H.P. (1972) 'An exposition of a Keynesian theory of investment', in Szego, G.P., and Shell, S. (eds) *Mathematical Methods in Investment and Finance*, Amsterdam: North-Holland, 207–33.
Minsky, H.P. (1974) 'The modelling of financial instability: an introduction', in Vogt, W.G. and Mickle, M.H (eds) *Proceedings of the Fifth Annual Pittsburg Conference held in April 24–26, 1974, Modelling and Simulation,* Vol. 5, Pittsburg, PA: School of Engineering, University of Pittsburg, 267–72.
Minsky, H.P. (1975) *John Maynard Keynes*, New York: Columbia University Press.
Minsky, H.P. (1978) 'The financial instability hypothesis: a restatement', *Thames Papers in Political Economy*, London: North East London Polytechnic, 1–26.
Minsky, H.P. (1980) 'Capitalist financial processes and the instability of capitalism', *Journal of Economic Issues*, 14(2), 505–23.
Minsky, H.P. (1982a) *Can 'It' Happen Again? Essays on Instability and Finance*, Armonk, N.Y.: M.E. Sharpe.
Minsky, H.P. (1982b) 'Debt deflation processes in today's institutional environment', *Banca Nazionale del Lavoro, Quarterly Review*, 143(4), 375–94.
Minsky, H.P. (1986) *Stabilizing an Unstable Economy*, New Haven, CT: Yale University Press.
Minsky, H.P. (1991) 'Financial crises: systemic or idiosyncratic?', Working Paper no. 51, Amandale-on-Huston, NY: Levy Economics Institute, Bard College.
Minsky, H.P. (1992) 'The capital development of the economy and the structure of financial institutions', Working Paper no. 72, Amandale-on-Hudson, NY: Levy Economics Institute, Bard College.
Minsky, H.P. (1993a) 'Schumpeter and finance', in Biasco, S., Roncaglia, A. and Salvati, M. (eds) *Market and Institutions in Economic Development: Essays in Honour of Paolo Sylos Labini*, NY: St Martin Press; London: Macmillan Press, 103–15.
Minsky H.P. (1993b) 'Community Development Banks: an idea in search of substance', *Challenge*, 36(2), 33–41.
Minsky, H.P. (1996) 'Uncertainty and the institutional structure of capitalist economics', Working Paper no. 155, Amandale-on Hudson, NY: Levy Economics Institute, Bard College.
Minsky, H.P. and Whalen, C.J. (1996) 'Economic insecurity and the institutional prerequisites for successful capitalism', Working Paper no. 165, Amandale-on-Huston, NY: Levy Economics Institute, Bard College.
Minsky, H.P. and Whalen, C.J. (1996–97) 'Economic insecurity and the

institutional prerequisites for successful capitalism', *Journal of Post Keynesian Economics*, 19(2), 155–71.

Schumpeter, J.A. (1934) *The Theory of Economic Development*, Cambridge, MA: Harvard University Press.

Wray, L.R. (2010) 'What do banks do? What should banks do?', Working Paper no. 612, Amandale-on Huston, NY: Levy Economics Institute, Bard College.

10. Keynes's views in financing economic growth: the role of capital markets in the process of funding

Noemi Levy-Orlik[1]

John Maynard Keynes rewrote the economic theory of his time and, more importantly, was highly concerned with economic policies to overcome unemployment. In terms of financing economic growth, we argue that Keynes had two versions, not entirely different, but in slight conflict, which prevented him from constructing a full and coherent explanation of the function of banks in financing economic growth and of capital markets' role in the capitalist system. One vision can be found in the *General Theory of Employment, Interest, and Money* (hereafter *GT*), in which his main purpose was to convince his fellow economists of the lack of clarity of the mainstream assumptions and, as a result, their inadequate economic policies. In doing that, the role of capital markets was overemphasized. The other vision can be found in the post-*GT* papers and in his *Treatise on Money*, in which he expands the explanation of the functioning of the banking structure, highlighting the importance of bank money and the role of central banks in the banking structure.

In his first proposition, he assumes that investment creates its own savings, therefore finance is a matter of liquidity, highlighting that the transition from savings to finance can be disrupted because of capital market operations, specifically due to agents' liquidity preference instability. In his second proposal, he outlines a monetary circuit theory in which the banking structure has a central role in financing investment and production. Keynes argues that although speculative activity dominates the capital market, investment finance needs to be *funded* in the capital market.

In this chapter, we argue that Keynes's analysis on finance is not fully developed on three counts. First, contradictions arise because of the different explanations of the relationship between the interest rate and investment. On the one hand, the long-term rate of interest, determined by the speculative motive of money demand (with a given money supply), is seen as the decisive variable in the determination of investment (*GT*). On the other hand, the central bank discount rate is the key variable since it can indirectly modify short- and long-run interest rates (*Treatise on Money*). According to Keynes, the main purpose of the central bank discount rate is to activate investment spending, despite its low elasticity with respect to interest rate changes. Second, the *endogeneity* of money is not fully analyzed, since the implications of bank money (debts created as a result of granting credits) are not thoroughly discussed; restricting the possibility of unlimited bank finance, under conditions that credits are channelled to the production sector, which increase income, savings and profits; creating the conditions of cancelling credits.

Third, we argue that capital markets' main function is not the provision of finance to increase investment spending. Instead, finance is supplied by banks, and debt payments are the main limitation to the creation of additional liquidity.

The chapter is divided in four sections. After this introduction, Keynes's arguments about finance in the *GT* are put forward. This is followed by a third section, where we discuss his unfinished theory of the monetary circuit. Finally, in the fourth section, we examine the main contradictions in Keynes's conceptions of capital markets, finance and interest rates.

KEYNES'S ANALYSIS OF FINANCE IN *GT*

In the introduction of *GT,* Keynes states that one of the major objectives of the book is to communicate with economists of the classical school,[2] to address their theoretical limitations and false assumptions and, more importantly, to convince them that economic policy ought to be modified. Keynes writes:

> This book is chiefly addressed to my fellow economists . . . Its main purpose is to deal with the difficult questions of theory . . . For if orthodox economics is at fault, the error is to be found in the lack of clearness and of generality in the premises' (1936: V).

Keynes begins by stating that capitalist economy's main feature is its monetary character. This was a fact not understood by mainstream economists of his day. He writes:

> it is my belief that the far-reaching and in some respects fundamental differences between the conclusions of a monetary economy and those of the more simplified real-exchange economy have been greatly underestimated by the exponents of the traditional economics; with the result that the machinery of

thought with which real-exchange economics has equipped the minds of practitioners in the world of affairs, and also the economists themselves, has led in
practice to many erroneous conclusions and policies. The idea that it is com-
paratively easy to adapt the hypothetical conclusions of a real wage economics
to the real world of monetary economics is a mistake. It is extraordinarily difficult to make the adaptation . . . Accordingly I believe that the next task is to
work out in some detail a monetary theory of production . . . [T]hat is the task
on which I am now occupying myself. (*CW*: 408–411, cited by Chick, 1992: 3)

The main contrasting views in terms of finance between Keynes and
the *classical* are related to the characteristics of money, money's price (the
rate of interest), and the role of capital markets in financing investment.
We begin with a discussion of Keynes's treatment of the characteristics of
money.

Money is a Special Commodity

Money in Keynes's analysis merits special consideration. He assumes
from the start that money is merely a symbol and has no value (discussed
more in the third section, following the chartalist theory). In *GT,* however,
the difference between Keynes and other classical economists is made by
assuming that money is a commodity with very special characteristics:
zero (or negligible) elasticity both of production and of substitution, total
liquidity (equal to one), and negligible net returns (quasi-rents minus
costs).

In this context, higher money demand (and more money production)
doesn't require the use of production factors, leaving income unchanged,
thus creating unemployment. Likewise, if money demand goes up and no
other commodity can perform its liquidity function equally well, money
prices rise, and the rate of interest will always be positive, undermining the
assumption of price flexibility. Hence, whenever investment and savings
are in disequilibrium, market mechanisms cannot reach equilibrium and
income becomes the accommodating variable. Finally, hoarding with-
draws money from circulation and deters effective demand, from which
emerges one of the major differences between the streams of thought
considered: money is not neutral. In Keynes's words:

> The first condition means that demand may be predominantly directed to
> money, the second that when this occurs labour cannot be employed in produc-
> ing more money, and the third that there is no mitigation at any point through
> the same factors being capable, if it is sufficiently cheap, of doing money's
> duty equally well . . . Thus a rise in money-rate of interest retards the output
> of all the objects of which the production is elastic without being capable of
> stimulating output of money. (1936: 234)

To which is added:

> Unemployment develops, because people want the moon; – men cannot be employed when the object of the desire (i.e., money) is something which cannot be produced and the demand for which cannot be readily choked off. There is no other remedy but to persuade the public that green cheese is practically the same thing and to have a green cheese factory (i.e., a central bank) under public control. (1936: 235)

According to Keynes, if market mechanisms do not operate and the velocity of money is unstable (discussed next) the only alternative policy to avoid economic stagnation is to run a fiscal deficit, with monetary policy serving two functions. First, it needs to provide stable liquidity for financing the fiscal deficit; and second, income distribution should operate against wealth holders, lowering the rate of interest to reduce debt burdens. Also, central banks can execute credit policies for the fringe of unsatisfied borrowers;[3] and monetary policy on its own cannot restore equilibrium, especially in stagnant periods.

A second crucial difference is the discussion on money velocity. Classical economists, based on Fisher (1930) and Marshall (1923), argue that money velocity is not very variable or unpredictable[4] and conclude that macroeconomic policy's main objective is the control of the money supply. Consequently, the quantitative theory of money maintains that inflation is explained in terms of money demand pressures (*i.e.*, higher spending), assuming that money is neutral. Contrary to these views, in *GT*, Keynes argues that money demand, which is a function of income, depends on transaction, business[5] and precautionary motives; and like the classicals he believes that the velocity of money is relatively unchanged in the short-run.[6] The main difference between Keynes and the classicals then stems from the speculative motive for money demand which is determined by assessments today of future interest rate movements. These assessments depend on the sentiments and feelings of agents about the future, from which is derived the belief that the velocity of money is highly unstable (Keynes 1936: 194–204).

The inclusion of the speculative motive turns the demand function for money into a liquidity preference schedule, with a given money supply (an assumption rejected by horizontalists and circuitists).[7] This makes the money rate of interest highly unstable, limiting the amount of liquidity that capital markets can channel towards the productive sector.

The Rate of Interest is a Monetary Variable

Following from the previous discussion, another important topic that differentiates Keynes and the classicals is the nature of the rate of interest.

According to classical economists, it is a real variable, relatively constant, and determined by real factors (investment and saving) in capital markets; while Keynes assumes that it is a monetary variable, highly volatile, due to agents' changing liquidity preferences, unrelated to savings. Keynes therefore believes that the interest rate can indirectly modify finance and investment. Consequently, the rate of interest, instead of determining the temporal composition of consumption (present and future), modifies the composition of savings and rewards agents for not hoarding. Keynes writes: 'It should be obvious that the rate of interest cannot be a return to saving or waiting as such' . . . rather 'it is the reward for parting with liquidity for a specified period' . . . 'It is the price which equilibrates the desire to hold wealth in the form of cash with the available quantity of cash' (1936: 166–167).

Second, Keynes argues that the representative variable of the rate of interest is the long-term rate. But, unlike the classicals, he believes that the long-term interest rate depends on future expectations and, more importantly, on conventions. In other words, the actual value of the rate of interest 'is largely governed by the prevailing view as to what its value is expected to be. Any level of interest which is accepted with sufficient conviction as likely to be durable will be durable' (1936: 203).

In *GT*, and especially in the *Treatise on Money*, Keynes acknowledges that central banks can influence short-term interest rates through the discount rate (further discussion in the next section), which can have an important influence on the long-term rate, undermining the importance of the speculative motive (this is also discussed further in the next section).

The relevant aspect of Keynes's discussion of the rate of interest, however, is that this variable is unlinked to the volume of savings, arguing instead that investment determines its own savings, which can be turned into finance (*i.e.,* through increasing profits). Therefore, investment finance is restricted by institutional arrangements rather than the lack of savings. Hence, the long-term rate of interest can modify the composition of savings (or *ex post* investment) since they can be held in either financial assets or in liquid forms (hoarding). The latter (hoarding) deters investment and economic growth and induces unemployment, while the former can finance productive investment, as long as the long-term rate of interest is not very volatile. Another view of this discussion is that enterprises' internal funds (profits of previous periods) are the main source of investment funding since external financing of investment spending is limited.[8]

It is interesting to note that Keynes did not include the finance motive in the *GT* (highly criticized by Hawtrey, Robertson and Ohlin)[9] because he was extremely keen to point out that investment spending is followed by higher savings that *can be converted* in finance, as long as speculation is under control. Taking in to account the importance that Keynes gives to the long-term rate of interest, we shall next analyse the workings of capital markets.

Capital Markets and Uncertainty

The connection between investment and capital markets takes place through bond and share prices, which are subjected to expectations and different rates of confidence. This may induce 'wrong prices'. In this way, Keynes dismisses the concept of the marginal productivity of capital, because the value of capital can change independently of its physical productivity as the desire (profitability) of its use changes relative to its availability. This means that the value of capital goods is determined by their 'scarcity'.[10]

The relation between investment decisions and speculation is explained by investment prices of demand and supply, the former determined in the capital market (*GT*: Chapter XI), in which future prospective yields in present values (discounted by the long-term rate of interest) are equal to the reposition price of capital assets.[11] Alternatively, investment decisions are determined by the internal rate of return (marginal efficiency of capital[12]) and the long-term rate of interest, the latter being determined in the capital market.

The reasons that bond and investment prices are 'incorrect' are discussed in detail in chapter XII of *GT*. Keynes highlights that the main source of instability lies in the future prospective yields because of fundamental uncertainty about the future. He argues:

> It would be foolish, in forming our expectations, to attach great weight to matters which are very uncertain . . . it is reasonable to be guided to a considerable degree by the factors about which we feel somewhat confident, even though they may be less decisively relevant to the issue than other facts about which our knowledge is vague and scanty. (1936: 143)

He adds 'The element of real knowledge in the valuation of investment by those who own them or contemplate purchasing them has seriously declined' (1936: 154).

The main distortion of the valuations of investment prices is the intervention of expert professionals that, instead of possessing judgment and knowledge beyond that of the average private investors that would correct the vagaries of ignorant individuals, use their energies to speculate. In his words:

> The speculator or expert professionals are largely concerned, not with making superior long-term forecast of the probable yield of an investment over its

whole life, but with foreseeing changes in the conventional basis of valuation a short time ahead of the general public. They are concerned ... with what makes the market will value it at, under the influence of mass psychology, three months or a year hence (Keynes 1936: 154–155).

From this it can be inferred that deep and broad capital markets can be detrimental for economic growth, especially in periods of high capital mobility since long-term irrevocable macroeconomic decisions (investment) can be turned into revocable individual decisions. Keynes, highly influenced by the events of the (first) big financial crisis of the 1930s, argues that uncertainty is one of the main features of investment valuation, especially when 'professional' investors (instead of 'entrepreneur' investors) dominate capital markets' decision-making.[13] Thus, capital markets are a limited source of finance if capital mobility is not restrained.

The argument that investment finances itself, limited mainly by the lack of liquidity because of capital market instability, sets aside the discussion of the relation between banks and finance. Keynes, in *GT*, makes a small number of references to banks, among them the discussion of the state of credit can be highlighted. This is defined as the confidence of the lending institutions towards those who seek to borrow from them. The collapse of the financial system is also explained in light of the state of credit (Keynes 1936: 158).

REVOLVING FUND, FINANCE, MONEY AND THE RATE OF INTEREST

The discussion of banks' performance can be found in various papers that Keynes published in the *Economic Journal* in 1937 and 1939, which were reprinted in *The Collected Writings of John Maynard Keynes* (hereafter *CW*), edited by D. Moggridge. The discussion is based on previous findings that Keynes developed in *A Treatise on Money* (hereafter *TM*), where he argued that bank money is a means of increasing liquidity that need not generate instability if debts are cancelled and/or central banks have a key role in banking operations through the impact of the rediscount rate on short-term and long-term interest rates and credit policies.

This section is divided into three headings in order to analyze these ideas. First, the *revolving fund* concept is analysed, in which it is argued that banks can create their own money, transferring uncertainty of agents operating in capital markets to bankers (Kregel 1984). Under the second heading, Keynes's ideas of debt and its connection with money and the state (central bank) will be discussed, from which the concept of bank-money is developed. Finally, central bank policy and its effect on investment financing are considered.

Revolving Fund and Finance

The first issue points out that the concept of a revolving fund is not present in *GT*, because it is assumed (as referred to previously) that investment creates its own savings, which can cancel previous debts. It is important to highlight that savings and finance are different concepts and, in terms of volume, need not be equal. Savings is a function of income while finance depends on future expectations of investment returns, and it can be affected by speculative activity.

The business motive of money demand, referred to in the *GT*, is a relevant consideration for short periods, such as the interval between the planning and execution of investment,[14] and it depends on planned income.[15]

Keynes (1937*a*: 109) begins the discussion by accepting Robertson's critique that higher money demand, because of increased economic activity, can put upward pressure on interest rates and produce economic cycles, following the *GT* theory spirit (Chapter 13). Keynes (referring to Robertson) writes:

> I fully agree with the important point he makes that the increased demand for money resulting from an increase in activity has a backwash which tends to raise the rate of interest; and this is indeed a significant element in my theory of why booms carry within them the seeds of their own destruction. (1937a: 109–110)

He adds: 'I did not allow for the effect of an increase in *planned* activity, which is superimposed on the former, and may sometimes be the more important of the two, because the cash which it requires may be turned over so much more slowly.' (1937c: 220)

Keynes, however, continues the discussion, relaxing the assumptions of the 'given money supply' in the determination of the rate of interest, highlighting the idea that credits related to finance (another motive of money demand) require money advances (not savings); they are subject to fluctuations of their own and, as shown before, these fluctuations can modify the rate of interest. Therefore, the business motive (linked to active balances) is transformed into the finance motive that lies half-way between active and inactive balances, therefore the rate of interest can be altered.

Following Robertson's concept of a revolving fund, Keynes argues that financial institutions can provide liquidity without modifying the price of money in order to meet the temporary demand for money, for which special techniques are required. Concerning banks, overdrafts are the main mechanism to meet temporary money demand, based on a continual process of debt creation and destruction, in which borrowers repay previous debts, and lending is granted to new borrowers that ought to be paid in future periods.[16] If aggregate investment remains constant (*ex ante* investment equals *ex post* investment) there are no financial pressures, the rate of interest remains unchanged, and liquidity provision is undisturbed. Keynes points out:

> If investment is proceeding at a steady rate, the finance (or the commitments of finance) required can be supplied by a revolving fund of a more or less constant amount, one entrepreneur having his finance replenished for the purpose of a projected investment as another exhausts his on paying for his completed investment. (1937b: 209)

and

> Credit, in the sense of 'finance,' looks after a flow of investment. It is a revolving fund which can be used over and over again. It does not absorb or exhaust any resources. The same finance can tackle one investment after another. But credit, in Professor Ohlin's sense of 'saving,' relates to a stock. Each new net investment has a new savings attached to it. (1937b: 209)

There is, however another scenario when investment spending (*ex ante*) is higher than savings (*ex post* investment). The immediate effect is congestion in the money market, due to the reduced liquidity provisions in the revolving fund. There are two ways that liquidity can rise without the rate of interest increasing: either the banking system is prepared to augment the supply of money or savers' liquidity preference shrinks.

The argument regarding banks is straightforward since they are the only institutions that can issue monetary debts against themselves that increase liquidity. Specifically:

> If the banking system chooses to make the finance available and the investment projected by the new issues actually takes place, the appropriate level of income will be generated out of which there will necessarily remain over an amount of savings exactly sufficient to take care of the new investment. (1937b: 210)

Consequently, if bankers decide to meet higher credit demand related to the finance motive, investment and savings rise. It should be noticed that agents' liquidity preference is transferred to bankers that decide whether or not bank advances will be increased (money supply). In Keynes's words:

> the main point remains that the transition from a lower to a higher scale of activity involves an increased demand for liquid resources which cannot be met

without a rise in the rate of interest, unless banks are ready to lend more cash
or the rest of the public to release more cash at the existing rate of interest. . . .
This means, in general that banks hold the key position in the transition from a
lower to a higher scale of activity. (1937c: 222)

Having said that, it can be noted that there is an alternative way of
increasing liquidity for financing economic activity without exerting pressures on the rate of interest (amply discussed in *GT*). Specifically, wealth
owners (families) can reduce their liquidity preference, and thereby more
ex post investment is transformed into financial savings. Actually, as discussed below, it is assumed that banks' decisions to increase cash need to
be endorsed by higher provisions of liquidity in capital markets, which
Keynes called the *funding* process. In Keynes's words:

> The entrepreneur when he decides to invest has to be satisfied on two points:
> firstly, that he can obtain sufficient short-term finance during the period of
> producing the investment; and secondly, that he can eventually **fund** his short
> term obligations by a long-term term issue on satisfactory conditions . . .
> Occasionally, he may be in a position to use his own resources or to make his
> long-term issue at once (1937c: 217; author's emphasis).

This well-known assertion led to the argument that financial systems can
finance economic growth as long as short-term debts are transformed into
long-term debts, matching debts with income flows, overcoming temporal
asymmetries between spending and returns. This process takes place as
long as the short-term and long-term rate of interest remains unchanged;
this is known as *funding* (Davidson 1986, Chick 1983, Studart 1995, Levy
2001).

It should be noticed that, although banks have their own mechanisms to
expand and destroy liquidity, they continue to be linked to capital market
operations and to long-term interest rates, which Keynes regarded as the
dominant price of money. Therefore, it can be argued that in Keynes's
analysis of finance, capital markets are overemphasized and banks' capa-
bility of creating bank-money is not fully developed. The effects of money
endogeneity and *non neutrality* are not entirely considered.

The Origin of Money

The previous discussion shows that banks, through overdrafts, can
increase liquidity to finance spending. These arguments are based on
Keynes's concept of money, which is based on the notion of contracts
that require the recognition of a state or a community power that, on the
one hand, recognizes debts and, on the other hand, enforces the means of
discharging them. Therefore, the state power is a centrepiece of the money

theory. The starting point is the money-of-account concept (contracts to defer payments and price lists), which requires the endorsement of the state. This takes place through the creation of *money-proper*, which itself exists in relation to the money-of-account. Keynes writes:

> Money of account is the *description* or *titles* and the money is the *thing* which answers to the description . . . The state . . . comes in first of all as the authority of law which enforces the payment of the thing which corresponds to the name or the description in the contract . . . [It also] claims the right to determine and declare what *thing* corresponds to the name, and to vary its declaration from time to time. (1930a: 3–4)

Once the state can name what thing should answer as money to money-of-account, money is converted into a state creature, reaching what Knapp named *Chartalism*. Money-proper guarantees the acknowledgments-of-debts and also has the power to discharge them.

On the basis of debt and contract recognitions and releases, new forms of money are created, particularly bank money, which is defined as the 'acknowledgment of a private debt, expressed in the money-of-account, which is used by passing from one hand to another, alternatively with Money-Proper, to settle transactions' (1930a: 6).

Bank money and fiat money are converted into representative-money. This latter category includes state or central bank money that 'undertakes to accept in payments to itself or to exchange for compulsory legal-tender-money' (1930a: 7). An alternative classification takes place between bank-money (non-legal tender money), private money and bank notes, in which central banks' deposits are incorporated, which are, in turn, transformed into currency money.

The diverse forms of money, especially the bank-money, leads us to Keynes's discussion of a banking system that 'consists of a Sun, namely the Central Bank, and Planets, which, following the American usage, are conveniently called Member Banks' (1930a: 9).[17]

Modern banks issue bank money, whose main distinctiveness is to create monetary claims against themselves (*i.e.,* deliver money), which are called deposits and take two forms:

> In the first place it creates them in favour of individual depositors against value received in the shape either of cash or of an order (i.e., cheque) authorizing the transfer of a deposit in some bank (either another bank or itself) . . . But there is a second way in which a bank may create a claim against itself. It may itself purchase assets, i.e., adds to its investment, and pay for them, in the first instance at least, by establishing a claim against itself. Or the bank may create a claim against itself in favour of a borrower, in return for his promise of subsequent reimbursement; i.e., it may make loans or advances. (1930a: 24)

The central feature of this discussion is that both forms of deposits release money, in opposition to the causality put forward by the classicals that runs from liabilities to assets. The main argument of Keynes (found in both post-Keynesian and heterodox) is that assets create their own liabilities. Therefore, banks' deposit creation is either an exchange for values received or against future promises, while the cancellation of deposits takes place once claims against them are being exercised in cash or transferred to other banks (1930a: 24). Moreover, the banking system can create money with no limits under certain circumstances. Keynes describes it as follows:

> If we suppose a closed banking system . . . in a country where all payments are made by cheque and no cash is used, and if we assume further that the banks do not find it necessary in such circumstances to hold any cash reserves but settle inter-bank indebtedness by the transfer of other assets, it is evident that there is no limit to the amount of bank-money which the banks can safely create *provided that they move forward in step.* The words italicised are a clue to the behaviour of the system. (1930a: 26)

The banking process of money creation is the settlement of debts which requires two important institutions. The *clearing house,* whose main function is to 'calculate each day how much is due on balance to (or from) any bank from (or to) other banks' (Keynes 1930a: 28), and the central bank that provides deposits, which are universally accepted debt that settles bank imbalances and closes their balance sheet, provided bank debts are settled:

> as a matter of convenience the banks generally accept for the purpose of day-to-day settlements a claim on a single bank – which is usually the Central or State Bank. Moreover a Central Bank deposit is not only available to meet Clearing House differences, but can also be cashed when the cash portion of a bank's reserves need replenishment (Keynes 1930a: 28).

Therefore, banks can increase debts, having no more limits than borrowers' solvency that will guarantee debt repayment. Thus, bank chairmen need not be passive agents as long as central banks are willing to accommodate bank reserves, without modifying their rate of interest. Keynes's analysis of debt-money and the revolving fund, along with central banks providing means (reserves) for temporally balancing banks' balance sheets, can increase economic activity, provided debts are cancelled.[18] Therefore, central banks play a very active role in promoting financial stability or instability, thus increasing the scope of their activities from lender of last resort to daily bank surveillance.

The next issue deals with the effects of central bank limits on the banking structure, ranging from rigid rules to loose monetary policy, expressed through short-term rates of interest and credit facilities.

Central Bank Performance in Financing Growth

In this discussion, Keynes does not pursue the ability of a central bank to accommodate banks' reserves in order to equilibrate banks' balance sheets. His main concern goes back to the determination of the interest rate and its impact on investment spending and employment.

An important instrument that central banks have to modify prices is the discount rate, through which they may modify the whole interest structure.[19] Keynes notes:

> it is broadly true to say that the governor of the whole system is the rate of discount. For this is the only factor which is directly subject to the will and *fiat* of the central authority, so that it is from this that induced changes in all other factors must flow. (1930b: 211)

And, more importantly, he claims:

> experience shows that, as a rule, the influence of the short-term rate of interest on the long-term rate is much greater than anyone who argued on the above lines expected. We shall find, moreover, that there are some sound reasons, based on the technical character of the market, why it is not unnatural that this should be so. (1930b: 353)

The basis of the last assertion are the statistics provided for the United States economy,[20] which show a high relation between the movements of the rate of discount determined by the central bank and the short-term and long-term rates of interest. Therefore, monetary policy modifies both the cost of bank credit and securities' returns.

Additionally, and setting aside the liquidity preference argument, Keynes argues that there are different ways in which low interest rates (cheap money) can affect credit costs and securities' returns (1930b: 356–362). If the running yield on bonds is greater than the rate payable on short-term loans, it will be profitable to borrow short to buy long-term securities. Another situation occurs when short-term yields are low, financial institutions will hasten to move into long dated securities, increasing their prices. Finally, and most strikingly, he claims that the rate of discount affects even 'professional investors' expectations, who have no intentions of holding securities long enough for the influence of distant events to have its effects. This takes place by lowering the: 'cost of borrowing and still more by their expectations on the basis of past experience of the trend of mob psychology . . . the apparent certainties of the short period, however deceptive we may suspect them to be, are much attractive' (1930b: 361).

The extensive analysis put forward by Keynes in *GT* Chapter XII is here undermined and central bank monetary policy turns powerful since it can modify the cost of bank credit and securities' returns in the financial markets.

In spite of this, Keynes argues that the rate of interest has a weak influence on investment spending, due to the inelasticity of investment in relation to interest rate movements. Specifically:

> the banking system has failed to change the market rate so as to keep in pace with changes in the natural rate. It is certain, therefore that hitherto the Banking System has not succeeded in controlling the Rate of Investment with sufficient success to avoid serious instability. (1930b: 363)

Again, Keynes opposes the classical economists by arguing that even if monetary policy can control short and long-term interest rates, it is unable to counter economic cycles, especially when economic activity is very low. In opposition to the arguments of his fellow economists, Keynes put forward the idea that the rate of interest has no direct impact on investment since it can only affect profit margins. Thus, as long as the demand price is above the supply price (or the marginal efficiency of capital is above the interest rate), discount rate movements only modify net returns. Hence, only large interest rate changes may impact investment spending. Considering the discussion above, Keynes restates his central argument: the only way to recover from economic stagnation is through monetary policies that accommodate the required liquidity of anti-cyclical fiscal policies. This entails lower discount rates so that entrepreneurs' debt burden goes down, and central bank credit policy that channels liquidity to specific productive sectors and agents.

CAPITAL MARKETS, FINANCE AND THE RATE OF INTEREST

This section summarizes the previous arguments and presents some ideas for further discussion. The first claim is that the capital market does not provide finance. In Keynes's terms in Chapter 12 of *GT*, this is due to capital market instability; and even if market interest rates are controlled by monetary policy, investment elasticity is low. Additionally, if it is accepted that debts are cancelled by inter-bank settlements and if there is no money hoarding, changes of interest rates only affect indirectly investment spending, through profits margins.

A second argument is that financial instability is not caused by money being taken out of circulation, but rather by borrowers' inability to cancel debts due to incorrect future profit predictions. Additionally, the central bank can modify discount rates from what is expected, or channel credit to financial activities, which induces higher debts that are unable to be paid, causing stock prices to fall below that which had been expected (financial deflation). It follows that net profits are the main investment determinants, setting the pace of economic growth and, if spending (investment) decreases, income and savings shrink reducing economic growth. Keynes fully understood that demand instead of supply determines the pace of income.

Third, there are multiple explanations in Keynes's work of the determination of interest rates and its effect on investment. It is assumed that interest rates, in general, are monetary variables, including the long-term rate of interest. This rate is determined in capital markets and supposedly affects investment spending, but cannot provide finance; since the commerce of bonds and stocks is related to financial gains[21] that modify income distribution in favour of financial wealth owners and against workers' income share, in periods of high capital mobility. The short-term interest rate, reflecting the cost of bank advances, has limited effects on investment spending both because inter-bank settlements are fully developed and central banks accommodate banks' reserves. Furthermore, investment spending need not be affected if profit margins are above the rise of short-term rate of interest or investment spending is financed through internal funds. Finally, higher short-term interest can be neutralized through the new instruments provided by derivates and securitization that, as stated above, induce financial stability.

Fourth, the funding process, which is the transformation of short-term into long-term interest rates, does not stabilize the finance of investment, since the movements of investment prices are not related to profits of the productive sector (it moves independently of the capital physical productivity). Even more, since investment generates its own savings that provides the means of cancelling debts, there is no requirement for capital markets to provide long-term debts.

We can conclude by stating that the banks are the main finance providers, and there is no instability if finance is channelled to increase spending, especially investment. This increases income and profits, allowing the cancellation of previous debts. The most important element is ongoing investment spending. The main problem arises if credits are channelled to financial activities that induce a Minskian financial cycle or if the central bank increases interest rates above the expected returns of investment. Capital markets have proven to be incapable of providing long-term finance for productive activity. Instead, these markets induce financial gains, which indirectly have an impact on economic activity, reducing liquidity if financial gains are above expected returns. Therefore, when teaching Keynes's views on finance, banks and capital markets should be analyzed separately, highlighting that financial market liquidity can induce economic instability.

NOTES

1. The author wants to thank Tracy Mott for his comments on this paper and Jeff Powell for the enormous help in the edition of this paper. The contents of this paper are the author's responsibility, applying all the usual disclaimers. This paper is part of the project IN 307111-3 sponsored by the Research Council of UNAM (PAPIIT).
2. Keynes used 'neo-classical' and 'classical' in a unique way. On page 1 of *GT* classical economists are considered the followers of Ricardo, that is to say those who adopted and improved the theory of *Ricardian* economics, including for example J.S. Mill, Marshall, Edgeworth and Professor Pigou. However in later writings he includes every teacher of the subject in this county (referring to the UK) besides Hawtrey and Hayek, who were classified as *neo-classicals* because they accepted the predominance of the monetary aspect of economics and tended to endorse classical conclusions in terms of economic policy (Tily 2007: 10, footnote 2). We follow the latter definition.
3. The point is highlighted in Toporowski, 2011.
4. This view is oversimplified in economic textbooks by stating that money velocity is constant.
5. The business motive, different from the finance motive, is held to bridge the interval between the time of incurring business costs and that of the sale proceeds. Cash held by dealers to bridge the interval between purchase and realization is included under this heading (Keynes 1936: 195). From this statement Davidson (1978) argues that investment depends on expected income.
6. Keynes clarifies, 'there is no reason for supposing the V is constant. Its value will depend on the character of the banking and industrial organization, on social habits, on the distribution of income between different classes and on the effective cost of holding money. Nevertheless, if we have a short period of time in view and can safely assume no material change in any of these factors, we can treat V as nearly enough constant' (1936: 201).
7. The monetary circuit theory, developed by the French and Italian schools and followed by horizontalists and circuitists, assumes that since bank money is debt, which can cancel monetary debts, the main constraint on higher levels of economic activity (and finance) is borrower's solvency and the creation by some banks of more debts than others. In this context, central bank liquidity proviso in at constant rate of interests is crucial for the banking sector stability, see Le Bourva (1992), Moore (1988), Parguez and Seccareccia (2000), Rochon (2006), among others.
8. A very interesting discussion of finance sources for investment spending can be found in Mott (2009) in which it is argued that internal funds are the principle supply of finance and external finance is limited, an argument that was taken up by Minsky in his Financial Instability Hypothesis (1986).
9. Keynes considered those economists as being the main representatives of the neo-classical school.

10. I owe this clarification to Tracy Mott.
11. 'The prospective yield from an asset at time r, and dr, is the present value of £1 deferred r years at the current rate of interest. $\Sigma Q r dr$ is the demand price of the investment; and investment will be carried to the point where $\Sigma Q r dr$ becomes equal to the supply price of the investment' (1936: 137).
12. The marginal efficiency of capital is defined 'as being equal to the rate of discount which would make the present value of the series of annuities given by the return expected from the capital assets during its life just equal to its supply price' (1936, p. 135).
13. In light of the financial crisis in the 1930s, Keynes put forward the idea of introducing a substantial government transfer tax on all transactions, with a view to mitigating the predominance of speculation over investment in enterprise.
14. A similar concept was put forward by Kalecki (1971: Chapter, X), when analyzing the time period between the decision of investment and the actual investment, highlighting that there is lag between these two variables.
15. Davidson (1978) and Minsky (1975) separate both activities when discussing the money demand determinants.
16. According to Chick (1983) the revolving fund is completely different from the theory of loanable funds, because in the former there is a process of ongoing liquidity issuance and payment, involving different borrowers, while in the latter, credit issued to one borrower needs to be repaid by the same agent for new credits to be created, producing a very close link between investment, credit and the rate of interest.
17. This analysis does not consider that money can be a real commodity which has its own value, *i.e., gold.* The discussion is based on the view that money is a social form, that: 'in the primitive age, before man had attained to the conception of weight or the technical contrivance of the scales, when he had to depend for measurement upon *counting* barley-corns or carats or cowries, it may still have been the State or the Community which determined what kind or quality of unit should be a due discharge of an obligation to pay which has been expressed by the numerals one or two or ten.' (Keynes 1930a: 13)
18. An interesting analysis of debts needing to be settled is found in Wray (2010).
19. This assertion has been highly debatable in periods of financial capital dominance, when financial inflation dominates capital markets (Toporowski 2000).
20. This analysis is based on the conclusions presented by W. Riefler, 'Money Rates and Money Markets in the United States' (Keynes 1930b: 353).
21. Minsky (1991) put forward an interesting argument in terms of how capital markets operate in periods when financial capital dominates the workings of capital. In contrast to Keynes's views that securities can supply finance, Minsky argues that financial markets' operations have been modified. At present derivatives and financialization are not related to enterprises' financial needs.

REFERENCES

Chick, V. (1983) *Macroeconomics after Keynes*, Cambridge MA: MIT Press.
Chick, V. (1992) 'The Evolution of the Banking System and the Theory of Saving, Investment and Interest', in Arestis P. and S.C. Dow (eds) *Money, Method and Keynes, Selected Essays*, New York: St. Martin Press, 193–205.
Davidson, P. (1978) *Money and Real World*, London: Macmillan Press.
Davidson, P. (1986) 'Finance, Funding, Saving, and Investment', *Journal of Post Keynesian Economics*, Fall, 9(1), 101–110.
Fisher, I. (1930) *The Theory of Interest*, London: Macmillan, available at http://www.econlib.org/library/YPDBooks/Fisher/fshToI.html (last accessed May 18, 2012).

Kalecki, M. (1971) *Selected Essays on the Dynamics of the Capitalist Economy, 1933–1970*, London: Cambridge University Press.

Keynes, J.M. (1930a) *A Treatise on Money*, London: Macmillan (reprinted 1935), Book I.

Keynes, J.M. (1930b) *A Treatise on Money*, London: Macmillan (reprinted 1935), Book II.

Keynes, J.M (1964[1936]) *The General Theory of Employment, Interest, and Money*, New York: Harvest/Harcourt, Inc.

Keynes, J.M. (1937a) *The General Theory of Employment*, reprinted in D. Moggridge (ed.) *The Collected Writings of John Maynard Keynes*, Vol. XIV, London: Macmillan, 109–124.

Keynes, J.M. (1937b) *Alternative Theories of the Rate of Interest*, reprinted in D. Moggridge (ed.) *The Collected Writings of John Maynard Keynes*, Vol. XIV, London: Macmillan, 201–214.

Keynes, J.M. (1937c) *The 'Ex Ante' Theory of the Rate Interest*, reprinted in D. Moggridge (ed.) *The Collected Writings of John Maynard Keynes*, Vol. XIV, London: Macmillan, 215–223.

Keynes, J.M. (1939) *The Process of Capital Formation*, reprinted in D. Moggridge (ed.) *The Collected Writings of John Maynard Keynes*, Vol. XIV, London: Macmillan, 279–284.

Keynes, J.M. (1973) *The Collected Writings of John Maynard Keynes*, D. Moggridge (ed.) London: Macmillan.

Kregel, J. (1984) 'Constraints on the Expansion of Output and Employment: Real or Monetary', *Journal of Post Keynesian Economics*, VII(2), 139–152.

Le Bourva, J. (1992) 'Money Creation and Credit Multipliers', *Review of Political Economy*, 4(4), 447–446.

Levy, N. (2001) 'Cambios Institucionales en el Sector Financiero y su Efecto Sobre el Fondeo de la Inversión, México, 1960–1994', Facultad de Economia, UNAM, Dirección de Asuntos del Personal Académico, Universidad Autónoma 'Benito Juárez' de Oaxaca, México.

Marshall, A. (1923) *Money, Credit and Commerce*, London: Macmillan.

Minsky, H. (1964), 'Financial Crises, Financial System, and the Performance of the Economy' in *Private Capital Markets, Research Study Two*, Englewood Cliffs, NJ: Prentice Hall, Inc, 173–380.

Minsky, H. (1975) *John Maynard Keynes*, New York: Columbia University Press.

Minsky, H. (1986) *Stabilizing an Unstable Economy: A Twentieth Century Fund Report*, New Haven and London: Yale University Press.

Minsky, H. (1991) 'The Endogeneity of Money', in E. Nell and W. Semmler (eds), *Nickolas Kaldor and Mainstream Economics*, New York: St. Martin's Press, 207–220.

Moore, B. (1988) *Horizontalists and Verticalists: The Macroeconomics of Credit Money*, Cambridge: Cambridge University Press.

Mott, T. (2009) *Kalecki's Principle of Increasing Risk and Economics*, London: Routledge.

Parguez, A. and M. Seccareccia (2000) 'The Credit Theory of Money: the Monetary Circuit Approach', in Smithin, J. (ed.) *What is Money?* Canada and USA: Routledge, 101–123.

Rochon, L.P. (2006) 'Endogenous Money, Central Banks and the Banking System: Basil Moore and the Supply of Credits', in M. Setterfield (ed.) *Complexity,*

Endogenous Money and Macroeconomic Theory, Essays in Honour of Basil J. Moore, Cheltenham UK and Northampton MA: Edward Elgar, 170–186.

Studart, R. (1995) *Investment Finance in Economic Development*, London and New York: Routledge.

Tily, G. (2007) *Keynes's General Theory, the Rate of Interest and 'Keynesian' Economics. Keynes Betrayed*, New York, USA: Palgrave Macmillan.

Toporowski, J. (2000) *The End of Finance, Capital Market Inflation, Financial Derivatives and Pension Fund Capitalism*, London: Routledge.

Toporowski, J. (2011) 'The Monetary Theory of Kalecki and Minsky', paper presented at 'From Marx to Minsky: Marxian Monetary Theory and Capitalist Finance', UNAM Economic Faculty, April 12 and 13, 2011.

Wray, L.R. (2010) 'Money', working paper, Levy Economics Institute Bard College, available at http://www.levyinstitute.org/pubs/wp_647.pdf (last accessed May 18, 2012).

11. Nothing learned from the crisis? Some remarks on the stability programmes 2011–2014 of the Euro area governments

Gregor Semieniuk, Till van Treeck and Achim Truger

INTRODUCTION

The economic crisis in the Euro area continues to galvanize its member states' governments in 2011. In particular, Greece and increasingly other countries in the so-called periphery of the monetary union are facing the threat of defaulting on their debt.

Over and above the pressing default problem, which is exacerbated by the lack of country-level exchange rate flexibility and monetary policy, Euro area governments need to achieve the longer-term macroeconomic stability required for a functioning monetary union. This stability, which includes the reduction of external imbalances, is widely recognized as essential for the Euro area to achieve robust growth. Without growth it is feared that unemployment cannot be reduced, foreboding more social unrest and possibly threatening the very project of European integration.

In striving for stability, Euro area governments therefore face two challenges: the reduction of public deficits, and the reduction of external imbalances. However, while the public deficits have been in the limelight ever since the inception of the monetary union, the focus on external imbalances has been meagre. While the present crisis has finally alerted some European policy-makers, the governments still largely ignore the importance of reducing current account imbalances in a coordinated manner.

This is evident in their latest version of national Stability Programmes (SPs) from April 2011.[1] If these SPs roughly reflect both perceptions about economic developments and intended policies in European governments, then their analysis helps to evaluate whether the Euro area is on track to stability and, thereby, finding its way out of the crisis.

In this chapter, we argue that the projections for achieving stability in the current SPs are very likely too optimistic.[2] We aver that by ignoring the importance of external rebalancing and assuming an overly buoyant world economy, the SPs either forecast unrealistic growth rates or unrealistically successful fiscal consolidation. Towards this, we examine the interrelatedness of public deficit reduction and external imbalances reduction. We derive our argument mainly from evaluating the SPs against the logic of simple accounting identities, which clarify the connections of financial balances and thereby of the two challenges. Thus we transcend the SPs' narrow focus only on the government balance, and shed light instead on the SPs' projections of the financial balances of all three sectors in the economy (foreign, private and public) and how they are intertwined with the overall macroeconomic development. Merely the final brief sketch of feasible alternative policy recommendations to address both challenges (sustainability of public deficits and current account positions) requires a greater sophistication of the economic argument and thus involves more judgment.

The chapter is subdivided into eight short sections. In the next section, we discuss the relevance of the public deficit and external imbalances in the European context. In Section 3, we recall the accounting relationships of the three financial balances. Section 4 discusses the related notion of the 'sustainability' of government, private and foreign sector financial balances, concluding that one balance being 'sustainable' is contingent on the other two balances being 'sustainable', too. Section 5 analyses financial balances in the Euro area from 1999 until 2010. Section 6 considers the SPs' forecast of macroeconomic and balance development until 2014. We find that, individually, the SPs rely on optimistic assumptions about GDP growth; collectively, they require an improvement of the Euro area's current account with the rest of the world, the continuation of significant current account imbalances *within* the Euro area, and a steep drop of private balances in some countries. Section 7 simulates three scenarios with less optimistic but, in our view, plausible assumptions to adumbrate how the SP projections about balances (and growth contributions) would fare in such a case. The scenarios differ mainly in which countries have to bear the adjustment burden. Our results show that either deficit countries would find it impossible to realize their rebalancing plans; or that surplus countries would have to acquiesce into increasing their public spending, since rebalancing on their side would require greater domestic activity to uphold growth. Section 8 concludes that failure to consider external imbalances is likely to entrench existing instability in the Euro area and to lead to long-lasting economic stagnation. Further we conclude that a symmetric effort at rebalancing current accounts would slow down fiscal consolidation (in the current account surplus countries) but would be one important aspect of addressing both macroeconomic challenges. It would help achieve fiscal consolidation in the medium term and the desired stability.

TWO POSSIBLE MEASURES OF MONETARY UNION STABILITY: FISCAL CONSOLIDATION AND EXTERNAL BALANCING

Functioning monetary unions require a degree of homogeneity within member economies. In the European context, the aim to establish or maintain this homogeneity is usually subsumed under the codeword 'stability'. Hitherto, creating stability was associated with reducing public deficits and public debt-to-GDP ratios. This is enshrined in the Stability and Growth Pact (SGP). Recently, however, calls have been heard to also address external imbalances, that is, very positive and negative current account balances.

Reducing Public Deficits

The Stability and Growth Pact (SGP) for the Eurozone countries allows for government deficits of no more than 3 percent of GDP. Failure to comply may result in sanctions. Yet, in 2010 this limit was breached by all member countries save Estonia, Finland and Luxembourg. Greece, Portugal and Spain reported a public deficit of more than 9 percent of GDP, France ran a deficit of 7 percent. Ireland topped the list with a 32 percent deficit, owing to large bank bail-outs. The Euro area average measured 6.9 percent of GDP (see Table 11.1), deteriorating 0.4 percentage points from 2009. The Council of the European Union has stipulated time frames ranging from 2011 for Malta to 2015 for Ireland to return below the 3 percent threshold.

Furthermore, the SGP demands that the debt-to-GDP ratio does not surpass 60 percent.[3] Actual debt levels were never below that mark in Belgium, Greece and Italy. Moreover, the lowest debt-to-GDP level for the Euro area as a whole never dipped below 66 percent of GDP ever since the inception of the Euro in 1999. Due to large government deficits and guarantees notably for financial institutions at risk of default, debt levels across member countries surged further during the crisis. In 2010 the Euro area's average public debt level had increased by almost 20 percentage points to 85.4 percent of GDP. In addition, the current solvency crisis

Table 11.1 Financial balances, Euro area countries, 2010

	Balances as percentage of GDP			Balances in billions of Euro			Bal. as percentage of EMU GDP			nom GDP
	Public	Foreign	Private	Public	Foreign	Private	Public	Foreign	Private	
Austria	-4.6	-3.2	7.8	-13.2	-9.0	22.2	-0.1	-0.1	0.2	284.0
Belgium	-4.1	-2.7	6.8	-14.4	-9.5	23.8	-0.2	-0.1	0.3	352.3
Finland	-2.5	-2.8	5.2	-4.4	-5.0	9.4	0.0	-0.1	0.1	180.3
France	-7.0	3.5	3.6	-136.5	67.3	69.2	-1.5	0.7	0.8	1947.6
Germany	-3.3	-5.1	8.3	-81.6	-126.6	208.2	-0.9	-1.4	2.3	2498.8
Greece	-10.5	11.8	-1.3	-24.2	27.1	-2.9	-0.3	0.3	0.0	230.2
Ireland	-32.4	0.7	31.7	-49.9	1.1	48.8	-0.5	0.0	0.5	153.9
Italy	-4.6	4.2	0.4	-71.2	65.0	6.2	-0.8	0.7	0.1	1548.8
Netherlands	-5.4	-6.7	12.2	-32.0	-39.9	71.9	-0.3	-0.4	0.8	591.5
Portugal	-9.1	9.8	-0.7	-15.8	16.9	-1.1	-0.2	0.2	0.0	172.5
Spain	-9.2	4.5	4.7	-98.2	48.0	50.2	-1.1	0.5	0.5	1062.6
Other EMU*	-5.0	0.3	4.7	-9.1	0.5	8.6	0.0	0.0	0.0	181.8
Average / Sum	-6.9	1.2	5.7	-550.5	36.0	514.4	-6.0	0.39	5.6	9204.3

Notes:
* Cyprus, Estonia, Luxembourg, Malta, Slovakia and Slovenia.
The three balances may not sum to zero due to rounding.
We analyse the SPs' assumptions and conclusions based on May 2011 data from the European Commission's Annual Macroeconomic (AMECO) database, which largely correspond to the data used for the SPs.

Source: AMECO, authors' calculations.

gave a boost to demands to make the SGP's threat of sanctions credible; and to require countries to keep their government budget close to balance or in surplus over the medium term. Germany had already created such a mechanism independently. The constitution was amended by the 'debt brake' law in 2009. It states that the 'structural' deficit of the federal government must not exceed 0.35 percent from 2016 onwards. On the regional plane, governments will even face sanctions if they incur any 'structural' deficit in or after 2020.

Reducing Current Account Imbalances

The global imbalances characterized by large current account deficits and surpluses are widely held to be one of the major macroeconomic distortions that fuelled the global economic crisis starting in 2008. Many economists argue that the reduction in global imbalances is a central prerequisite for a global recovery and for the stabilization of the world economy more generally (e.g. Blanchard and Milesi-Ferretti 2009; Horn et al 2009; IMF 2009).

As a matter of fact, many sizeable economies had current accounts significantly different from zero in 2007: the US deficit stood at 5.2 percent of GDP, the UK's at 2.6 percent, Spain ran a 10 percent current account deficit. Conversely, China, Germany and Japan displayed surpluses of 11, 7.9 and 5.8 percent of GDP respectively.

Meanwhile, the Euro area as a whole has sustained a relatively balanced current account with the rest of the world since its creation in 1999. Yet, within the monetary union, individual countries display both large surpluses and deficits: Germany's 5.8 percent was topped by the Netherlands' surplus of 8.4 percent of national GDP by 2007. On the flipside, Greece, Portugal and Spain ran current account deficits of more than 10 percent of GDP by 2007. These imbalances are particularly vicious in a monetary union: while in the early stages, credit was available at attractive interest rates, the resulting foreign indebtedness in combination with the inability to adjust exchange rates is now a formidable obstacle to these countries servicing their debt on financial markets.

While the SGP does not address such imbalances, it is now being recognized that a reform of this pact should include avoiding 'excessive imbalances', in particular divergences in current account positions. This has been argued by the so-called Van Rompuy task force and has been incorporated into the European Commission's proposals for a reform of the SGP (van Rompuy 2010; see Hacker and van Treeck 2010 for a discussion). However, it is not yet reflected in the SPs as will become clear in what follows.

FINANCIAL BALANCES: A QUICK REMINDER

The Three Financial Balances

Before analysing the SPs with respect to reducing public deficits and external imbalances, we introduce the accounting relationships of public, private and foreign financial balances.[4] These will inform our analysis.[5] The following accounting identity holds:

(1)   Public sector financial balance + Private sector financial balance + Financial balance of the foreign sector $\equiv$ 0.

Hence, any particular sector in the economy can only run a surplus, if it is offset by a deficit of equal magnitude in the remaining two sectors of the economy. For the foreign balance, it moreover holds that if one country runs a current account surplus, then at least in one other country the government or the private sector has to sustain a financing deficit.

GDP and balances

Given certain assumptions, the (projected) evolution of the financial balances of the three sectors also has implications for the (projected) growth contributions of the different components of GDP (see Appendix for a more detailed discussion). In order to elucidate the link between the composition of GDP and the sectoral financial balances, recall that:

(2) $$GDP \equiv C + I + G + X - M,$$

where C = private consumption, I = private investment, G = government expenditures in final goods, X = exports, M = imports.
    Also recall that:

(3) $$GNI \equiv GDP + NIA,$$

where GNI = gross national income, NIA = Net income and current transfers received from abroad.
    Gross national income will be used to derive consumption, saving (S) and tax payments to the government net of government transfer payments and subsidies (NT).

(4) $$GNI \equiv C + S + NT.$$

It follows from (3) and (4) that

(5) $(NT - G) + (S - I) + [(M - X) - NIA] \equiv 0,$

where $(NT - G)$, $(S - I)$, and $[(M - X) - NIA]$ are the financial balances of the public, private and foreign sectors, respectively. Hence, changes in any of the components of GDP also impinge on the balances.

Desired and Actual Balances

Ex post, the financial balances of the three sectors must sum to zero. Clearly, any particular sector will only be able to adjust its financial balance in the desired way, if the other two sectors *wish* to adjust their joint financial balance by the same amount in the opposite direction. If this is not the case, and the sum of the *desired* balances exceeds, or falls short of, zero, then GDP will adjust to bring the *actual* balances in accordance with each other.

To illustrate, suppose a government desired to keep a balanced budget by cutting expenses. Then the ex post balances would still have to match. Given that foreign demand is insufficient to let government balance its budget, i.e. $(X - M) < (S - I)$, then it is likely that government would be forced into deficit by automatic stabilizers, for the cost cutting would result in involuntary unemployment. Private sector savings would also fall due to this. Thus, the actual balances would sum to zero but at a lower than the desired output level.

Since the onset of the current crisis in 2008, governments proactively sought to stabilize the economy and reduce unemployment by means of discretionary measures, thus increasing the public deficit and accommodating a desired surge in the private balance. Yet, over the medium term such a policy may imply that the government deficit and the public debt-to-GDP ratio eventually increase to what many fear (and the SGP posits) to be 'unsustainable' levels.

WHEN ARE FINANCIAL BALANCES 'UNSUSTAINABLE'?

While the SGP strictly defines allowed government spending to be maximally 3 percent of GDP, there is no clear-cut economic definition of 'unsustainable'. However, if one subscribes to the notion that public deficits can be too large and moreover recognizes that current account balances cannot grow without bound, it automatically follows that there must be an upper limit to the extent to which the private sector can be allowed to run a surplus.

One can furthermore conclude that not only private surpluses but also private deficits should be kept moderate: first, a large private deficit would increase the danger of a solvency crisis. Second, should such a solvency crisis set in, as seen in the subprime crisis, the government – through automatic stabilizers and discretionary measures – would subsequently incur large deficits. These may suddenly be deemed 'unsustainable' from the point of view of the SGP or the financial markets. This completes the argument: the government financial position cannot be considered 'sustainable' by itself, but only when simultaneously the private sector financial position is deemed 'sustainable' as well. Intriguingly, the SPs do not address this issue of linked balances but focus on the public sector deficit only. Similarly, 'the financial markets' seemed to consider the public finances of all Euro area member states 'sustainable' between 1999 and 2008/9, but then suddenly changed their minds in view of rapidly rising public deficits and debt. The current account balance is a much more accurate ex ante indicator of the sustainability of national debt, since it reflects the joint financing situation of the private and public sectors of the country in question. In conclusion, declaring the financial balance of any particular sector as 'unsustainable' necessitates calling the balances of the two other sectors equally 'unsustainable' – irrespective of how this term is defined.

FINANCIAL BALANCES AND MACROECONOMIC DEVELOPMENT IN THE EURO AREA, 1999–2010

Section 3.2 spells out the connection between financial balances and GDP. The macroeconomic development in the Euro area until 2010 illustrates these connections. Average real growth contributions of private, public and foreign sectors from 1999–2007 varied across countries: countries with relatively strong private demand growth on average displayed lower, partly even negative private financial balances (e.g. Spain or Greece). From the accounting relationships we know that the private balance is $(S - I)$, and high private demand growth, i.e., consumption and investment, would imply that saving (S) is low and investment (I) is high, depressing the balance. The evolution of public and private financial balances during the crisis differed sharply from the preceding period. In 2007, government deficits were still below 3 percent in most countries, but the private sector ran large deficits especially in the 'PIGS' countries,[6] reflected in large current account deficits. When the private debt bubbles burst and the private sector suddenly increased its net savings in all Euro area countries, government filled the gap as a consequence of rising unemployment and solvency problems in the private sector: the public balance fell and public deficits soared (see Table 11.1 for the 2010 balances).[7]

Moreover, the yields on 10-year government bonds indicate that financial markets deem public debt-to-GDP ratios to have reached 'unsustainable' levels in some countries. At the time of writing (July 2011), speculative pressures are focused on Greece, Ireland, and Portugal. Spain and Italy are increasingly threatened to be classified in this category, too. This development highlights the interrelatedness of the financial balances: until shortly before the crisis, the public financial balance and the public debt-to-GDP ratio used to be significantly lower in Spain or Ireland than, for instance, in Germany. Those two countries fulfilled the SGP rules for 'sound' government policy. Yet, in both countries public indebtedness has drastically increased during the past two years as a result of the sharp upward move in private financial balances (see note 7).

ASSUMPTIONS AND IMPLICATIONS OF THE NATIONAL STABILITY PROGRAMMES FOR 2011–2014

The SPs forecast the macroeconomic development until 2014. Based on assumptions about some variables such as growth in the rest of the world, they draw conclusions about Eurozone countries' GDP growth and the ability of the public sectors to reduce their deficits as well as the current account. The projections in the SPs about public financial balances and current account balances allow us to determine the private financial balance as the residual. Because the SPs also provide data on projected GDP growth, we can express the financial balances in euros as well as in percent of GDP. These projections create a system of equations with $3 * 17 = 51$ variables for each year. For 2014, it is depicted in Table 11.2. Each row sums to zero, satisfying the accounting identity in Section 3. In the middle three columns, the bottom line sums to the respective Euro area balance. The foreign balance in that row is the financial balance of the Euro area vis-à-vis the rest of the world.

Inspection of the projections for all SPs combined rather than only separately reveals three intriguing features.

1.   Overall projected GDP growth rates appear quite optimistic, given the degree of fiscal consolidation: by the end of the projection period, private financial balances in the current account deficit countries

Table 11.2   Financial balances, Euro area countries, 2014, according to the Stability Programmes

	Balances as percentage of GDP				Balances in billions of Euro				Bal. as percentage of EMU GDP			nom GDP
	Public	Foreign	Private		Public	Foreign	Private		Public	Foreign	Private	
Austria	−2.4	−4.7	7.1	Austria	−8.0	−15.7	23.7	Austria	−0.1	−0.1	0.2	334.1
Belgium	−0.8	−3.7	4.5	Belgium	−3.3	−15.3	18.6	Belgium	0.0	−0.1	0.2	414.3
Finland	−1.0	−2.0	3.0	Finland	−2.2	−4.4	6.6	Finland	0.0	0.0	0.1	219.9
France	−2.0	3.7	−1.7	France	−45.7	84.5	−38.8	France	−0.4	0.8	−0.4	2283.0
Germany	−0.5	−6.0	6.5	Germany	−14.0	−168.2	182.2	Germany	−0.1	−1.6	1.7	2803.6
Greece	−2.6	5.3	−2.7	Greece	−6.3	12.9	−6.6	Greece	−0.1	0.1	−0.1	244.1
Ireland	−4.7	−3.7	8.4	Ireland	−8.2	−6.5	14.7	Ireland	−0.1	−0.1	0.1	174.5
Italy	−0.2	3.0	−2.8	Italy	−3.5	52.7	−49.2	Italy	0.0	0.5	−0.5	1756.8
Netherlands	−1.4	−9.8	11.2	Netherlands	−9.4	−65.9	75.4	Netherlands	−0.1	−0.6	0.7	672.9
Portugal	−2.3	3.4	−1.1	Portugal	−4.2	6.1	−2.0	Portugal	0.0	0.1	0.0	180.7
Spain	−2.1	2.4	−0.3	Spain	−25.8	29.5	−3.7	Spain	−0.2	0.3	0.0	1230.3
Other EMU*	−1.8	−0.8	2.5	Other EMU*	−4.0	−1.7	5.8	Other EMU*	0.0	0.0	0.0	229.9
Average	−1.6	−0.6	2.3	Sum	−134.7	−92.0	226.7	Average	−1.3	−0.87	2.2	10544.0

Note: * Cyprus, Estonia, Luxembourg, Malta, Slovakia and Slovenia.

Source: Stability Programmes (authors' calculations; we use an extrapolation of the AMECO forecast as Luxembourg's foreign balance).

would have worsened dramatically, in some cases by more than 5 or 6 percentage points (to -1.7 percent of GDP in France, -2.7 percent in Greece, -2.8 percent in Italy, -1.1 percent in Portugal and -0.3 percent in Spain).[8] If the private sector does not desire to reduce saving by as much, the adjustment process between a consolidating government and a cautious private sector will cause frictions in the economy and loss of growth. This relationship is frequently not explicitly discussed, but movement in the remaining balances is a necessary consequence of fiscal consolidation. The next two points discuss whether it is likely that the foreign balance could act as a buffer.

2. Adding up the national current accounts in 2010 and 2014, the Euro area as a whole has to improve its current account position by 1.3 percentage points of GDP from 2010 until 2014. This requires that exporters in the Euro area benefit from strong global demand, while imports grow less. It also runs contrary to efforts at global rebalancing. Hence, if global rebalancing is nonetheless to take place and the large deficit countries, in particular the US and the UK, attempt to reduce their deficits, the SP projections shift the surplus adjustment burden entirely on the other world's large surplus countries, in particular China and Japan.

3. Despite the Euro area-wide upward trend in current accounts *within* the Euro area, current accounts continue to diverge significantly in 2014. At first look, the improvement in current account of the 'PIGS' countries looks promising. Greece, Portugal and Spain would rebalance but still run deficits of more than 2 percent. Note, however, that part of this improvement in projections rests on the assumption of slow or even negative growth. The surplus countries Germany and Netherlands would augment their current account surpluses from roughly 5 to 6 and 8 to 10 percent of GDP in the period 2010 to 2014. The only two countries that fare badly with their balances according to the projections are Italy and France. Italy never reduces its current account deficit below 3 percent while France's actually steadily deteriorates to 3.6 percent. This is all the more worrying as this might produce 'new pigs', but of an order of magnitude larger than the current ones.

In short, the GDP growth projections and the fiscal consolidation may be jeopardized by non-realization of the optimistic assumptions about private sector's ability to drive GDP growth and Euro area current account development.

The contemplation of the private financial balance projection necessitates another word of caution: the deterioration of private financial balances in those countries, in which the increase in private indebtedness has been also strong during the years prior to the financial crisis, is remarkable. The deterioration would be triggered by renewed private demand booms, implying zero or even negative net private saving. The development of relatively good public balances with negative private balances was last witnessed in Ireland and Spain and flipped with the onset of the crisis. Against this backdrop, the implicit assumption about negative private financial balances for 2014 looks worrying, in particular for France, Greece, Italy and Portugal.

THREE ALTERNATIVE SCENARIOS FOR THE EVOLUTION OF THE EURO AREA CURRENT ACCOUNTS

Returning to the assumptions for the Euro area as a whole, we examine the sensitivity of the projections to a deterioration in one assumption. This seems justified by the assumptions' optimistic nature. Moreover, it underscores our argument of the importance of heeding not only public deficits but also current account imbalances. In particular, we simulate what would have to happen to the financial balances of all Euro area countries in 2014, if the Euro area failed to improve its current account vis-à-vis the rest of the world. The failure of Euro area current account improvement might happen for a number of reasons at the time of writing (see e.g. IMF 2011): growth may slow in China among fears of overheating and a housing-bubble, depressing world economic activity as a result; fears of a double-dip recession in the US are substantiated by dismal economic data from the world's largest economy and continuing partisan arguments about the speed of fiscal consolidation (deemed too slow by many) and the public debt ceiling (which many argue should be raised no further); volatile food and oil prices may also pose threats especially to emerging markets' health; and financial market turbulences in Europe and elsewhere may further increase should current growth projections turn out to be overly optimistic. All of these threats make a strong case for the Euro area to develop a growth strategy that is less reliant on 'the upturn in the volume of world trade' as optimistically projected in the German SP (2011: 8).

We carry out three counterfactual exercises. In all of them, we assume that in 2014 the Euro area foreign financial balance (the negative of its current account) continues to be at 0.4 percent of Euro area GDP instead of improving to -0.9 percent. Further, we continue to take government deficits and GDP growth rates from the SPs' projections. Thus we ensure comparability with the SP baseline and can check whether the adjusted current accounts and growth contributions would let such growth rates and consolidation still appear plausible. The scenarios differ merely by who bears the adjustment burden. In Scenario 1, the adjustment burden is borne by each deficit country proportional to its share of the 2010 Euro area gross deficit in 2010. In Scenario 2, the same takes place but the burden is distributed according to the projected deficit shares in 2014. This is to take heed of the governments' belief about the performance of their export industries. In Scenario 3, surplus countries share the adjustment burden, which is distributed according to the size of their share of the surplus in 2010. Meanwhile, deficit countries reduce their deficit to like projected in the SPs but at least to 2 percent of GDP.

The results of the simulations are shown in Tables 11.3, 11.4 and 11.5 for the three scenarios respectively. Obviously, the implications of Scenario 1 in Table 11.3 for the balances of the burden-bearing deficit countries are devastating: In Greece and Portugal, private sector and current account deficits would once more soar to above 10 percent of GDP. Italy and Spain would both run current account deficits of over 5 percent and incur private deficits of respectively almost 5 and over 3 percent. Note that France's current and private accounts do not budge much from their SP values: France projects a drastic deterioration of its balances anyhow.

Scenario 2 shows the emergence of 'new pigs' in Table 11.4: France and Italy would incur huge deficits and drastically reduce their private financial balances.

Scenario 3 has Germany and the Netherlands starkly reduce their balances. Altogether the figures in Table 11.5 look less outrageous. Yet, as Germany bears the lion's share of the adjustment burden, its growth contribution from net exports is not a driver of GDP growth any more. Figure 11.1 shows the ramifications of the rebalancing simulation for Germany's balances and sectoral growth contributions. The foreign sector's steady growth contribution stems from our assumption that adjustment takes place in equal steps, i.e. every year one fourth of the entire current account deterioration is credited to Germany's balance. Clearly, Germany would require even stronger private domestic demand (as government spending is taken over from the SP) than in the baseline. 2011 and 2012, in particular, would necessitate a veritable demand boom: Figure 11.1 shows the private growth contribution would be at almost 3 and 2.5 percentage points. Historically, the private sector had much lower demand contributions. The average 1999–2007 was 0.7 percentage points! Thus, Scenario 3 clearly shows that growth would fall in Germany in case of adjustment of the current account, if government kept on its course for spending.

Scenario 3 looks more stable than the other two scenarios, which would

Table 11.3 Simulated financial balances of Scenario 1: Euro area countries, 2014

	Balances as percentage of GDP				Balances in billions of Euro				Bal. as percentage of EMU GDP			nom GDP
	Public	Foreign	Private		Public	Foreign	Private		Public	Foreign	Private	
Austria	-2.4	-4.7	7.1	Austria	-8.0	-15.7	23.7	Austria	-0.1	-0.1	0.2	334.1
Belgium	-0.8	-3.7	4.5	Belgium	-3.3	-15.3	18.6	Belgium	0.0	-0.1	0.2	414.3
Finland	-1.0	-2.0	3.0	Finland	-2.2	-4.4	6.6	Finland	0.0	0.0	0.1	219.9
France	-2.0	4.0	-2.0	France	-45.7	92.4	-46.8	France	-0.4	0.9	-0.4	2283.0
Germany	-0.5	-6.0	6.5	Germany	-14.0	-168.2	182.2	Germany	-0.1	-1.6	1.7	2803.6
Greece	-2.6	15.3	-12.7	Greece	-6.3	37.2	-30.9	Greece	-0.1	0.4	-0.3	244.1
Ireland	-4.7	0.9	3.8	Ireland	-8.2	1.5	6.7	Ireland	-0.1	0.0	0.1	174.5
Italy	-0.2	5.1	-4.9	Italy	-3.5	89.3	-85.8	Italy	0.0	0.8	-0.8	1756.8
Netherlands	-1.4	-9.8	11.2	Netherlands	-9.4	-65.9	75.4	Netherlands	-0.1	-0.6	0.7	672.9
Portugal	-2.3	12.9	-10.6	Portugal	-4.2	23.2	-19.1	Portugal	0.0	0.2	-0.2	180.7
Spain	-2.1	5.4	-3.3	Spain	-25.8	65.9	-40.1	Spain	-0.2	0.6	-0.4	1230.3
Other EMU*	-1.8	0.6	1.2	Other EMU*	-4.0	1.3	2.7	Other EMU*	0.0	0.0	0.0	229.9
Average	-1.6	1.5	0.1	Sum	-134.7	41.3	93.4	Average	-1.3	0.4	0.9	10544.0

Notes:
* Cyprus, Estonia, Luxembourg, Malta, Slovakia and Slovenia.
The three balances may not sum to zero due to rounding.
Given surplus countries realize their plans, but the Euro area as a whole fails to improve its current account – adjustment is borne by deficit countries according to 2010 deficit shares.

Source: Authors' calculations.

199

Table 11.4 Simulated financial balances of Scenario 2: Euro area countries, 2014

	Balances as percentage of GDP				Balances in billions of Euro			Bal. as percentage of EMU GDP			nom GDP
	Public	Foreign	Private		Public	Foreign	Private	Public	Foreign	Private	GDP
Austria	−2.4	−4.7	7.1	Austria	−8.0	−15.7	23.7	−0.1	−0.1	0.2	334.1
Belgium	−0.8	−3.7	4.5	Belgium	−3.3	−15.3	18.6	0.0	−0.1	0.2	414.3
Finland	−1.0	−2.0	3.0	Finland	−2.2	−4.4	6.6	0.0	0.0	0.1	219.9
France	−2.0	6.3	−4.3	France	−45.7	144.4	−98.7	−0.4	1.4	−0.9	2283.0
Germany	−0.5	−6.0	6.5	Germany	−14.0	−168.2	182.2	−0.1	−1.6	1.7	2803.6
Greece	−2.6	9.1	−6.5	Greece	−6.3	22.1	−15.8	−0.1	0.2	−0.1	244.1
Ireland	−4.7	−3.7	8.4	Ireland	−8.2	−6.5	14.7	−0.1	−0.1	0.1	174.5
Italy	−0.2	5.1	−4.9	Italy	−3.5	90.1	−86.6	0.0	0.9	−0.8	1756.8
Netherlands	−1.4	−9.8	11.2	Netherlands	−9.4	−65.9	75.4	−0.1	−0.6	0.7	672.9
Portugal	−2.3	5.8	−3.5	Portugal	−4.2	10.5	−6.3	0.0	0.1	−0.1	180.7
Spain	−2.1	4.1	−2.0	Spain	−25.8	50.5	−24.6	−0.2	0.5	−0.2	1230.3
Other EMU*	−1.8	−0.1	1.9	Other EMU*	−4.0	−0.3	4.3	0.0	0.0	0.0	229.9
Average	−1.6	0.4	1.2	Sum	−134.7	41.3	93.4	−1.3	0.4	0.9	10544.0

Notes:

* Cyprus, Estonia, Luxembourg, Malta, Slovakia and Slovenia.
The three balances may not sum to zero due to rounding.
Given surplus countries realize their plans, but the Euro area as a whole fails to improve its current account – adjustment is borne by deficit countries according to 2014 deficit shares projected by the stability programmes.

Source: Authors' calculations.

Table 11.5 *Simulated financial balances of Scenario 3: Euro area countries, 2014*

	Balances as percentage of GDP				Balances in billions of Euro				Bal. as percentage of EMU GDP			nom GDP
	Public	Foreign	Private		Public	Foreign	Private		Public	Foreign	Private	GDP
Austria	−2.4	−0.9	3.3	Austria	−8.0	−3.1	11.2	Austria	−0.1	0.0	0.1	334.1
Belgium	−0.8	−0.8	1.6	Belgium	−3.3	−3.3	6.6	Belgium	0.0	0.0	0.1	414.3
Finland	−1.0	−0.8	1.8	Finland	−2.2	−1.7	3.9	Finland	0.0	0.0	0.0	219.9
France	−2.0	2.0	0.0	France	−45.7	45.7	0.0	France	−0.4	0.4	0.0	2283.0
Germany	−0.5	−1.6	2.1	Germany	−14.0	−44.3	58.3	Germany	−0.1	−0.4	0.6	2803.6
Greece	−2.6	2.0	0.6	Greece	−6.3	4.9	1.5	Greece	−0.1	0.0	0.0	244.1
Ireland	−4.7	−3.7	8.4	Ireland	−8.2	−6.5	14.7	Ireland	−0.1	−0.1	0.1	174.5
Italy	−0.2	2.0	−1.8	Italy	−3.5	35.1	−31.6	Italy	0.0	0.3	−0.3	1756.8
Netherlands	−1.4	−2.1	3.5	Netherlands	−9.4	−14.0	23.4	Netherlands	−0.1	−0.1	0.2	672.9
Portugal	−2.3	2.0	0.3	Portugal	−4.2	3.6	0.5	Portugal	0.0	0.0	0.0	180.7
Spain	−2.1	2.0	0.1	Spain	−25.8	24.6	1.2	Spain	−0.2	0.2	0.0	1230.3
Other EMU*	−1.8	0.1	1.6	Other EMU*	−4.0	0.3	3.8	Other EMU*	0.0	0.0	0.0	229.9
Average	−1.6	0.2	1.4	Sum	−134.7	41.3	93.4	Sum	−1.3	0.4	0.9	10544.0

Notes:
* Cyprus, Estonia, Luxembourg, Malta, Slovakia and Slovenia.
The three balances may not sum to zero due to rounding.
Given symmetric rebalancing (maximum 2 percent of GDP current account deficits) but the Euro area as a whole fails to improve its current account.

Source: Authors' calculations.

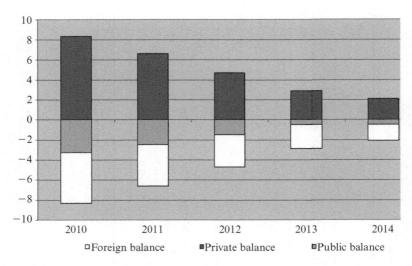

Figure 11.1   Simulated pattern of financial balances and GDP growth in Germany, 2010–2014 from Scenario 3: Financial balances, in percent of GDP

entirely undermine the project of stability in the Euro area. However, what would likely happen in the surplus economies is that the *ex ante* plans of both the public and foreign sectors to improve their respective financial balances in the surplus countries would harm GDP growth, as Section 3.3 details, unless the private sector *desires* to worsen its balance by an equivalent amount.

The alternative to a collapse in growth rates would be for the government to *willingly accept* higher public deficits over an extended period of time. In such a scenario, it is clear from the analysis above that the German government may well have to accept deficits of significantly more than 3 percent of GDP for several years, if the officially projected GDP growth rates and current account rebalancing are to be achieved within the Euro area. Although such a policy would currently be considered a breach of the 'debt brake' rule, the deficit would still appear quite modest by international standards.

CONCLUDING DISCUSSION

This chapter has evaluated whether the 2011 national Stability Programmes (SPs) of the Euro area countries are instrumental in achieving

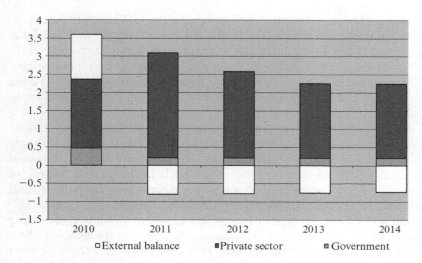

Source: Authors' calculations.

Figure 11.2   Simulated pattern of financial balances and GDP growth in Germany, 2010–2014 from Scenario 3: Real growth contributions, in percentage points

economic stability in the monetary union. In particular, we analysed how the SPs tackle the double challenge of public deficits and external imbalances. Our analysis rests, first, on the accounting identities of the public, private and foreign financial balances and, second, on the consideration of all SPs at once rather than separately. We found that conclusions are optimistic regarding GDP growth and fiscal consolidation, while current account rebalancing is neglected. The SP conclusions are arrived at by assuming strong global export markets, entrenched current account imbalances within the monetary union as well as the deterioration of private financial balances in the current account deficit countries. By means of our simulations we conclude, on the one hand, that the failure of favourable global macroeconomic developments to materialize may lead to the opposite of the desired stability by exacerbating imbalances in the Euro area. On the other hand, given symmetric efforts at rebalancing, such exacerbation could be avoided. If the rebalancing surplus countries were to hold on to their fiscal consolidation strategy, however, growth rates are likely to fall. For Germany as a case in point we reason that maintaining forecast GDP growth would presuppose a private sector demand boom unprecedented in recent history. Admitting to the unlikelihood of such a boom, the only alternative way to achieve the GDP growth rates projected in the SPs by means of domestic economic activity would be higher government activity for Germany and the surplus countries in general. In terms of the financial balances this could be achieved by running higher deficits and thus a deterioration in the public sector balance; or by taxing away private sector savings and thus a deterioration in the private sector balance.

Our approach to presenting our argument is overwhelmingly simple. Focussing on accounting identities we say little about economic theory that would explain the behaviour causing changes in desired financial balances or the adjustment process that leads to the ex post balance of zero. We do not attempt to explain how macroeconomic policies, unit labour cost differentials, demographic factors, productivity growth differentials or financial market turbulences etc. play a role in determining actual financial balances. For instance, we eschew a discussion in how far it is realistic to assume that Euro area countries with current account deficits would benefit from a reduction in the current account surpluses of Germany and other surplus countries (Scenario 3). While these questions merit closer attention, they would also necessitate more assumptions than we deemed necessary for the purpose of this chapter. Also, we admit to different conceptions of 'unsustainable' balances. However, given our aim of elucidating the interrelatedness of financial balances in the Euro area context, it was beyond the scope of this chapter to address these more nuanced issues. And we could show that by focusing on the accounting identities, it can be revealed that the project of achieving the stability necessary for a functioning of a monetary union is jeopardized.

Our counterfactual exercises involve several assumptions, which are appropriate when considering the approximate medium term effects of the change of current account adjustments, but may not appear realistic for every single year. This is in line with our aim to provide qualitative conclusions about the direction in which Euro area economies are headed until 2014 rather than with estimating precise annual numbers.

Subject to the qualification inherent in our approach, our straightforward calculations suggest that Euro area governments should not be surprised to see real macroeconomic developments diverge substantially from their SP projections. In particular, barring higher public deficits on the part of current account surplus and low debt-to-GDP ratio countries, a continued breach of the Euro area stability rules by countries with current account deficits is to be expected. In fact, realization of the interrelatedness of the financial balances and sustained government deficits and aiming for symmetric rebalancing while accepting higher than 3 percent public deficits in surplus countries may prove to be the only way to effectively stabilize the European Monetary Union without worsening the growth projections.

NOTES

1. SPs project macroeconomic developments and government plans for achieving stability over the next four years. The April 2011 version of the SPs, on which this paper focuses, makes forecasts for 2011–2014. They are submitted annually by each member government to the European Commission.
2. A similar argument for the stability programmes of the previous reporting period can be found in Brecht et al (2010). The present contribution is a shortened version of our more comprehensive analysis of this year's SPs (Semieniuk et al 2011).
3. Given a government deficit of 3 percent and nominal GDP growth of 5 percent every year, the public debt-to-GDP ratio converges to 60 percent in the long run.
4. The balances are annual flow variables. The public financial balance is the negative of the government deficit. The foreign financial balance is the negative of the current account. The private financial balance is net savings of households and firms.
5. See Godley et al (2008) and Hatzius (2003) for more detailed expositions of the financial balances approach.
6. It should be obvious from our analysis that we reject the one-sided blaming of the current account deficit countries as being responsible for the current euro crisis. We use this term here simply to remember that the projected current account surpluses by Germany and the Netherlands (and some other smaller member states) necessitate the existence of a certain number of 'PIGS' countries, i.e., countries with worryingly large current account deficits.
7. As an example, in Ireland the public debt-to-GDP ratio was very low until recently, but it almost quadrupled between 2007 and 2010 as a result of the current crisis. Similarly, over the past two years, the Spanish government had to run very large deficits and substantially increase the public debt relative to GDP, after it had run surpluses for several years before (while the private sector had very high deficits during the real estate boom).
8. The surplus countries forecast private net saving to fall but remain at high levels of 7.1 percent in Austria, 4.5 percent in Belgium, 6.5 percent in Germany, and 11.2 percent in the Netherlands.

REFERENCES

Blanchard, O. and Milesi-Ferretti, G.M. (2009) 'Global Imbalances: In Midstream?', IMF Staff Position Note, December 22.

Brecht, M., Tober, S., Truger, A. and van Treeck, T. (2012) 'Squaring the Circle in Euroland? Some Remarks on the Stability Programmes 2010–13', in Papadimitriou, D. and Zezza, G. (eds) *Contributions to Stock-flow Modeling. Essays in Honor of Wynne Godley*, Palgrave Macmillan.

Godley, W., Papadimitriou, D., Hannsgen, G. and Zezza, G. (2007) 'The U.S. Economy: Is There a Way Out of the Woods?', The Levy Economics Institute of Bard College, Strategic Analysis, 11/2007.

Hacker, B. and van Treeck, T. (2010): 'What Influence for European Governance', International Policy Analysis, Friedrich Ebert Stiftung, December.

Hatzius, J. (2003) 'The Private Sector Deficit Meets the GSFCI: A Financial

Balances Model of the U.S. Economy', Goldman Sachs, Global Economics Paper, 98.

Horn, G., Joebges, H. and Zwiener, R. (2009) 'From the Financial Crisis to the World Economic Crisis (II) Global Imbalances: Cause of the Crisis and Solution Strategies for Germany', IMK Report, 40/2009.

IMF (International Monetary Fund) (2009) World Economic Outlook, October 2009: Sustaining the Recovery, Washington DC.

IMF (International Monetary Fund) (2011) 'World Economic Outlook, April 2011: Tensions from the Two-Speed Recovery: Unemployment, Commodities, and Capital Flows', Washington DC.

Semieniuk, G., van Treeck, T. and Truger, A. (2011) 'Reducing Economic Imbalances in the Euro Area: Some Remarks on the Current Stability Programs, 2011–14', Levy Economics Institute of Bard College Working Paper No. 694.

SPs (Stability Programmes) (2011), available at http://ec.europa.eu/economy_finance/sgp/convergence/programmes/2011_en.htm (last accessed 22 May 2012).

Van Rompuy (2010) 'Strengthening Economic Governance in the EU. Report of the Task Force to the European Council', Brussels, 21 October 2010, available at http://www.consilium.europa.eu/uedocs/cms_data/docs/pressdata/en/ec/117236.pdf (accessed on 22 May 2012).

12. European economic policy and the problem of current account imbalances: the case of Germany and Spain

Jorge Uxó, Jesús Paúl and Eladio Febrero

INTRODUCTION

The Great Recession has highlighted a problem generated since the launch of the European Monetary Union (EMU) that had not received preferential treatment from the authorities until recently: current account imbalances in several Member States.

The Euro area[1] as a whole has remained relatively close to external balance with the rest of the world since 1999, with an average net lending of 0.3 percent of GDP.[2] This balance has swung from a current account surplus of 1.2 percent (2004) to a deficit of -0.6 percent (2009). However, within EMU there have been significant and growing external imbalances.[3] According to the dynamics of current accounts and their situation before the crisis, in 2007, we can broadly distinguish between three groups of Euro area Member States:

- Large-surplus countries: Netherlands (8.2 percent of GDP), Germany (7.7 percent), Finland (4.3 percent), Austria (4.1 percent) and Belgium (3.6 percent). Compared with their initial position in 1999, Germany and Austria significantly improved their balance (they started with a small deficit), the Netherlands also increased its external surplus, whereas Belgium and Finland recorded a little reduction of their surplus. In 2010 they all remained in surplus.
- Countries experiencing large and growing current account deficits: Greece (−13.5 percent in 2007), Spain (−9.6 percent), Portugal (−8.9 percent) and Ireland (−5.6 percent). These deficits gave rise to a progressive deterioration in their international investment position. In Spain, for example, its value changed from -35.6 percent of

GDP in 2001 to −78.1 percent in 2007, and it reached −89.5 percent in 2010. And the accumulated debt held by residents of the rest of the world rose from 45 percent in 2001 to 110 percent of GDP in 2007. Since the beginning of the crisis, the net borrowing of these countries has been reduced substantially, except in Portugal.

● Finally, France (−2.1 percent) and Italy (−1.7 percent) also had current account deficits at the beginning of the crisis, but more moderate ones.

In this chapter we will analyse, specifically, the German surplus and the Spanish deficit, for four main reasons.

The first one is their importance in explaining the total amount of current account imbalances in the whole of the Euro zone. Their external balances have registered an opposite behaviour, and in 2007 amounted, respectively, to 71 percent of the sum of the surpluses of all lending countries of EMU and 45 percent of the total deficit of all borrowing countries.

Secondly, Spain had sound public finances before the crisis: it never had an excessive deficit according to the definition of the Stability and Growth Pact and in 2007 registered a fiscal surplus and its public debt (36 percent of GDP) was clearly below the average in the Euro zone. This fact shows clearly that, in order to explain the current crisis, the imbalances accumulated since the outset of the monetary union, particularly private and external debt, are much more relevant.

The third reason is that Germany has pursued an export-oriented growth strategy, based on stagnating domestic demand and wages. This economic policy can only succeed, and avoid high unemployment rates, if other countries have large domestic demand and imports growth, and hence a current account deficit. So, deficit and surpluses must be considered together.

And the last reason has to do with the economic policies implemented during the Great Recession by both countries. On the one hand, Germany tries to retain its trade surplus, without taking any significant step to correct the depression of its own domestic demand. On the other hand, Spain has reduced its current account deficit to -3.7 percent in 2011. However, this is mainly due to the contraction of GDP and imports and the development of strong austerity policies with a high cost in terms of unemployment. In our opinion, this shows that although large current account imbalances and unsustainable foreign debt accumulation should be avoided, a non-recessive adjustment mechanism is necessary, with a symmetrical treatment of surplus and deficit. Both export and import surplus countries should share the re-balancing effort.

GERMANY AND SPAIN: EXPORT-LED GROWTH, CREDIT-LED GROWTH AND THE MONETARY UNION

An outstanding characteristic of the conventional analysis of external imbalances is its focus on deficit situations, forgetting that, by definition, associated with a current account deficit there is always a surplus – a disequilibrium of the opposite sign – in other places.

If the problem is approached in this way, the consequence is that it is usually concluded that the imbalance is the result of a 'lack of competitiveness' by the deficit country, where unit (labour) costs grow faster than abroad, or it is caused by overspending ('the country is living beyond its means'). On the contrary, the surplus is frequently considered as the consequence of a virtuous and appropriate economic policy, fiscal and wage discipline and efficiency: a demonstration of success.

This point of view is clearly maintained for example by Axel A. Weber, the former President of the Deutsche Bundesbank, when he says that the real problem of the Monetary Union:

> is that a number of countries have obviously failed to meet the obligations and requirements of a currency union. The persistent problems of countries in refinancing their debt are only the symptoms of the problems, not the problem itself. The financial crisis has revealed unsustainable developments in some member countries – developments which were already in existence before the crisis: too much public spending, unproductive use of capital inflows, losses of competitiveness. Those were just some of the shortcomings which had been carelessly neglected, not least by the financial markets. Painful adjustment processes, including structural reform and budget consolidation, are essential to restore the ability of the countries concerned to live up to the demands of the single monetary policy. (Weber 2011: 238–239)

However, neither the global current account imbalances accumulated in recent decades, nor those recorded inside the Euro zone, can be understood without taking into account the deliberate policy of some other countries that base their growth on the external surplus, achieved by increasing exports, wage restraint and the sluggishness of domestic demand. This policy can only succeed if another imbalance, identical and opposite, is taking place simultaneously in other countries: strong growth of imports and current account deficit. From this perspective, it cannot be said that the root cause of the imbalances are (only) on the side of the deficits that, at the end of the day, fill in the demand gap created by those countries which spend less than they produce ('they live below their means').

This alternative approach is consistent with Stockhammer (2011), who analyzes the current account imbalances in the context of the shift in economic policy that occurred in the early 1980s. These policies are characterized by the retrenchment of the welfare state, a worsening of income distribution and an intense process of financialization. While the first two factors reduce consumption and lead to a problem of lack of global demand, financial liberalization offers the means to solve it temporarily through the growth of debt.

But this finance-dominated accumulation regime has given rise to notable divergences across countries in terms of the pattern of demand. Some countries have offset their weak domestic demand with the strength of their exports ('export-led growth'), while in others growth is based on expanding domestic demand funded with increasing debt ('credit -led growth'). In the case of EMU, Germany is the best example of the first case, and Spain and other peripheral countries such as Greece, Portugal and Ireland are in the second group.

Both patterns are interdependent (the exports of the first group are only possible thanks to the demand from the periphery which, at the same time, needs surplus countries to fund their imports) but their continuity is threatened by the accumulation of imbalances. Therefore, the solution to the problem of lack of demand is only temporary, and the crisis appears just as lenders begin to have doubts about the creditworthiness of borrowers.

Germany and Neo-mercantilism

Regarding the case of the monetary union, a way to balance the emphasis on external deficits and surpluses is to highlight, first, the policy of wage restraint put into place by Germany and its effects on domestic demand and competitiveness.

Following Hein and Truger (2009), we can use the sum of the growth in productivity per employee plus the inflation target as a benchmark to determine whether the wage policy is too restrictive in a country. This amount represents the scope available for nominal wage increases, without changing the wage share and with the inflation rate equal to the target ('neutral wage policy'). Given that between 1999 and 2007 (from the start of EMU until the onset of the crisis) the average productivity per worker in Germany grew annually by 1.1 percent, and considering an inflation target of 2 percent, the scope for wage growth was 3.1 percent per year. However, in this period the compensation per employee (in nominal terms) rose in Germany at an annual rate of 1 percent. This means that in those years, nominal wages in Germany grew 16 percent less than permitted by increasing productivity without compromising the inflation target.

This wage growth is not only low compared to the aforementioned benchmark, but also in comparison with the German experience during the previous decades: the nominal unit labour cost registered a cumulative growth of 21.5 percent between 1980 and 1990, 16.4 percent between 1990 and 2000, and only 6 percent during the last decade.

As a consequence, real wages were brought down (in 2007 they were almost 5 percent lower than at the beginning of EMU) and the share of wages in income also fell, from 59.6 percent to 55.1 percent. Although the declining wage share is a common trend throughout the whole Euro zone, this 4.5 percentage points of reduction in Germany are the largest between all the Member States (the average was -2.6).

According to Horn et al, who present a complete analysis of the changes in income distribution in Germany, these tendencies had a strong contractive impact on aggregate demand:

> the majority of the population has reacted to declining real wages and social spending cuts (especially in the state pension system) in recent years by reduced consumer spending. As statistical analyses show a large part of the increase of the household savings ratio is due to changes in the distribution of income and increased old-age provisions in connection with the recent pension reforms . . . Almost half of the increase of the savings ratio between 2001 and 2008 can be attributed to the shift in the income distribution from wage to profit incomes. The other half seems to be due to the effects of the pension reform. (Horn et al 2009: 25)

The average annual growth rate of domestic demand reached only 0.7 percent between 1999 and 2007, versus the 1.4 percent that had been achieved between 1995 and 1998. This is due, partly, to the effect of the low growth in wages on private consumption. But it is important to underline that the increase in the share of profits in income did not provoke a more dynamic investment, which even registered a lower contribution to the increase of GDP than in previous years. Instead, the net saving of non-financial corporations and of the total economy grew by 7.9 and 9.0 percentage points of GDP respectively. Actually, this is not surprising because outside the export-oriented sectors of the economy, demand was weak.

In this context, the foreign sector was the main source of economic growth, well above the historical experience of Germany in the decades before. For example, the annual average contribution to the increase of GDP of net exports was 1.1 percent between 2001 and 2007, when the average contribution during the decade before had been 0.4 points.

One of the factors that gave rise to the increase in German net exports was the increase in the competitive position of Germany: unit labour costs remained almost constant throughout this period, while in the rest of EMU they grew 14 percent, and 30 percent in Spain. However, the repressed domestic demand in Germany and the strong dynamism of demand in other European countries, like Spain, also play a decisive role. Indeed, according to Schröder (2011) demand dominates prices, in the sense that the relative strength of demand explains the development of the German trade balance while factors determining relative prices did not contribute significantly to the observed trade balances.

In 2007 the value of the exports of goods and services from Germany to the rest of the Euro area was 80 percent higher than in 1999 while, in the same period, imports had only grown 51 percent. In terms of GDP, the trade surplus with the rest of EMU countries rose from 0.5 percent of GDP in 1999 to 3.8 percent in 2007. However, it should be noted that, despite these positive contributions of external demand to the growth of GDP, the German economy recorded a growth rate of 1.5 percent in these years which is low when compared with other Euro zone countries (2.1 percent), with Germany's previous experience (1.9 percent between 1994 and 1999), and with the growth rate required to prevent a rise in unemployment, which rose from 8.2 percent in 1999 to 11.2 percent in 2005. This means that, in spite of the high trade surpluses recorded, the export-led model only partially offset the depressive effects on domestic demand of wage suppression.

Some authors have defined the economic policy developed in Germany as 'neo-mercantilist'. In principle, export-led growth and mercantilism are not equivalent, because it is possible to have exports as the main driving force of growth and, at the same time, use them as a means to increase imports and raise the level of consumption. As Chandrasekhar and Ghosh (2010) say, what is characteristic of mercantilism is the failure to perceive that the purpose of increasing exports is precisely to be able to import more. The economic policy we have described above fits this definition completely because it implies suppressing domestic wages and consumption and, then, it requires positive net exports to avoid unemployment.

Cesaratto (2010: 5) also thinks that 'Germany seems a good example of a mercantilist economy: focus on trade surplus, production and productivity; wage moderation and compression of internal consumption; concern about a competitive real foreign exchange rate', although he emphasizes the difference between benign mercantilism and malevolent or aggressive mercantilism. In his opinion, if the economic policy put in practice by Germany after World War II was a good example of the first, Germany became a 'malevolent mercantilist' country after the first oil shock. Instead of cooperating internationally, Germany has pursued wage stagnation and productivity growth to gain competitiveness with respect to her European competitors and to increase her own share in world activity.

In similar terms, Hein and Truger (2009: 31) define the German economic policy strategy as 'dysfunctional mercantilism' and emphasize its restrictive effects on national and European economies: 'This ill-designed strategy has not only harmed the German economy, it has also put severe pressure on the Euro area member countries and runs the serious risk of competitive wage deflation in near future.'

Domestic Demand and the Housing Bubble in Spain

If we take into account that the Euro zone as a whole registered a close to balance current account with the rest of the world, for Germany to run a large surplus, Spain (and the other peripheral countries) had to run similar deficits. This is the other side of the coin.

These deficits came from a buoyant domestic demand funded with private debt. If the German economy grew at an average annual rate of 1.5 percent between 2000 and 2007, Spain was growing at 3.6 percent. This high rate was mainly driven by private sector construction spending. Between 1997 and 2007, the building of more than 6 million dwellings was underway and one out of every five new jobs was created by the construction industry. At the end of the period, the weight of the building industry in the generation of value added was much larger in Spain than the average for other countries in EMU (11.8 percent versus 6.5 percent) and its growth had been offset by a similar fall in the manufacturing sector (19.0 percent of value added in 1997 and only 15.0 percent in 2007).

Private and public consumption also remained high, like productive investment. However, the latter made a lower contribution to GDP growth because a great portion of this demand was covered by imports (48 percent in 1995, and nearly 60 percent in 2005).

The strong growth in residential investment was driven by several factors, among which there are some demographic and social changes that increased the demand for housing (Dejuán and Febrero 2010).

However, real wages remained almost constant in Spain during these years, the labour share declined 4 percentage points (from 59.6 percent to 55.6 percent) and housing prices multiplied by 2.8. Therefore, this potential increase in housing demand could only materialize in more effective spending thanks to the mass access of families to credit. This was made possible by the coincidence of a strong decrease in interest rates and the change in the financial institutions' credit policy.

Regarding interest rates, both long term and short term nominal rates experienced an important reduction in Spain before the start of EMU (more than six points between 1995 and 1999) due to the convergence of the official rates and the disappearance of risk premium associated, for example, with variations in exchange rates. And real interest rates were negative between 2002 and 2006, because of a higher inflation than the Euro zone average.[4]

On the other hand, the strong growth of banking credit was also partly due to the policy of banks of offsetting the effect on the benefits of narrowing interest margins derived from the fall of interest rates. The average length of a mortgage grew from 19 to 28 years, there was a significant increase in the value of credit with respect to housing and the effort of the debt – percentage of income that a representative household has to devote to debt service – rose by more than 12 points. Then, as Onaran explains, financialization and the worsening of income distribution are decisive factors in explaining the development of this growth model:

> The debt-led growth model was facilitated by the deregulation in the financial markets and the consequent innovations in mortgage backed securities, collateralized debt obligations and credit default swaps. However, without the unequal income distribution the debt-led growth model would not have been necessary or possible. (Onaran 2011: 52)

The increase in housing credits provoked a rise in house prices, and the increased wealth then served as collateral for further credit, inflating the housing bubble and fuelling consumption.

Along with strong demand growth, the current account deficit in Spain is also explained by a higher rate of inflation than its competitors. Relative unit labour costs between Spain and Germany in 2007 were 30 percent higher than in 1998, and if the comparison is with the Euro area, the loss of competitiveness was 14 percent. However, although competitiveness is not irrelevant, we think that the differential in the rates of growth of domestic demand is the main explanatory factor. Wage inflation and loss of competitiveness in the periphery is more a by-product of its strong domestic demand.

Besides this, the growth in nominal unit labour costs in Spain has been accompanied by a declining labour share of wages in income (an increase of profit margins). Therefore, the increase in nominal wages is not the result of a change in the distribution of income in favour of wages, but of a higher inflation rate and the attempts to compensate – not totally successfully – its effects on the real wage (relative to productivity). As noted by Felipe and Kumar (2011), reducing the problems of the external sector to a measure of competitiveness centered on unit labour costs puts the burden of adjustment on workers, and ignores that the unit capital costs (ratio of the nominal profit rate to capital productivity) has also grown in the peripheral countries, and faster than labour costs.

It is also noteworthy that the changes in external net borrowing recorded in Spain (an increase of 6.4 points of GDP between 2000 and 2007) are explained mainly by private sector behaviour, and not by the public sector. Specifically, between 2000 and 2007, the financial balance of corporations deteriorated by 6.9 percent of GDP and households by 3.8 percent, while the net lending of general government increased by 2.9 percent of GDP, reaching a budgetary surplus of 1.9 percent of GDP in 2007.

Net borrowing of households and corporations has translated into large debt levels: the total debt of the non-financial private sector rose from 132 percent of GDP in 2001 to 214 percent in 2007. Again, the Spanish debt problem appeared in the private sector imbalances and not in the public sector (which had, in fact, decreased during these years and reached 36.1 percent in 2007). Public debt in Spain is the consequence and not the cause of the current crisis.

In conclusion, the creation of EMU caused an expansionary shock in the Spanish economy, and the consequence of this surge in demand financed by debt and accompanied by a higher inflation rate than the average one was obviously a rise in imports, external deficit and external debt. But, as noted by Bibow (2009), the German model worked for Germany precisely because other countries behaved differently.

The Influence of the Design of the Monetary Union

Both the initial design and the subsequent operation of EMU have contributed to the emergence of these two patterns of growth, for several reasons.

Firstly, the evolution of the external balance received little attention in the design of the monetary union, as it is evidenced by the absence of any reference to the current account position in the convergence criteria. In fact, it was initially thought that the creation of the single currency would mean the virtual disappearance of the balance of payments constraint, since it would eliminate the risk of exchange rate and the liberalization of international capital movements, facilitating the financing of external deficits. Furthermore, it was considered that, with a single currency, foreign restriction would be no different from that faced by domestic borrowers against national lenders. According to this point of view, current account imbalances should not pose a concern for policy-makers or a source of instability for the Euro area, at least when they arise as a result of private decisions and not as a manifestation of high fiscal deficits.[5]

Once the single currency was launched, the emergence of large current account deficits, and the resulting accumulation of external debt in some countries, should have been detected from the outset as a fundamental problem for the functioning of EMU. However, it was considered to be a positive phenomenon, reflecting better access to foreign borrowing and expectations of greater productivity and future growth. Moreover, the high and growing current account deficits were seen as a collateral effect of the process of adjusting to the structural change caused by the creation of EMU itself and of real convergence.

This view of the external imbalances fails to take into account, however, other factors that may make the debt accumulation process unsustainable, as witnessed by the current problems of the Euro zone.

For example, the borrowing decisions of economic agents are decisively influenced by their expectations about future income, and these may be affected by psychological factors or related to the formation of bubbles in asset prices.

At the same time, these bubbles can lead to price rises that once the possibility of changing the nominal exchange rate has been lost, reduce competitiveness and, ultimately, the possibility of obtaining sufficient revenues to meet re-payments of past debt.

In surplus countries, on the other hand, there is a lack of demand and this problem must be solved at some point so that the loans to deficit countries can be recovered.

And above all, the continuity of the model depends crucially on the ability of debtors to obtain funding at a reduced cost in international financial markets. The creation of the monetary union, the elimination of the risk premium and increased financial integration enabled these resources to be channeled more easily and at a historically low cost to Spanish households and corporations, and this probably raised the threshold that the current account deficit can reach without problems for financing it. Nevertheless, if this flow is interrupted, as has happened in the current crisis, the model collapses, leaving behind a heavy burden in the form of private and external debt, deterioration in the solvency of financial institutions, cumulative loss of competitiveness and excessive weight of the housing sector.

Secondly, the impossibility of changing the nominal exchange rate implies that differences in inflation translate into gains and losses of competitiveness within the currency union. Without a strong political coordination, this encourages some countries to pursue policies that can only succeed at the expense of other Member States, such as the wage restraint policy implemented by Germany. This is not 'healthy competition' but 'competitive devaluation' and beggar-thy-neighbour policies.

It could be argued that, prior to the introduction of the euro, European economies running big trade deficits used to devaluate their currencies against the Deutschmark, and they had no incentives to search for increases in productivity to solve their problems of competitiveness. However, as Tilford (2010) points out, these devaluations facilitated rebalancing within European Union, because the devaluing economies recovered competitiveness and could continue to grow, the prices of imported goods fell to German consumers, increasing their disposable incomes, and Germany could not afford to ignore domestic demand. On the contrary, Germany's competitive devaluation within EMU helped to create imbalances; it is not an answer to them.

Finally, the single monetary policy also plays an important role in the development and maintenance of this unbalanced growth model, by applying the same nominal interest rate to countries with different behaviour in their domestic demand and rates of inflation. This results in a destabilizing effect and, in turn, gives rise to further increases in current account imbalances.

For example, the policy of moderate wage growth leads to lower growth in consumer demand in Germany, and consequently the interest rate should be reduced in this country. But as the European Central Bank can only apply one monetary policy and its objective is price stability in the Euro area as a whole, the decline in the rate of interest that occurs is too moderate for Germany, while for other countries where autonomous factors of demand have a more dynamic behaviour, as in Spain, it is excessive.

Indeed, the problem lies not only in the fact that the nominal interest rate established by the ECB may not be appropriate for all the countries, but that, as a result, the real interest rate may have a destabilizing effect. As inflation falls below the average in Germany and rises above the average in Spain, the real interest rate is higher in the former and lower in the second. Although there is also a stabilizing mechanism through changes in real exchange rates (real appreciation tends to reduce net exports and aggregate demand in Spain and increase them in Germany) it seems to act more slowly and, in any case, through higher external imbalances.

Saving Glut or Endogenous Money?

By definition, the current account surplus in Germany is accompanied by net capital exports, in the same way that the Spanish deficit implies net borrowing. This is simply an accounting identity. But looking more closely at the data we can also see that the net borrowing in Spain has been covered to a significant extent with the increasing net lending of Germany.

In 1998, the volume of foreign claims held by German banks was less than US$400 billion (about 20 percent of German GDP). A decade later, before the onset of the international financial crisis, these assets were close to US$5 trillion (180 percent of German GDP, or 70 percent of the overall amount of lending of surplus countries in the Euro zone). In the same period, the foreign assets of German banks against Spanish borrowers multiplied by more than six and they represented more than 6 percent of total foreign claims of German banks (Bank for International Settlements, *Consolidated Banking Statistics*, available at http://www.bis.org/statistics/consstats.htm (last accessed 5 March 2012)).

As a result of this process, according to BIS (2011), the external exposure of Spain against German banks reached US$242,000 million in the third quarter of 2010, equivalent to approximately 17 percent of Spanish GDP, or 22 percent of cross-border debt of Spanish banks.

This relationship between the strong growth of domestic demand in Spain, the sluggishness of German investment and consumption and abundant financial flows from Germany to Spain and other peripheral economies has been interpreted by some authors using the loanable funds theory. According to this point of view, one of the effects of the monetary union was that capital flowed out of Germany to the booming periphery, and this was the *leading cause* of current account imbalances. Specifically, German saving would have been channeled to Spanish banks, which would have increased credits to households and nonfinancial corporations. This would have boosted spending, leading to the expansion of demand and the housing bubble. At the same time, the outflow of this saving would be the cause of the sluggish investment in Germany and of the slow growth of its domestic demand.

For example, Sinn et al think that the German surplus is due to these net capital exports, because they meant that national savings were invested abroad, depressing domestic demand as a consequence:

> In the past few years, Germany was the world's second-largest capital exporter after China. From 2002 to 2010, Germany had exported two thirds of its aggregate savings, some 1,050 billion euros altogether. Only one-third was invested at home ... Due to the lack of growth in general and investment demand in particular, the scope for wage and price increases was low, resulting in Germany having the lowest inflation rate of all euro countries since 1995 ... The low rate of income growth dampened German imports, while the low prices stimulated German exports, both translating into a huge current account surplus. Thus, Germany's current account surplus resulted from the country's weakness. (Sinn et al 2011: 50–51)

On the other hand, the arrival of these savings in Spain would have been the cause of credit expansion and rising demand and imports: the euro

resulted in excessive capital inflows fuelling extremely rapid growth and ultimate overheating in the countries on Europe's south and western periphery . . .
The result was a building boom that ultimately developed into a bubble. The
rising incomes raised imports, and the increasing price level undermined the
competitiveness of the domestic economy, hurting exports. (Sinn et al 2011:
50–51)

For this to be true, saving should determine investment, while the post-
Keynesian economic theory states just the opposite. Because of this, we
think that it is more appropriate to interpret these data according to the
endogenous money theory. This interpretation is also consistent with our
explanation of current account imbalances in Germany and Spain.

To fund the increase in spending, households and non-financial corporations borrow from Spanish banks, which create deposits at the same
time. This makes GDP grow faster, but part of this money goes to fund
Spanish imports, it allows producers in the rest of the world to cancel
debts, and deposits remains on the liability side of foreign banks balances (German in our case). Now, Spanish banks are indebted to German
banks, and they postpone paying back this debt with the sale of mortgage
backed securities. Therefore, the hypothesis that surplus countries lend to
deficit countries (here Spanish banks) and then banks can lend once they
have collected deposits (the 'savings glut' hypothesis, an international
version of the loanable funds theory) cannot be accepted.

It should be borne in mind that Spanish banks' assets (mortgage loans)
have a much longer maturity than their liabilities. When the housing
bubble bursts in Spain in 2008, non-performing loans begin to rise dramatically and many small banks were strongly affected. As private indebted
agents cannot pay back part of their debts to Spanish banks, they cannot
settle debts to other banks. Hence, banks in the rest of the world do not
refinance Spanish banks and the latter stop lending to Spanish agents and
use collected liquidity (including ECB loans) to settle their debts.

All this has been reflected since 2007 in an increase in the liabilities of
the Banco de España (and other peripheral central banks) with the ECB
under the TARGET2 system, and of the claims of the Bundesbank on the
ECB. While during the previous years, central banks' TARGET2 positions had remained within fairly narrow boundaries, a sharp increase in
claims and liabilities has emerged since then. Specifically, at the end of
2010 the Bundesbank's claims on the ECB under TARGET2 stood at
€325.5 billion, and the sum of the liabilities of Spain, Portugal, Greece and
Ireland was €360.0 billion.

Cross-border payments that arise from foreign trade transactions or
from international capital transactions are usually carried out via the
banking system, and they are reflected in the corresponding interbank

claims or liabilities vis-à-vis to the rest of the world. Within the Euro area, these payments are settled using TARGET2.

If funds are transferred from a Spanish bank to a German bank, this results in a liability of the Bundesbank to this bank. These transactions generate a Bundesbank claim for the same sum to the Banco de España, which in turn debits the account of the originating commercial bank. This requires this private bank to have sufficient credit balance in central bank money. The outstanding claims and liabilities of all the national central banks participating in TARGET2 are transferred to the ECB at the end of the day, where they are netted out.

The sharp rise in the central bank's TARGET2 balances since 2007 is related to the financial crisis. While, because of the current account surplus, funds continue to flow into German banks from Spanish (and other countries') banks, the first are less willing to lend these funds to foreign institutions on the interbank market, and Spanish banks are receiving larger amounts of central bank money through the Eurosystem.

The increase in the liabilities of the Banco de España with the ECB under TARGET2 in 2011 has been even greater than the balance (negative, but decreasing in absolute terms) of the current account. This probably means that a relocation of funds from Spain to other countries of the monetary union is taking place.

IS A KEYNESIAN SOLUTION POSSIBLE FOR EUROPEAN CURRENT ACCOUNT IMBALANCES?

Orthodox analyses of the economic crisis within EMU focus on presenting the problems of public finances and the sovereign debt crisis, and the proposed solutions usually include as a critical component the tightening of the Stability and Growth Pact and the application of strict measures of fiscal austerity. In our view, however, the underlying reasons for the European crisis must be sought rather in the imbalances accumulated since the outset of the monetary union, particularly private and external debt, which in turn reflect the current account deficits and surpluses that were taking place between different members of the Euro zone.

On the other hand, the policies that are currently being implemented to correct these external imbalances only make reference to the adjustment of the competitiveness of the deficit countries, mainly through policies of wage restraint. The *Euro Plus Pact* (European Council 2011) is a clear representation of this type of economic policy, which includes the deregulation of labour markets, cutbacks in social spending and different actions to ensure proper development of labour costs in relation to productivity. But this approach ignores other alternative sources of current account imbalances and treats deficit and surpluses in a completely asymmetric way.

It is supposed that this 'internal devaluation' will adjust competitiveness in deficit countries, allowing an expansion of their exports which, in turn, will solve current account deficits and compensate for present weak domestic (private and public) demand. However, while one country may be able to boost its exports, all of the countries taken together cannot, because one's exports are always another's imports. Germany seems to want the peripheral countries to be as similar to itself as possible, but this is not possible, because its deficient domestic demand cannot be universalized. This 'solution' only works through cutting real wages and driving down national income to such a degree that imports contract drastically – and a recession on the deficit side deep enough to significantly reduce imports necessarily contracts export-dependent sectors in surplus countries.

Moreover, the German government continues to hold large and increasing trade surpluses as a goal for its economic policy, unaware that this export-led growth may be an obstacle to Euro area stability. Hence, if peripheral countries intend to engage in competitive reductions of wages, German producers will have an incentive to 'defend' their present competitive advantage, and rebalancing will be very difficult. It is not clear that this 'race to the bottom' would be an improvement in competitiveness of peripheral countries if surplus countries maintain a policy of low wages and slow growth in domestic demand. And it will be impossible to solve current account imbalances, except at the expense of a deep recession and deflation, which would actually end up endangering the repayment of past debts.

In order to avoid this deflationary bias, European authorities and national governments should look at the problem of current account deficits 'with Keynesian glasses' (Buzaglo 2011).

First of all, Keynes already pointed out in the *General Theory* (p. 382), that in a context of inadequate aggregate demand, some countries could try to avoid unemployment through international trade. If this was successful, this policy would simply shift the problem of lack of demand to other countries:

> If nations can learn to provide themselves with full employment by their domestic policy . . . there need be no important economic forces calculated to set the interest of one country against that of its neighbours . . . There would no longer be a pressing motive why one country need force its wares on another or repulse the offerings of its neighbour . . . with the express object of upsetting the equilibrium of payments so as to develop a balance of trade in its own favour. International trade would cease to be what it is, namely, a desperate

expedient to maintain employment at home by forcing sales on foreign markets and restricting purchases, which, if successful, will merely shift the problem of unemployment to the neighbour which is worsted in the struggle. (Keynes 1936)

Second, the ideas expressed by Keynes in the preparatory work of the Bretton Woods Conference could be used to facilitate a cooperative and symmetric solution for the current account imbalances within the Euro zone.

According to Skidelsky (2010), Keynes realized that, although the international gold standard was supposed to provide for an automatic and symmetrical adjustment of current account imbalances, it was compulsory for the debtor and voluntary for the creditor. Keynes's Clearing Union plan of 1941 was designed to avoid this, and its essential feature was that creditor countries would not be allowed to sterilize their surpluses, or charge punitive rates of interest for lending them out; rather these surpluses would be automatically available to debtors. Persistent surplus countries would be charged rising rates of interest and, in turn, persistent deficit countries would be allowed or required to depreciate their currencies, and they would also be charged interest.

Keynes's insights are highly relevant today, because adjustment pressures are concentrated on the deficit countries and the surplus countries can get off without adjustment. In this sense, Davidson says that:

> an essential improvement in designing any international payment system requires transferring the major onus of adjustment from the debtor to the creditor nation. This transfer of responsibility for ending persistent trade imbalances to those nations that persistently experience exports that exceed their imports would, Keynes explained, substitute an expansionist, in place of a contractionist, pressure on world trade. (Davidson 2011: 9)

Specifically, he proposes an International Monetary Clearing Union with the following objectives: to prevent a lack of global effective market demand for the products of industry occurring due to a liquidity problem whenever any nation(s) holds excessive idle reserves by saving too much of its internationally earned income; to provide an automatic mechanism for placing a major burden of correcting international trade imbalances on the nation running persistent trade surpluses; and to provide each nation with the ability to monitor and, if desired, to control capital movements out of the nation.

This plan implies a mechanism that encourages any nation that runs persistent trade surpluses to increase its spending, on the understanding that these resources are funds that the creditor nation could have used to buy the products of foreign industries rather than creating unemployment problems or excessive indebtedness abroad.

Of course, we cannot ignore the political difficulties which the reforms proposed here face. These difficulties are institutional (the objectives and even the design of fundamental aspects of economic policy instruments, like the independence of the ECB or fiscal austerity, are currently part of the European Union Treaty) as well as ideological (associated with the neo-liberal agenda). But, as Arestis and Sawyer (2010, p. 14) highlight, without these changes the outlook for the next years is not very rosy:

> The faults lie in the neo-liberal design of the euro Project, now embedded in the Treaty of Lisbon, and where there is little prospect of serious change because of the unanimity requirements for change. But without basic and fundamental change, many (perhaps all) Euro area countries face a bleak economic future. (Arestis and Sawyer 2010: 14)

CONCLUSIONS

Current account imbalances in the Euro area are usually interpreted as the result of problems of competitiveness, lack of efficiency and economic policy mistakes made by the deficit countries. The central idea of this chapter, however, is that the genesis of these imbalances is in the growth pattern that has characterized European economies since the creation of the euro, and that surpluses and deficits are interdependent.

Consequently, the resolution of current imbalances cannot come only from the side of the deficit countries, trying to regain competitiveness through wage restraint, but also from the side of the surplus countries. What is needed is to address the root causes that have resulted in the lack of demand in the whole system, and a more balanced pattern of growth within EMU, in which countries do not base their growth on stimulating exports by means of wage competence.

In this sense we find the reflection by Blanchard and Milesi-Ferreti very interesting, when they ask if, 'from a multilateral viewpoint, countries should be allowed to pursue export-led growth strategies' and then they write the following:

> An export-led growth strategy – that is, a policy combination of a depreciated real exchange rate and enforced low domestic demand (through high saving and/or low investment) – is formally equivalent to a combination of tariffs on imports cum subsidies on exports, and low domestic demand to maintain internal balance. This second, equivalent combination is illegal under the World Trade Organization. Should the first one be as well? (Blanchard and Milesi-Ferreti 2011: 8).

We would answer 'Yes'.

In short, the current 'asymmetrical approach' is not adequate to correct the current account imbalances and the problems related to the workings of EMU, and it should be replaced by a 'symmetrical approach' in which the core countries also contribute to the recovery of domestic demand and the adjustment of competitiveness within the Euro zone.

NOTES

1. We will only refer to EMU-12, with the exception of Luxembourg.
2. In this chapter the data source is Eurostat, unless otherwise stated.
3. For a thorough analysis of current account positions within the Euro area see Arestis and Paúl (2009).
4. In 2000 the rate of inflation in the Spanish economy was 3.4 percent versus 2.3 percent in the Euro area and 1.5 percent in Germany. The average inflation rate since then has remained at 2.8 percent in Spain compared to 2 percent of the whole monetary union and 1.5 percent in Germany.
5. This economic logic is consistent with the so-called Lawson doctrine and with the theoretical approach developed for example by Corden (1994).

REFERENCES

Arestis, P. and J. Paúl (2009) 'Déficits en cuenta corriente en la Unión Económica y Monetaria Europea y crisis financiera internacional', *Ola Financiera*, September–December, 1–43.
Arestis, P. and M. Sawyer (2010) 'The problems of the Economic and Monetary Union: is there any escape?', *Journal of Economic Issues*, 1(1), 1–14.
Bibow, J. (2009) *The American-German Divide*, New America Foundation, available at http://www.newamerica.net/publications/policy/american_german_divide (last accessed 5 March 2012).
BIS (2011) 'The international banking market in the third quarter of 2010', *BIS Quarterly Review*, March, 14–19.
Blanchard, O. and G.M. Milesi-Ferreti (2011) '(Why) Should Current Account Balances Be Reduced?', *IMF Staff Discussion Note*, March 1.
Buzaglo, J. (2011) 'The Eurozone Crisis: Looking through the financial fog with keynesian glasses', *Real-Word Economics Review*, 8, 77–82.
Cesaratto, S. (2010) 'Europe, German Mercantilism and the Current Crisis', *Quaderni del Dipartimento di Economia Politica, Università degli Studi di Siena*, 595.
Chandrasekhar, C.P. and J. Ghosh (2010) 'The New Mercantilists', *IDEAS*, available at http://www.networkideas.org/news/sep2010/news07_Mercantilists.htm (last accessed 5 March 2012).
Corden, W.M. (1994) *Economic Policy, Exchange Rates and the International System*, Oxford: Oxford University Press.
Davidson, P. (2011) 'The Keynes Solution for Preventing Global Imbalances', Paper presented at conference on 'From Crisis to Growth? The challenge of

imbalances, debt and limited resources', Berlin, Germany: Research Network Macroeconomics and Macroeconomic Policies.

Dejuán, O. and E. Febrero (2010) 'The failure of a path of growth driven by household indebtedness (Spain, 1997–2009)', *Économie Appliquée*, LXIII(1), 63–78.

European Council (2011) Conclusions of the Presidency, 24–25 March, available at http://www.consilium.europa.eu/uedocs/cms_data/docs/pressdata/en/ec/120296.pdf (last accessed 5 March 2012).

Felipe, J. and U. Kumar (2011) 'Unit Labor Costs in the Euro Zone: The Competitiveness Debate Again', *Levy Economics Institute Working Papers*, 651.

Hein, Eckhard and Achim Truger (2009) 'How to Fight (or Not to Fight) a Slowdown', *Challenge*, 52(3), 52–75.

Horn, G., K. Dröge, S. Sturn, T. Van Treeck and R. Zwiener (2009) 'From the financial crisis to the world economic crisis. The role of inequality', Berlin: IMK (Institute für Makroökonomie und Konjunkturforschung) Report, 41.

Keynes, J.M. (1936) *The General Theory of Employment, Interest and Money*, Cambridge: Macmillan.

Onaran, Ö. (2011) 'From wage suppression to sovereign debt crisis in Western Europe: who pays for the costs of the crisis?', *International Journal of Public Policy*, 7(1/2/3), 51–69.

Schröder, E. (2011) 'Trade Balances in Germany and the United States: Demand Dominates Price', Paper presented at conference on 'From Crisis to Growth? The challenge of imbalances, debt and limited resources', Berlin, Germany: Research Network Macroeconomics and Macroeconomic Policies.

Sinn, H.-W., T. Buchen and T. Wollmershäuser (2011) 'Trade Imbalances – Causes, Consequences and Policy Measures: IFO's Statement for the Camdessus Commission', CESIfo Forum, 1/2011, 47–58.

Skidelsky, R. (2010) 'Keynes, Global Imbalances and International Monetary Reform, Today', in S. Claessens, S. Evenett and B. Hoeckman (eds) *Rebalancing the Global Economy: A Primer for Policymaking*, London: Centre for Economic Policy Research, 173–180.

Stockhammer, E. (2011) 'Peripheral Europe's Debt and German Wages. The Role of Wage Policy in the Euro Area', *International Journal of Public Policy*, 7(1/2/3), 83–96.

Tilford, S. (2010) 'Germany's Euro Advantage', *The New York Times*, available at http://www.nytimes.com/2010/07/14/opinion/14iht-edtilford.html (last accessed 5 March 2012).

Weber, A. (2011) 'Challenges for monetary policy in EMU', *Federal Reserve Bank of St. Louis Review*, July/August, 93(4), 235–42.

Index